The Economics of Income Distribution

The Economics of Income Distribution

Heterodox Approaches

Edited by

Joep T.J.M. van der Linden

and

André J.C. Manders

Department of Social Economics,
Utrecht University, The Netherlands

BELGIAN–DUTCH ASSOCIATION FOR POST-KEYNESIAN STUDIES

Edward Elgar
Cheltenham, UK • Northampton, MA, USA

Published by
Edward Elgar Publishing Limited
Glensanda House
Montpellier Parade
Cheltenham
Glos GL50 1UA
UK

Edward Elgar Publishing, Inc.
6 Market Street
Northampton
Massachusetts 01060
USA

A catalogue record for this book
is available from the British Library

Library of Congress Cataloguing in Publication Data

The economics of income distribution: heterodox approaches / edited
by Joep T.J.M. van der Linden and André J.C. Manders.
    "In association with the Belgian–Dutch Association for Post–
Keynesian Studies."
    Includes index.
    1. Income distribution. I. Linden, J.T.J.M. van der.
HC79.I5E24   1999
339.2—dc21   98–45768
                                                          CIP

ISBN 1 84064 029 4

Printed and bound in Great Britain by Bookcraft (Bath) Ltd.

Contents

List of Figures		vi
List of Tables		vii
List of Contributors		viii
Acknowledgements		ix

1. The Economics of Income Distribution: Heterodox Approaches. An Introduction — 1
   Joep T.J.M. van der Linden and André J.C. Manders
2. Bronfenbrenner Revisited — 9
   Martin Bronfenbrenner
3. An Institutionalist Approach to Income Distribution — 15
   Warren J. Samuels
4. Beyond Income Distribution: An Entitlement Systems Approach to the Acquirement Problem — 29
   Bas de Gaay Fortman
5. Deflation and Distribution: Austerity Policies in Britain in the 1920s — 77
   Victoria Chick
6. Income Distribution in the Transition: Some Reflections and Some Evidence — 127
   Jan A. Kregel
7. Income Distribution and Environmental Policy Instruments — 143
   Bouwe R. Dijkstra and Andries Nentjes
8. Looking Back — 173
   Yehojachin S. Brenner

Index — 205

Figures

5.1	Wages and prices	102
5.2	Unemployment	103
5.3	Yield on consols	104
5.4	Retail price index	105
5.5	The debt	106
5.6	Exchange rate ($/£)	107
5.7	Money supply, advances (£m)	108
5.8	Wholesale prices	109
5.9	Bank rate	110
5.10	National debt (£m)	111
5.11	Revenue and expenditure (£m), budget balance (% of GDP)	112
5.12	Interest rates	113
5.13	Revenue and debt service	114
5.14	GDP and its components at 1938 prices (£m)	115
5.15	Factor income shares	116
5.16	Interest and dividends as a percentage of gross profit	117
5.17	The Strakosch diagram	118
5.18	Shares of potential income	119
5.19	Interest payments and non-trading income of the corporate sector	120
7.1	No environmental policy	149
7.2	Standards	150
7.3	Charges	153

Tables

5.1	War loan, nominal returns	101
6.1	Offical estimates of the private sector contribution to GDP 1990–1995	134
6.2	Composition of final demand in current prices % GDP 1993–1995	135
6.3	Selected indicators of transition economy performance 1989–1994	139
7.1	Preferences for instruments in the neoclassical model	147
7.2	Income impacts of bubble and charge	154
7.3	Income impacts of grandfathering	155
7.4	Preferences for instruments in the post-Keynesian model	158
7.5	Workers' preferences in the post-Keynesian model	158
7.6	Harmony and conflict in instrument choice	159
7.7	Shareholders' and workers' payoffs and government revenue	162

Contributors

Yehojachin S. Brenner,	Utrecht University, Utrecht
Martin Bronfenbrenner,	Duke University, Durham NC
Victoria Chick,	University College London, London
Bouwe R. Dijkstra,	University of Groningen, Groningen
Bas de Gaay Fortman,	Institute of Social Studies, The Hague
Jan A. Kregel,	University of Bologna, Bologna
Joep T.J.M. van der Linden,	Utrecht University, Utrecht
André J.C. Manders,	Utrecht University, Utrecht
Andries Nentjes,	University of Groningen, Groningen
Warren J. Samuels,	Michigan State University, East Lansing MI

Acknowledgements

The editors of this volume, also organizers of the Conference on Heterodox Economics and Income Distribution of the Belgian–Dutch Association of Post-Keynesian Studies gratefully acknowledge the financial and logistical support of the Department of Social Economics of Utrecht University and the Netherlands School for Social and Economic Policy Research (AWSB) Utrecht.

Many thanks to the contributors to this volume for complying with the editors' requests and meeting deadlines so efficiently.

A special message of thanks goes to Mrs. Maiumi Sadler, Loes van der Heijden and Carina Kok for their patience and dedication in preparing a camera-ready copy of the original manuscript of this book.

1. The Economics of Income Distribution: Heterodox Approaches.
An Introduction

Joep T.J.M. van der Linden and
André J.C. Manders

This volume comprises a set of essays on income distribution. The collection of articles stems from the Annual Conference of the Belgian–Dutch Association of Post-Keynesian Studies on *Heterodox Economics and Income Distribution*, held at Utrecht University in 1996. The conference was organized with the intent to honour Professor Y.S. Brenner on the occasion of his retirement.

The subject of income distribution is in the centre of most issues related to social change. It is no exaggeration to say that considerations of income and wealth distribution are the driving force behind many if not all questions of public policy.

Despite its importance the study of income distribution appears not to be high on the economists' agenda. One reason for this may be that a discussion on income and wealth distributions is a sensitive matter. Another important reason can be that factors which govern the distributions of income and wealth, and the way distribution affects economic performance, are very complex. Indeed they often seem impenetrable (Samuels and Kelsey, 1991, p. 119).

The purpose of the conference was to promote discussion on the positive and normative aspects of research on income distribution. It was the intention of the organizers to show that the study of distribution ought not to be marginalized in the intellectual discourse, and that questions of distribution are an appropriate subject for research and public discussion.

Many deplore the lack of agreement among economists about the interpretation of economic phenomena in general, and of income and wealth distribution in particular. In their opinion this 'pluralism' impedes the development of a cumulative coherent body of knowledge. Others believe that the diversity of thought shows the discipline's vitality.

Considering that economic theory is developing in a constantly changing social and economic environment, 'plurality' is hardly surprising. Any historical reconstruction of phenomena and of their consequences is inevitably incomplete. Seldom *all* determining variables can be traced. Moreover, economics deals with only part of social reality and its interpretation of events depends on insights obtained from other social and cultural sciences. Society is always in a process of transformation which renders reality unstable. The formulation of economic theories therefore depends on fundamental postulates which are outside the strict limits of economics proper. The postulates involve normative elements and are rarely open to 'falsification'. The point is that economic theories are consciously or unconsciously influenced by ideas about how society *ought* to be, and this accounts for much of the profession's disagreement. It seems to us more fruitful that the economic discussion about how to avoid socially undesirable developments between the different schools of thought, should reach across paradigmatic boundaries and not be confined to expressions of mutual contempt as often happens. Such open-mindedness is particularly necessary when dealing with issues like income distribution. According to several contributions in this volume it is not only the controversy about the explanatory powers of the basic model of neoclassical theory, but also about other analytical tools which should be sought for a better understanding of social reality.

In his *Income Distribution Theory* (1971) Bronfenbrenner critically commented on the theoretical contributions of 'dissidents particularly in Western Europe'. He was thinking of economists like Kalecki, Kaldor, and Joan Robinson.

> These dissidents appear to have little in common, beyond sceptical doubts, sometimes extending to contempt, for the Good Old Theory in general, and for certain particular pieces of the apparatus like the production function and the marginal productivity concept (p. 407; see also the Postscript by Pen in his book *Income Distribution*, 1971).

Bronfenbrenner added to his critical evaluation that it could be possible '...that a later generation of dissident theory may overcome these deficiencies and take over the field' (p. 438).

The contributors to this book belong to different schools of economic thought. Except for Bronfenbrenner himself, they may well fit into his category of dissidents. He himself, Samuels, Brenner and de Gaay Fortman discuss the state of the art, while the contributions by Chick, Kregel, Dijkstra and Nentjes discuss the empirical findings on income distribution, and consider how these distributions are effected by the different stages of economic development.

In 1996, as he already wrote in 1971, Martin Bronfenbrenner appears still to be unwilling 'to discard neoclassical economics, either marginalism or the production function, either at the micro-economic or the macro-economic level. Unlike the ultra-Keynesians I do not believe that distribution is determined wholly or even primarily in output markets making the input markets shadow-boxing arenas' (p. xi).

In his contribution to this volume Bronfenbrenner discusses several develop- ments which in his opinion are important expansions to his earlier book. Among others he mentions the works by Atkinson, Williamson and Lindert, and also the writings of Rawls and Nozick on distributive justice. In his paper he explains that certain alternatives (to neoclassical economics) yield more sympathetic implications for the interventionist position. Two of these rivals to neoclassical orthodoxy are bargaining theories, and the post-Keynesian theory. He grants that both these theories deserve fuller treatment than they received in his book of 1971.

In the last paragraph of his paper he comments on the Brenners' *Theory of Full Employment* (1996). He does not agree with the Brenners about government intervention, and their predilection for progressive taxation and rejection of wage moderation. In his discussion of the same problem in the *Journal of Income Distribution* (1991) he pointed out that conservative warnings against 'redistributional tinkering' usually seem to be based on two conceptually-distant propositions. One of these is a 'general equilibrium' proposition, with which neoclassical economists (including himself) would be happy because one cannot in general change income distribution by itself without changing production, income, and other aspects of the macroeconomy as well. The second proposition is a 'cost-benefit' proposition, which means that the particular changes in production and income that one can expect from massive equalization of income and wealth will reduce the rate of growth of national output and the living standard. In his opinion this proposition can neither be proven nor disproved by appeal to standard economics.

My personal hope is that adequate factual evidence against it can accumulate from experimentation now underway in Northern and Western Europe, chiefly the Netherlands, Sweden, and Norway and largely under social democratic auspices, for our children or grandchildren to consider it disproved – at least under the special conditions of such countries – within the next generation or two. Not, alas, within my own lifetime (1991, pp. 202–3).

As an economist working in the Michigan State University tradition of institutionalist law and economy Warren Samuels considers distribution a function of institutions, especially law, and institutions a function of distributions, and thereby of the use of government. Assuming that human assumptions enter into laws which help govern the distribution of income and wealth, he states that distribution is an artefact and not something transcendental and independent of human decision. (1991, pp. 215–9). The economy is a system of organization and control which means that it is not only an artefact but also the changing product of the social reconstruction of economic reality. He points out that the distribution of income, wealth, and opportunity is partly a matter of who controls government and the uses to which government is put. The critical question is not whether there will be 'intervention' but what forms it will take, and with what purposes, or whose interests it will promote. Changing the distribution of income, wealth, and opportunity is the ideal of important groups in society. These groups realize that these distributions and related social arrangements (specially legal arrangements) are a matter of human choice, and can be changed.

With regard to this argument it may be relevant to recall a discussion at the Annual Meeting of the Dutch Royal Association of Economics in 1995. On this occasion the Dutch former Cabinet-minister of Social Affairs and Employment, De Vries, argued that in most OECD countries income inequality has increased during the 1980s, and that a further increase of inequality in the primary incomes would seriously affect the social cohesion in society. To sustain social cohesion the government of the Netherlands pursued tax-policies to mitigate inequality in the secondary distribution of income. This argument was criticized on the grounds that such policy would hinder growth and employment. It was argued that taxation discourages economic activities. It was suggested that instead of taxation a better policy preventing income inequality would be to promote education and vocational training, technological innovation, and work. This view was supported by the argument that a more equitable primary distribution of income has positive effects on economic growth (De Vries, pp. 1–22; Van Sinderen and Bergeijk, pp. 83–103).

In his essay Bas de Gaay Fortman explains the importance of legal arrangements with regard to the distribution of income and wealth. He discusses the significance of entitlement – having legitimate claims based on rights. Entitlement should be regarded as a structural process by which individuals try to improve their positions. This process is always an interrelationship between rights and obligations. Concerning the access to resources he distinguishes primary and subsidiary, and formal and informal, entitlements. He refers to Samuels's and Kelsey's distinction (1991, p. 126) between the productivity, exploitation and appropriation paradigms, and thinks that the latter will be useful to explain Sen's 'acquirement problem'. This appropriation paradigm locates 'the factors at work which determine income distribution'. In his view the institutionalist approach to entitlement and acquirement gives insight into the disputes which arise about the problems between rights and obligations and their settlement by law. These disputes originate from claims legitimized by rights only insofar as there are corresponding obligations on the part of others to respect them. It is in the dialectics of law and power that people's entitlements get actually determined.

With regard to the development of the Third World, de Gaay Fortman applies the entitlement systems approach to the acquirement problem under conditions of structural deficiency. He discusses different requirements of structural development, namely the challenge to increase productivity, the challenge to reduce dependency, and the challenge to promote individual and collective empowerment. He argues that the development strategy of Western countries based on direct resource-connected entitlement within an universalist legal system is in complete contrast to the predominantly particularistic legal culture and traditional structures of entitlement in developing countries. Changes in traditional structures, according to the Western way of thinking, lead to marginalization of the weaker members of less developed societies. He points out that customary sources of law (and traditional entitlement structures) should not be regarded as constraints on the process of development, but rather as a guarantee against increasing inequality and marginalization. He concludes that the transition from traditional institutions based entitlement, and entitlement rooted in novel institutions will be promoted by a strategy of empowerment- participatory types of development.

The problem of transition and its consequences for the distribution of income and wealth are the main theme of Victoria Chick's contribution on the austerity policies in Britain in the 1920s, and of Jan Kregel's article on the developments in Eastern Europe.

Chick discusses the UK policy of 1919, to return to the gold standard at pre-war parity, in order to restore 'sound money' and fiscal deflation. Though the aim was to reduce British prices to bring them into line with processes abroad, this was achieved only through high unemployment and hitherto unprecedented interest rates in peacetime. These results significantly altered the distribution of income in favour of fixed income recipients. However desirable sound money may seem, there are classic results, repeated in the Thatcher recession of the early 1980s. The same principles are now again enshrined in the Maastricht criteria for joining the single currency and in the Stability Pact. She is of the opinion that the operation of these principles cannot fail to be damaging to growth and to favour recipients of rentier income at the expense of labour income.

In his essay Kregel discusses the process of transition in Eastern Europe and its consequences for the distribution of income and wealth. In these societies the enrichment of the few goes with poverty for many (see also Nuti, 1996).

He comments on the argument that the changes in the economic system in Eastern Europe can be compared to those after the stock market crash of 1929. He thinks it impossible to determine the impact of change. 'It represents a comparison across socio-economic systems, and thus across incompatible distribution categories and theories.' He suggests that a more appropriate way of looking at the transition in general is to focus on the transformation from State ownership of capital to ownership by individual private capitalists. The privatization of State capital reaffirmed the distribution of income (see also Van Brabant, 1992). It appears that the distribution of income did not become more uneven than it was before the change. The benefits from the transition fell to those who also belonged to the privileged class in the socialist era. The transformation of a class of state bureaucrats into a class of capitalist does not create a new entrepreneurial class but creates arbitrageurs and speculators in capital assets. Private investment did not take over the role which was prior to the transition held by the state in domestic investment, and consequently economic development stagnated.

Kregel concludes that 'the rapidity of the decline in equality and the extent of the decline in the face of so little industrial restructuring' is surprising.

A difficult question is how ecological factors can be included in economic theory. There is one theoretical position which holds that to ascertain whether or not a society is actually striving for sustainable development can only be learned from observing the actual behaviour of economic subjects in and outside markets. From this behaviour it becomes clear whether they are prepared to make sacrifices for ecological conservation or not. Another position is that the conventional assumptions behind economic analyses are too simplistic about the absolute limits of economic growth. According to this point of view there is an excessive optimism about the variability of the technical coefficients of production and about the direction and rate of technological progress. Given the urgency of ecological problems and our responsibility for global development and our obligation to future generations, radical measures need to be taken. This implies government intervention, and the realization that major decisions cannot be left to the market alone.

In their contribution Bouwe Dijkstra and Andries Nentjes discuss if it is possible to explain actual political decision-making, specifically the choice of instruments for environmental policy, as the outcome of a struggle about the distribution of gains and losses between interested parties; and whether the controversy inevitably leads to the choice of inefficient policies or instruments. They begin from the assumption that governments are susceptible to the influence of interest groups and therefore that regulation may not be designed to maximize social welfare. With others, they feel that a policy that increases aggregate welfare by inflicting large losses on a small group of individuals will not be realized, because losing agents have a strong incentive to form powerful lobbies. Their rent-seeking analysis focuses on the interests of capital owners (shareholders) and labour in polluting industries. It appears that regulation leads to lower profits and loss of employment. They prefer market instruments, for example agreements between government and enterprises which reduce pollution, and find them more efficient and less expensive than by regulation – standards/sanctions and/or taxation.

The last essay is Brenner's farewell lecture to his students and colleagues. In his contribution he *Looks Back* at the ideas he has held and elaborated during the years he worked at Utrecht University. An important theme of his concerns the explanation of the mechanisms by which the national income is distributed between groups and individuals in the economy. He takes a firm stand for the restoration of the humane ideals of the founders of the welfare state against the opportunism of politicians striving for re-election and power who place trust in rhetoric more than in truth. But most of all he reproaches his fellow economists for ignoring Keynes's proposition that 'it is employment that generates savings and induces investment, and that the level of employment determines the height of real wages'. He accuses them of flexing with the fashion of the time, and trying to find remedies for the symptoms of the malaise that plagues the Welfare State, by monetary measures to contain inflation and to cut back government expenditure, which he believes to be paving the way into a social, economic and moral morass. They disregard that 'the entire economic structure is in a process of rapid transformation'. He points out the need for a revival of the public's political engagement, and for revision of economic theory. 'Instead of holding on to the idea that economic growth provides employment, and "small government" is good for financial stability, it must be recognized that growing employment produces economic growth and that financial stability depends on the judicious regulation of income distribution. Hence, the prime objective of economic policy should be *full employment*, in the conventional sense of this term.'

REFERENCES

Brabant, J. van (1992), 'Economics in Transition and Privatisation – The Case of Eastern Europe', in J. van den Broeck and D. Van Den Bulcke (eds), *Changing Economic Order*, Groningen: Wolters-Noordhoff, 161–202.

Brenner, Y.S. (1988), 'The tricky problem of Distribution', in Y.S. Brenner, J.P.G. Reijnders and A.H.G.M. Spithoven (eds), *The Theory of Income and Wealth Distribution*, Brighton/New York: Wheatsheaf Books, 11–53.

Bronfenbrenner, M. (1971) *Income Distribution Theory*, Chicago/New York: Aldine Atherton.

Bronfenbrenner, M. (1991), 'Editorial', *Journal of Income Distribution*, **1**(2), 199–207.

Nuti, D.M. (1996), 'The Role of the State in Post-Communist Economies', in C. Naastepad and S. Storm (eds), *The State and the Economic Process*, Cheltenham/Brookfield: Elgar, 159–176.

Pen, J. (1971), *Income Distribution*, Harmondsworth: Penguin Books.

Samuels, W. J. (1991), 'Editorial: A Statement of Orientation, Purpose and Policy', Journal of Income Distribution, **1**(Spring), 1–3.

Samuels, W.J. (1991), 'An Essay on the Philosophy and Psychodynamics of Income Distribution', *Journal of Income Distribution*, **1**(Fall), 210–220.

Samuels, W.J. and T.W. Kelsey (1991), 'Some Fundamental Considerations on the Positive Theory of Income Distribution', in J.T.J.M. van der Linden and W.L.M. Adriaansen (eds), *Post-Keynesian Thought in Perspective*, Groningen: Wolters-Noordhoff, 119–138.

Sinderen, J. van, and P.A.G. van Bergeijk (1995), 'Inkomensverdeling, economische groei en werkgelegenheid: een modelmatige verkenning', in A.Knoester and F.W. Rutten (eds), *Inkomensverdeling en economische activiteit*. Pre-adviezen, Koninklijke Vereniging voor Staathuishoudkunde, Utrecht: Lemma, 83–102.

Vries, B. de (1995), 'Inkomensverdeling en arbeidsparticipatie', in A. Knoester and F.W.Rutten (eds), *Inkomensverdeling en economische activiteit*. Pre-adviezen, Koninklijke Vereniging voor Staathuishoudkunde, Utrecht: Lemma, 1–22.

2. Bronfenbrenner Revisited

Martin Bronfenbrenner

Unfortunately the late Martin Bronfenbrenner was no longer able to send us the full and revised version of his presentation. He died on 2 June 1997. As this was probably his last public address, we publish it here as it was spoken in Utrecht. Little did we expect him to leave us so soon after the meeting. The Editors of this book and the Editors of the Journal of Income Distribution as well as his many friends will sadly miss him. His great scholarship and humour were a constant encouragement to all of us.

These festivities are for Joe Brenner, not for me, and rightly so. I did not choose this title for my remarks, and I had best begin this so-called 'contribution' by disclaiming any desire to 'rain on Joe's parade' as we say in America. I come at the invitation of our Utrecht colleagues, perhaps because this year is the 25th anniversary of my fat but nearly-forgotten book on *Income Distribution Theory* (1971).

Please let me begin by indicating some of the things I recognize as mechanical defects in my book and what I might consider doing about them were I not both lazy and superannuated. Then, if time permits, I propose to indicate briefly why I have not been entirely converted by Joe Brenner's *magnum opus* on *The Theory of Full Employment* (1996). That 1971 book, culminating nearly 25 years of work, was written perhaps 10 years too late, in an unfortunate style, and from the viewpoint of a single developed (industrialized) economy largely isolated from the rest of the world. A bigger and more advanced Tokugawa Japan, perhaps, rather than from either Kennedy-Johnson's or Richard Nixon's America. It is also 90 per cent micro-economics and 10 per cent macroeconomics; it might better have been the reverse, although I cannot see quite how. And finally, its animus may have been a reaction to my University of Wisconsin colleagues' general assumption that the public interest was whatever the leaders of its 'democratic' trade unions said it was, and that this movement, together with governments which it dominated, could bring the U.S. more than half-way to Utopia without relapsing into either Communist- or fascist-type dictatorship.

There is surely a middle ground for academic monographs of serious

9

intent, neither 'over the heads' of the 'intelligent layman' nor beneath the contempt of the up-to-the minute specialist suckled in a creed of 'algorithmic corner solutions for amphoteric matrix equations of the Thunder-ten-Trockh type'. I tried for a middle ground, and remain confident of its existence. But for myself, my 'happy landing' was between two stools. And that, I very much fear, is that.

In addition, an unusual flowering of distribution theory occurred, I think, in the late-60s and the 70s of the disappointing century now drawing to its close. Had my book somehow managed to appear 10 years earlier, it might have had 10 or 15 years of useful life before sinking into obsolescence. As things were, instead, it went out of date while still under editorial review, or still in press. So much for bad timing.

Occasional well-intentioned publishers have innocently asked whether I might attempt a second edition of *Income Distribution Theory*. I have refused, pleading old age, flagging ambition, and failure to keep up with advances of technique. But let me indicate ten alterations – mostly, alas, expansions! – of my 1971 treatment, which I now consider decidedly in order.

1.–3. The first three of these points pertain primarily to my Chapter 3, entitled 'Topics in Personal Income Distribution'. One is the inter-relation between functional and personal distributions. My principal creditor here is Anthony Atkinson, whose work, I must confess, I have thus far been unable to follow in its technical aspects. A second point is the causation problem conventionally summarized as 'heredity versus environment' or 'nature versus nurture', where the English-language literature, at least, has been expanded tremendously by the Richard Herrnstein-Charles Murray volume on *The Bell Curve* (1994) and by its critics. Thirdly and finally, sections 22–23 of that chapter, entitled 'An Income Revolution?' must be completely rewritten, since this 'revolution' in the direction of greater equality, if it actually occurred, seems to have been reversed by a counter-revolution which apparently began soon after my study appeared.

4. Jeffrey Williamson and Peter Lindert have introduced a new 'Topic in Functional Income Distribution' omitted in my Chapter 4. They do this by sub-dividing the labour share into 'skilled labour' and 'unskilled labour' categories. They go on to explain much American 'distributional history' to fluctuations in the relations between the shares of these sub-classes.

5. John Rawls and Robert Nozick, both of Harvard University's Department of Philosophy, propounded in the 1970s rival theories of distributive justice. Rawls' *Theory of Justice* (1971) implied a highly-negative view of things-as-they-are in capitalist distribution, while Nozick's *Anarchy, State, and Utopia* (1974), seemed more tolerant of the

status quo – indeed, to almost any status quo in which the legal niceties of transfer have been observed for a substantial period. I should certainly be happy to add my two cents' worth of economic contribution to this ethical controversy in my 'Maldistribution?' Chapter 5. Another recent tendency – leading names include Hal Varian and William Baumol – identifies 'fairness' as the absence of envy. This seems to me, if taken literally, to make any distribution unfair and to make fairness impossible in the real world, but this view may be 'a libel on the human race'.

6. My 'marginal productivity' chapters, particularly Chapter 6, assume maximizing behaviour (with information a free good) on the part of employers. They are accordingly silent about rules-of-thumb in average-cost and average-productivity terms, which might usefully approximate the corresponding marginal quantities. I had discussed such matters previously in 'Imperfect Competition on a Long-Run Basis' (*Chicago Journal of Business*, 1950), but did not apply them in my larger book, let alone make use of the subsequently developed 'multiple-goals' and 'aspiration levels' insights of Herbert Simon and Oliver Williamson. In any revision, I should try to do better.

7. Many economists of many persuasions, including many who know better, refer to distribution-theory orthodoxy as 'marginal productivity', when in fact marginal productivity refers only to the demand side of input markets and becomes 'the whole story' only when input supplies are absolutely price-inelastic. I tried and failed to clarify this distinction, and wish I had entitled or at least sub-titled all or part of my Chapter 9 'The Labor-Leisure Choice,' especially as regards labour markets. Of course, there are plenty of problems here, especially when the choices or preferences of a spouse, a parent, or oneself when young (at time t_0) have bound one's preferences at time t_1. I suspect that much of the 'joylessness' of Tibor Scitovsky's *Joyless Economy* (1976) arises from this source, not to mention the 'harrying' of Staffan, Burenstam Linder's *Harried Leisure Class* (1970). How much of A's bored satiety of 'comfort' or B's 'rat race' or 'squirrel cage' feeling can be traced to 'wrong' labour-leisure choices made by someone (not always someone *else*) 15–20 years ago and irreversible in practice either today or in the foreseeable future? In the words of a Scottish folk song:

My heart's in the Highlands, my heart is not here.
My heart's in the Highlands, a-chasing the deer.
A-chasing the wild deer and following the roe.
My heart's in the Highlands wherever I go.

8. Numerous economic historians, and also Joe Brenner, have objected to a conventional assumption, which I too have made, that unregulated input and output quantities and prices are set in contemporary and impersonal

markets. The dissidents think today's quantities and prices are determined largely by what they were yesterday, the day before, and so on back to the first syllable of recorded time. Today's fancy label for this view is 'path-dependency'; it makes better sense for quantities than it does for prices. I have one additional quibble with it, as it refers to the quantities of inputs supplied and demanded. If a quantity q_0 today (t_0) is determined largely by the prior quantities (q_{-1}, q_{-2}, . . .,q_{-n}) and if the initial term in time, namely q_{-n} at t_{-n} was itself determined by market forces such as supply and demand, how are the influences determining today's q_0 to be allocated between 'the market' and 'path-dependency'? Actually this issue came up in a disagreement between myself and my editor-cum-referee Harry Johnson, in connection with the 'rent' Chapter 14 of *Income Distribution Theory*. My semi-final draft had argued that Henry George's single tax, or any similar differential or discriminatory taxation of land as against other forms of fixed capital, would force land into premature and inferior uses in the short term, and hence, by path-dependency, into sub-optimal uses in the long term as well. Johnson managed to convince me that my argument implied not only poor foresight but actual irrationality on the landholders' part. I now think I was right: 'A man convinced against his will of the same opinion still'.

9. My 'macroeconomic' Chapter 16 is very weak in its treatment of the dissidents. Particularly neglected is Piero Sraffa's *Production of Commodities by Means of Commodities* (1960, 1975) in its 'disequilibrium' implications calling for controls. I was also too hasty and superficial in attacking other dissents as confusing the effects with the causes of distributional change. At the very least, I should have the time sequences and transmission mechanisms which continue to lead me to my preference for the Good Old Theory.

10. In these days of globalization led by multinational companies, it seems peculiar to have completely ignored the internationalization aspects of income distribution in a monograph on *Income Distribution Theory*. Omission of at least one 'international' chapter is, I have now come to feel, the single most glaring sin of my book. The unwritten 'international' chapter should, I believe, have concentrated on the Stolper-Samuelson and especially the factor-price-equalization (f.p.e.) theorems, both the quantitative importance of the assumptions behind them and the reasons why f.p.e., in particular, has not led in practice to income convergence between countries – rather the reverse. (Is this a matter primarily of flaws of the theory, unreality of its assumptions, non-economic [political or demographic] influences, advanced-country protectionism, or of the big bad neoimperialists and multinationals?)

So much for old Bronfenbrenner, at least one generation out of date. As an appendix, I request your kind permission to turn to Joe's *Theory of Full Employment* (1996), as a *dernier cri*. If I understand him correctly, he proposes a regime of guaranteed full employment without either real or nominal wage cuts. The government would employ on socially-useful projects the 'employable' private-sector rejects, and provide the education and training required to make the 'unemployable' employable next year. The scheme is to be financed at minimal inflationary risk by progressive taxation of business profits and of the incomes and wealths of rich and upper-middle classes. I presume, though I haven't found it in my desultory reading of Joe's manuscript, that wages would rise over time, *pari passu* with average labour productivity, and that this would suffice to keep the John L. Lewis and Arthur Scargill elements of the trade unions reasonably satisfied.

Even in the reactionary Reaganite America of the 1980s, I have run across several proposals something like this, circulating in various intellectual undergrounds. Some are advocated by intelligent laymen, some by 'horny-handed sons of toil', some by self-styled 'intelligentsia' of the university campuses, and some even by economists!

At my advanced age of over 80, I could certainly live under this scheme in the brief period permitted to me, but I would not be so sanguine at age 20. I suspect the ratio of government to private employment would rise quite steadily over time. I would also expect the amount and degree of trade protection in aid of the existing employment structure to rise over time. I would also anticipate chronic divisive conflicts within the heterogeneous labour force about the ratio of skilled-labour to unskilled-labour wages, about the differentials between white-collar and blue-collar workers, about the special problems of the upper and lower extremities of the age range, about 'parity' between traditionally male and traditionally female occupations, and so on. Conflicts more serious than we have now, because of greater centralization of age decisions. But all these are, in John Stuart Mill's words, 'dust in the balance.'

My chief worry at age 20, however, should be the long-term dynamics of proposals like Joe's. To explicate these doubts, I should like this audience to imagine that the revolutions of 1848, nearly 150 years ago, had succeeded to such an extent that Joe's plan had been installed both in the Netherlands of that year and also in such leading industrial countries as Britain, France, and the northern states of the U.S. How, under such conditions, could Holland have progressed from wooden shoes to leather ones, from water transport to road and rail and airplane, from wind-power to internal combustion engines and, yes, from minuet and waltz to rock and roll? (Remember, foreign sources of technical knowledge and know-how, military matters excluded, are cut off both by domestic protectionism and by equivalent 'reforms' abroad.)

Bad as we are, and notwithstanding my fuddy-duddy distaste for rock and roll, I prefer the present to all but the ultra-idealized past. Even more than for the present, I prefer a capitalist, market-dominated future, despite all that future threatens for computer-illiterates like myself. (But my teenage grandson is a 'computer nerd'.) I can even put my pessimism into doggerel verse, parodying a section of Oliver Goldsmith's 'Deserted Village':

Ill fares the laud, in stale stagnation's sway,
The sedentary Civil Service way.

Well, think about it.

3. An Institutionalist Approach to Income Distribution

Warren J. Samuels[1]

1 INTRODUCTION

This autumn marks the forty-second anniversary of my enrolment in and successful completion of the great Martin Bronfenbrenner's wonderful course on income distribution at the University of Wisconsin. Although I have never taught a course on the subject, I have included topics from it in my lectures on the history of economic thought. More important, the subject has never been out of my own thought. I have published several articles directly on the subject (Samuels, 1982, 1985, l991, 1992; see also 1981, Samuels and Kelsey, 1991), two of which I consider among my best, at least my favourite, work (Samuels, 1982 and 1992) (and perhaps would have published more if I had regularly taught a course in the field). Since 1991 I have joined with Joep van der Linden, Y.S. Brenner and Bronfenbrenner in editing the *Journal of Income Distribution*.

Although I have been known as a heterodox/institutional economist, I have been eclectic, borrowing insights and knowledge from all schools of thought. My institutionalism has bothered some mainstream neoclassical economists (though not all who have known me and my work) and my eclecticism has bothered, even severely agitated, some doctrinaire institutionalists. I generally have considered such annoyance to be their problem, not mine. My principal area of work other than the history of economic thought and methodology has been the economic role of government, sometimes called by me the interrelations between legal and economic processes, and more recently the legal-economic nexus. While absorbing some neoclassical and perhaps even some Marxist ideas (though I do not think that attention to power necessarily makes one a Marxist), this work has been principally institutionalist and has included considerations of income and wealth distributions as a central category. The work of A. Allan Schmid and James D. Shaffer and me – along with some by Nicholas

Mercuro, Steven G. Medema and others, including Harry M. Trebing – have constituted something of a Michigan State University tradition in institutionalist law and economics. We have been fully aware that we work in the tradition initiated and carried on by such scholars as Richard T. Ely, John R. Commons, Martin Glaeser, Martin Groves and Edwin Witte, all constituting the venerated University of Wisconsin tradition in the field. In all this work, the question of the distribution of income has never been far from the centre of attention – typified by Richard T. Ely's magisterial two-volume 1914 work, *Property and Contract in their Relation to the Distribution of Wealth.*

In this article I outline one institutional economist's approach to the distribution of income.[2] Several constraints apply: first, I am concerned with functional and not personal distribution, though much of what I say about the former applies to the latter. Second, I largely omit epistemological, empirical (descriptive statistical) and ideological considerations. Third, it is not my intention to present my approach to distribution as either a doctrinaire and exclusive institutionalist approach or a critique of either neoclassical or Marxist theory. My eclectic inclusion of ideas from both schools should be more or less evident. Fourth, I have not tried to address every question ensconced within the field of distribution and of interest to those specializing in the field. Fifth, although much of my work in the field of law and economics – including property, the compensation problem, regulation, public utility regulation, and the legal-economic nexus – relates to distribution, I will bring very little of it to bear on my major theme, that *distribution is a function of institutions, especially law, and institutions are a function of distribution, and thereby of the use of government.* Sixth, it should be evident to anyone who knows my work that I have attempted neither a general theory of institutional economics nor an elaborate institutionalist theory of distribution. The present article is an imperfect substitute for the latter but it is all that my other commitments and to some extent my expertise will permit. Seventh, in some of what I write, but by no means all, the term 'institution' is used synonymously with 'organization'. Eighth, some, but only some, of what I have to say is programmatic.

2 A VIEW OF THE PROBLEM OF DISTRIBUTION IN ECONOMICS

One – but only one – of the motivating forces driving the history of economic thought since at least the eighteenth century has been distribution. It is not surprising that this should have been so. With due regard to the difficulties of historical dating, the eighteenth century witnessed the clear beginnings, at least the clear perception, of modern industrial and commercial capitalism. As the later controversy over the English Corn Laws evidenced, for example, the institutions governing distribution under the old agrarian and manorial post-feudal system were being gradually replaced by new institutions. The middle or business class was gradually replacing or accompanying the landed class at the zenith of the social structure. The controversy between Thomas Robert Malthus and David Ricardo over the proper application of the theory of rent was a microcosm of the grand struggle over distribution which itself was both a proxy and manifestation of the centuries long contest over social system and structure and over the control and use of government relating to the conflicts between classes. Eventually the interests of the landed and non-landed properties coalesced in response to the claims of the working classes and their spokesmen. For all these people, the distribution of income within some social system and structure and some distribution of wealth was critical for their well-being; and the human concern with knowing, explicating and legitimizing their social world increasingly came to focus on issues of distribution, however much distributional issues were obfuscated by the political semantics of the day. It is indeed no wonder that theories of wages, profits, rent, and interest were developed: such theories constituted some or much of the rhetoric deployed in arguments over socioeconomic and political systems, government policy, and class interest. Theories developed for other purposes were brought to bear on questions of distribution and the critique and defence of distributional institutions. Arguments over distribution comprised one part of the vast debates between landed and non-landed property interests and between property and non-property interests over the nature and institutional structure of the economic system. The contest over distribution was one facet of what Joseph Spengler called the problem of order and of the working out of the problem of the organization and control of the economic system; not only one facet, to some extent the driving motivation and surely a proxy for the larger problem of systemic and structural change as a whole.

The history of modern economic thought with regard to distribution, therefore, can be seen as comprised in part of a series of efforts, on the one hand, to provide explanations and legitimations of profit and, on the other hand, to provide different explanations, ones which would cast negative lustre on profits and on those who receive profits.[3] One important aspect is the human tendency to accept a theory which ostensibly correctly describes or explains something as a legitimation of the existence of that which is explained. David Hume may have conclusively demonstrated that 'is' propositions are different from 'ought' propositions and that one cannot derive an 'ought' from an 'is' alone, but throughout the history of modern economic rhetoric, theories of the explanation of profits – and property, and... – have been taken to be and used as justification of the existence of profits, even if perhaps less self-consciously than in earlier epochs.[4] To say, for example, that profit is a return for the successful bearing of uncertainty, is not only to explain but to normatively ground or sanction profits. It is no wonder, then, that in the late nineteenth and twentieth centuries, opponents of labour unions were critical of those who would study labour unions; after all, to study labour unions is to presume that they are worth studying, which further implies some social value, whereas to their opponents no such presumptions were justified. The difference between explanatory theories and analytical proofs, on the one hand, and justificatory theories, on the other, in matters of distribution has been well expressed by Lionel Robbins:

> In this connection, I would like to go out of my way, here and now, to repudiate certain uses to which this analysis has been put. It has sometimes been argued – J.B. Clark is perhaps the chief culprit – that a proof that, under competitive conditions, productive agents are paid according to the value of their marginal physical product is a proof that such a system is just. This of course is a complete *non sequitur*, and one which is a temptation to tendentious usage. Before we can begin to discuss distributive justice in this connection, we must investigate the arrangements – the distribution of property, the accessibility to appropriate training, the availability of appropriate information and so on – which bring it about that a man's marginal product is what it is and not otherwise; and that involves many considerations quite outside the range of the kind of analysis I am discussing. It is to be noted, however, that the leading exponents of this idea, with the exception of von Thünen, have made no such claims. If we take Marshall as providing the *locus classicus* of its prudent application, we find that he definitely goes out of his way to deny that it affords a complete theory of distribution, even in the narrow sense, and throughout puts it in its proper place as a partial explanation of derived demand and as an essential ingredient of the idea of substitution. (1970, pp. 19–20)

Theories of distribution therefore have had at least two coefficients of meaning: one, with regard to their neutral, scientific usefulness; the other, with regard to their serviceability as argument in controversy over government policy. Much the same can be said, of course, with regard, for example, to theories of macroeconomics and John R. Commons's theory of the legal foundations of capitalism.

The importance of this should be obvious. To the extent that the economy is socially constructed, the construction is predicated in part upon some operative definition of reality. Theories of distribution serve to provide a definition of reality useful for the policies through which social construction is deliberatively pursued. So what satisfies the human needs to explain and to justify their arrangements also provides a basis for the social (re-)construction of those arrangements – even, and perhaps most fundamentally, when those arguments are formulated in an absolutist manner. Theories of distribution – both those which are used to defend and those used to criticize present arrangements and results – are part and parcel of these processes.

To say all this, in my view, is decidedly not to say that the pursuit of theories of income distribution has been essentially suspect if not nefarious. It is to say, first, that the quest for 'satisfactory' theories or principles of distribution is very human and very expectable; second, that the theories are socially conditioned; and third, that their use and misuse in argument is also very human and very expectable. Of course, even to talk about these matters either this way or at all is suspect to some people; but that is their problem, not mine.

One final preliminary consideration: the neoclassical treatment of distribution takes place within the conventional neoclassical research protocol. That protocol stipulates the production of unique determinate optimal equilibrium solutions. It is a useful research strategy, especially with regard to its equilibrium analysis, which is a useful technique for working out abstractly the consequences of a change in a variable. The protocol itself has several sources. One is a belief in scientific determinism. Another is the desire for the status of science, with 'science' understood in part as generating unique as well as determinate results. Still another is the desire for social status, a correlative of which is the avoidance of unsafe topics, one of which is distribution. But that research protocol or strategy has analytical limits. One of them is directly pertinent to the institutionalist approach to distribution: it tends to largely avoid consideration of the operative factors and forces which govern resource allocation and distribution insofar as they do not fit neatly into the microeconomic theory of the firm and the household. The problem is that consideration of such factors and forces would challenge the *raison d'être* of producing unique determinate optimal equilibrium solutions by showing and giving effect, for example, to the fact that resource allocation and income distribution are a function of the distribution of wealth and past income distribution, such that there is no unique allocative or distributional solution or that such solution is reached only by ruling certain variables out of analytical bounds. And one key variable thus eliminated and rendered invisible is the inexorable control and use of government for distributional and redistributional purposes. To the extent that neoclassical writers treat that factor at all, as in the case of the rent-seeking literature, it is treated as a common aberration if not abomination rather than, as we will see, a fundamental process. On the other hand, neoclassical practice often diverges from its canonical expression. The actual practices of neoclassicists are broader and more diverse than the conventional research protocol, however much that protocol is its standard expression and badge of scientific honour (see Medema and Samuels, 1996).

3 AN INSTITUTIONALIST VIEW OF DISTRIBUTION

The fundamental institutionalist view of distribution is this: distribution is in part, perhaps a large part, a function of institutions and institutions are in part, perhaps a large part, a function of distribution, in a process of what the institutionalist calls cumulative causation, some Marxists call over-determination, and some others call general equilibrium. Institutions help govern the asset portfolios of individuals, that is, their wealth position. Institutions help form, structure, and operate through markets; if the term 'market' is a metaphor, as has been claimed (correctly, in my view), it is a metaphor for the institutions which make markets what they are and which operate through them. Institutions govern who has access to and can participate in markets and other processes. Institutions govern whose interests will be registered and valorized in markets, in politics, and in other social processes and thereby both enter into price formation and become costs to others (see Samuels and Schmid, 1997). And, to complete the circle, the distributions of income and wealth influence the formation, path dependence and evolution of institutions.

   In order to both understand and place those themes in perspective, one has to appreciate that institutional economists often approach markets and other economic phenomena differently from neoclassical economists. The difference is between the neoclassical conception of pure abstract markets – 'the market' – as utterly devoid of institutional content *and* the institutionalist emphasis on working with actual markets and the institutions which form, structure and operate through them. The difference is also between the neoclassical conception of the economy as an abstract, given a transcendent process in which prereconciled prices operate and in which unique determinate optimum prereconciled, or ergodic (to use Paul Davidson's felicitous term), equilibrium positions are reached; *and* the institutionalist conception of working with actual markets and human behaviour in those markets, that is, through the institutions which form and operate through them, and in which the allocation of resources is worked out. The distinction is between what George Shackle (1967, pp. 293–4) called three levels or worlds of thought. One is the 'world of what we take to be "real" objects, persons, institutions and events'. The second is 'the logical or mathematical construct or machine, a piece of pure reasoning, almost of "pure mathematics", able to exist in its own right of internal coherence, as a system of mere *relations* amongst undefined thought-entities'. The third is that which links 'the real world elements with the undefined entities of the abstract machine'. Much, but not all, of neoclassical economics is of the second type; much, but not all, of institutional economics is of the first type. Terribly underdeveloped is the self-conscious articulation of the third type of theory, the theory which links, for example, the market as a pure thought-entity with real-world markets given effect by real-world institutions and in which real-world people act.

Consider capital markets, the markets on which profit and interest rates, as well as the allocation of resources and growth over time, so much depend and from which they so much emanate. If there are no residential mortgage markets, people do not have access to housing credit. If there are no short-term, long-term, or intermediate-term credit institutions available to farmers, then they lack access to capital. If there are no investment banking and no commercial banking institutions and no security exchanges, then the major institutional modes of marshalling saving and generating new credit are lacking, not available to those who would be eager to invest those funds. If the people who control these institutions – which control is partly, perhaps largely, a function of their position in the distributions of income and wealth – create and manage them in their own interests, then the opportunity sets of others will be adversely affected. The formation of profit and interest would be vastly different.

The specific rules which govern such of these (and other) institutions as do exist, rules which emanate from or through government (often at the behest of the institutions themselves), govern who has access to these institutions and thereby to the funds available for one or another kind of investment. Rules governing insider trading and rules governing red-lining of neighbourhoods channel the allocation of income and the formation of profits and interest.

None of this is, in my view, necessarily or totally inconsistent with various conventional, neoclassical theories of capital markets and/or interest rates. One can accept the idea that interest rates are profoundly influenced, even determined, by the central bank, as well as by the rules just discussed, and still develop and deploy models of interest rates as a function of the demand and supply of money (or loanable funds, or whatever) and/or of IS-LM. These different models are simply useful for different purposes; they explore different, perhaps overlapping and interacting, aspects of interest-rate formation and therefore the formation and distribution of interest income.

In this connection, we should make clear the meaning of a model (and of a theory insofar as it is or approximates a model). A model is a group of variables structured in a particular way to permit analysis of the relationships among the variables. One variable may be the dependent variable, the variable determined in a functional way within the model; the others are the independent or determining variables. MV=PT, the equation of exchange is a model which is a truism. Restructuring it to read P=(MV)/T enables the conversion of a truism to the statement of a model giving voice to the quantity theory of money, in which that which is determined in the price level and it is said to vary directly with the quantity of money and the velocity of money and inversely with the level of transactions. Similar things could be said of Y=C+I+G, and so on, including the technology/institutions dichotomy of Veblen-Ayres institutionalists. No model, and no theory, can cover everything we might want to explain or to answer every question we might want answered on a subject. So it is with all distribution theories. Theories which explore the institutional foundations of interest, profit and wages are not mutually exclusive of theories which explore certain functional relationships among the more or less conventional monetary and fiscal variables. Theories ensconced within covering laws only cover the domain covered by the variables included within the law and only in the way provided for by the theory.

Consider the theory of rent. Define rent as the sum of the supra marginal increments. How rent so defined is distributed depends on the institutions which govern who has a claim to the rent, whatever the claims and the income may be called. Thus, the pure theory of rent developed by Malthus and Ricardo (and others) and the empirical study of the institutions governing the distribution of rent by Richard Jones are two different theories and one can prefer one or the other, but both pertain to the analysis of the formation and distribution of rent. They answer different questions, and while one can prefer one question to the other, both belong within the domain of the theory of rent. One theory explains the formation of rent as the sum of supra marginal returns; the other explains the distribution of that rent among various claimants. Neither theory, properly understood and applied, necessarily justifies either rent in the abstract nor rent in the particular forms which it takes under concrete institutions. (See Samuels, 1992, for details.)

Apropos of the question of justification, we must appreciate that differences exist between theories which describe and/or explain and those which justify, however much the two may be commingled. Theories of distribution inhabit different paradigms of which I have been able to identify three, two of which are normative and justificatory/critical and one of which is strictly positive. Theories with the productivity paradigm and the exploitation paradigm seek to explain and thereby also normatively to legitimize or to condemn, respectively, the generation and distribution of income within capitalist markets. The leading examples of these two paradigms, of course, are the variety of productivity theories and the variety of exploitation theories. But a third type of paradigm encompasses theories which attempt solely to describe and/or explain distribution without passing normative judgement on the distributional results. The leading examples of this type are those of Max Weber, Gustav Kleene, and the institutionalists – though I hasten to add that insofar as some institutionalists criticize the regnant institutions of capitalism as they have developed, they too normatively criticize distribution. (See Samuels, 1982, for details.)

Even among the conventional theories, different theories explain different things. Consider theories of interest. There is the question of what functions interest performs in addition to functional distribution. Among the functions are resource allocation among varying lines in the present and over time; instrument of monetary policy; and so on, in addition to serving as a source of income. Different theories and models of interest address these functions separately and differently. Among the questions relevant to functional distribution are why interest is paid, where interest comes from, and how high the rate of interest will be. Particular different theories of interest address these questions differently: the non-monetary theories, such as productivity, time preference, and monopoly; and the monetary theories, such as the classical saving and investment theory, John Maynard Keynes's liquidity preference theory, Dennis Robertson's loanable funds theory, and the Hicksian IS-LM theory. Straddling both are, for example, Knut Wicksell's combination of the natural rate (productivity of capital) and market rate (supply and demand for money) theories. These different theories and models of interest address the aforementioned questions quite differently. And in all cases, particular theories are used to answer the questions to which they are put quite differently by different writers.

It would be as foolish for an institutionalist to exclude from analysis such other variables as technology, the extent of the market, and the business cycle as to exclude the variables normally considered by mainstream, neoclassical theories. A 'complete' positive theory of distribution, to the extent that such is possible, not to say desirable, must be as wide-ranging as are 'complete' positive theories of resource allocation; the determination of the levels of income, output, employment and prices; and the organization and control of the economic system. Yet even technology, the extent of the market, and business cycles are influenced by institutions, and institutions are in turn influenced by those variables. A 'complete' theory would have to encompass analyses of the intersections, interactions, and aggregated effects of all relevant variables.

Perhaps most fundamental in analytic terms, a 'complete' positive analysis would have to include the dualism that income distribution is in part a function of institutions and that institutions are a function in part of income distribution.

All of which brings me to marginal productivity and bargaining theories (already touched on in the quotation from Robbins), apropos of which I want to make the following points:

1. Properly understood, positive marginal productivity theory only points to a condition of equilibrium: that, under certain (assumed) conditions, in equilibrium the value of the marginal product (or marginal value product) is equal to the wage rate, both being determined simultaneously in the process of adjustment leading to equilibrium. That and no more than that. The theory is trivialized and made to bear more explanatory load than it can properly and conclusively handle when it goes much if at all beyond that. More narrowly defined, marginal productivity theory is a theory only of factor demand.
2. Marginal productivity theory does not guarantee that workers will get the value of their marginal product. Some workers may well receive less and others more. Both the divergence and the opportunity for discretion are approached by efficiency wage theory.
3. Marginal productivity theory is nonoperational and nonpredictive for most purposes in any nontautological way, that is, outside the confines of a model. At best, it tells a story in terms of one category, productivity, rather than others (Samuels, 1982).
4. Bargaining theory, properly understood, points to the possibly skewed structure of the process of what I have called mutual coercion, governed by institutions, including law (see Samuels, 1971). Bargaining theory is trivialized when it is reduced to situations of collective bargaining. Accordingly, '*bargaining* theory' is misnamed. On the one hand, bargaining encompasses many things beyond collective bargaining; on the other, the overwhelming majority of contracts are standardized by one party, with the other prospective party able only to accept or reject (contracts of adhesion).
5. Bargaining theory is nonoperational and nonpredictive for most purposes in any nontautological way, that is, outside the confines of a model.
6. Both marginal productivity and bargaining theories of wage determination are useful in understanding (describing and explaining) distribution. Generally speaking, they concentrate on different variables and different

dependent variables. The use of the two theories, respectively, to attack and to defend labour unions is presently entirely beside the point, for reasons examined above.

The principal negative lesson of the foregoing is that there is no single governing law of distribution. There is no single governing law at the level of distribution as a whole, such as marginal productivity or exploitation, which are either technical matters carried to ideological extremes or pure ideology. There is no single governing law at the level of particular factors of production: no single governing law of wages, of profits, of interest, or, for that matter, of rent. In each case there are a multitude of factors and forces which influence distribution, not least of which are institutions. In each case, if one follows the nonnormative appropriation paradigm, the actual distribution is a function of the unregulated (by any single governing law) meeting of all the operative factors and forces, among which are those constituting and acting in the contest over the economic role of government.

If there is a single explanatory principle (as distinct from a story or paradigm), it has not yet been found. The closest perhaps that explanation has come may well be, cynically or not, in the perception that distribution is a function of power. For example, the distribution of wealth, which is itself a function of law, governs who controls government and thereby the future distributions of wealth and income; money not only speaks, it makes the rules.

A corollary to that negative lesson is that notwithstanding the motivations at work to transfer distribution to the realm of transcendental determination, distribution is a very human matter, something to be worked out; the same is true of institutions. One interesting twist in this regard is the use of theories which purport to render distribution independent of human action coupled with efforts to influence legislation to modify distribution. At any rate, the motivations for such transfer to the realm of transcendental determination are several. They include: ideological absolutist legitimation in the process of social control; the quest for psychic balm, in a sensitive and touchy area, including the desire to believe that one's income is justified; and the belief in and/or longing for a deterministic world.

The principal affirmative lesson of the foregoing is that insofar as distribution is a function of institutions, especially legal arrangements, it is a function of an incredibly wide-ranging array of statutes and court decisions. The story of distribution is in the details and the details include the entire range of government actions. The laws of property, contract, agency, negotiable instruments, business association (corporation, partnership, etc.), money, banking, protective labour legislation, labour relations legislation, consumer protection, environmental legislation, and so on, profoundly influence the formation of markets, the opportunity sets of and interactions among economic actors (including who has access to markets and on what terms) ... and the distributions of income and wealth. One day spent in a law library perusing state and federal court decisions and legislation will give an inkling of these details. Our individualist ideological definition of the world inclines us to think in terms of individual productivity, but what we accomplish takes place within the network of law which both enhances and restricts individual opportunity sets and incomes. These legal foundations/arrangements are not given to mankind but are artifacts socially constructed by man through a process driven in part by distributional and redistributional efforts (however much each is perceived as giving effect to the natural order of economic things).

Following the lead of Frank Knight, who likened the economy to a game, the analogy is with the results of a soccer, rugby, football, baseball or basketball game, which are a function of both what the players do and the rules which govern what they can do and with what effect. It is as if the Super Bowl or World Cup winner each year got to rewrite the rules for the next season to favour its strengths, and get the first draft choice as well. In this context, the performance result called 'distribution' is a function of another performance result called 'institutions' and vice versa. The actually achieved 'Pareto optimal' allocative result is a function in part of – and indeed contributes to – this dual process in which distribution and institutions are mutually determined. Institutions matter and distribution matters. Distributive outcomes, whether explicated in terms of marginal productivity or bargaining theory, are a function of institutions and are not uniquely determined. If the histories of economic thought and economic policy are driven by considerations of distribution, it is no wonder that part of this contest is efforts of various elites and (in the Paretian sense) sub-elites to control government in order to control the making and remaking of the laws which, in both detail and in the aggregate, control the distributions of income and wealth.

All this is what distribution is all about, at least from the perspective of the institutionalist approach. That is what it is all about, as a matter of positive analysis. Because of the fundamental normative importance of distribution, including the immersion of distribution theory in the absolutist legitimation processes of society, taking such an approach seems heretical, but it need not be so seen. Perhaps all economic theory has, at one time or another, been normatively either revolutionary or reactionary. Positive theory, however, should tell it like it is, period, with due regard to problems of selective perception and the hermeneutic circle.

NOTES

1. Warren Samuels is indebted to Jeff Biddle and Steven Medema for helpful comments on an earlier version of the paper.
2. I should like to incorporate by reference the two entries on distribution theory by James Peach in *The Elgar Companion to Institutional and Evolutionary Economics* (Peach, 1994a, 1994b). The literature on institutionalist distribution theory is both substantial and growing; for example, in the same number of the *Journal of Economic Issues* will be found Colander, 1996, Haggerty and Johnson, 1996, and Knoedler, 1996. *Inter alia,* see Brown, 1988.
3. The combination of legitimation and explanation has a long history. It includes, for example, debates over the just price, usury, profit from retail trade, etc., in Scholastic and other pre-classical literature. This is what is meant, in part, by the origins of economics being in moral philosophy. The contest over distribution is an aspect of the larger, perennial problem of order, namely, having to reconcile the forces of continuity and change, freedom and control, and hierarchy and equality – all evident in the oldest known human writings.
4. There may well have been a shift in the conscious (on the part of author's) ratio of explanation to justification/condemnation over time.

REFERENCES

Brown, C. (1988), 'Income Distribution in an Institutional World', in G. Magnum and P. Phillips (eds), *Three Worlds of Labour Economics,* Armonk, NY: M.E. Sharpe, pp. 51–63.

Colander, D. (1996), 'New Institutionalism, Old Institutionalism, and Distribution Theory', in *Journal of Economic Issues,* **30**(6), 433–42.

Haggerty, M. and C. Johnson (1996), 'The Social Construction of the Distribution of Income and Health', in *Journal of Economic Issues,* **30**(6), 525–32.

Knoedler, J. (1996) 'Coordination of Distribution in a Monetary Theory of Production', in *Journal of Economic Issues,* **30**(6), 579–90.

Medema, S.G. and W.J. Samuels (eds) (1996), *Foundations of Research in Economics: How Do Economists Do Economics?,* Brookfield, VT: Edward Elgar.

Peach, J. (1994a), 'Distribution Theory', in *The Elgar Companion to Institutional and Evolutionary Economics,* Brookfield, VT, vol. I, 166–71.

Peach, J. (1994b), 'Distribution Theory, Institutionalist Critique of Neoclassical', in *The Elgar Companion to Institutional and Evolutionary Economics,* Brookfield, VT, vol. I, 171–4.

Robbins, L. (1970), *The Evolution of Modern Economic Theory,* Chicago, IL: Aldine.

Samuels, W.J. (1971), 'Interrelations Between Legal and Economic Processes', in *Journal of Law and Economics,* **14**(10), 435–50.

Samuels, W.J. (1981), 'The Historical Treatment of the Problem of Value Judgments: An Interpretation', in R.A. Solo and C.W. Anderson (eds), *Value Judgment and Income Distribution,* New York: Praeger, pp. 57–69.

Samuels, W.J. (1982), 'A Critique of the Discursive Systems and Foundation Concepts of Distribution Analysis', in *Analyse & Kritik,* **4**(10), 4–12.

Samuels, W.J. (1985), 'The Wage System and the Distribution of Power', in *Forum for Social Economics*, (Fall), 31–41.

Samuels, W.J. (1991), 'An Essay on the Philosophy and Psychodynamics of Income Distribution', in *Journal of Income Distribution*, 1 (Fall), 210–20.

Samuels, W.J. (1992), 'Institutions and Distribution: Ownership and the Identification of Rent', in *Journal of Income Distribution*, 2 (Winter), 125–40.

Samuels, W.J. and T.W. Kelsey (1991), 'Some Fundamental Considerations on the Positive Theory of Income Distribution', in J.T.J.M. van der Linden and W.L.M. Adriaansen (eds), *Post-Keynesian Thought in Perspective*, Groningen: Wolters-Noordhoff, pp. 119–39.

Samuels, W.J. and A.A. Schmid (1997), 'The Concept of Cost in Economics', in W.J. Samuels, *The Economy as a Process of Valuation*, Brookfield, VT: Edward Elgar.

Shackle, G.L.S. (1967), *The Years of High Theory*, New York: Cambridge University Press.

4. Beyond Income Distribution: An Entitlement Systems Approach to the Acquirement Problem

Bas de Gaay Fortman

1 INTRODUCTION

...the distribution of income is a result
of the entire social fabric.
Samuels and Kelsey, 1991, p.135

In orthodox economics income is linked to *productivity*. Hence, the major
focus is *functional* income distribution, that is, the determination of payments
to factors following from their productive employment. Personal income
distribution would follow from individual human beings' command of
factors of production (land, labour, capital and technical and organizational
know-how).

If *homo sapiens* were, indeed, a pure *homo economicus*, would that
creature then be wise to focus all its energy on production and consumption,
merely attempting to maximize profits and satisfaction respectively? This is,
indeed, highly unlikely. In real life, as opposed to the hypothetical world of
neo-classical economics, productive activities do not result automatically in
income as a basis for claiming the goods and services one wants. Agents
would be well advised to continuously keep an eye on the relative strength of
their various claims. Behind income distribution are different claiming
positions that tend to change with processes of production, distribution and
consumption of goods and services. There are no pure economic processes.
Ignoring cultural, legal, political and other factors might lead to serious flaws
in our efforts to interpret reality.

Significantly, behind the same amount of income, we may find entirely
different claiming positions. In terms of socio-economic security $100 earned
by a farmer who owns the land, for example, is structurally worth a lot more
than the $100 of a seasonal agricultural worker. Looking beyond the

29

respective claims, we see different sets of rights and duties which might be typified as *entitlement positions*.

Entitlement is the possibility to make legitimate claims, that is, claims based on rights. It is a function of both law and power. Power means opportunity, actual command. Law legitimises and hence protects in case of dispute.

It is the combination of law and power that makes entitlement such a precious affair. Much more than the occasional claim, the entitlement situation as such is an object of desire. People continuously try to improve their entitlement positions. Hence, more than a given state of affairs, entitlement too, is a *process*. It is part of social processes in society. There is, indeed, always an interrelationship between rights and obligations within a socio-cultural context.

While there may be income without any structural improvement of a person's entitlement position – drawing a winning lot, for instance, or wage earnings in purely temporary employment – the reverse can also obtain. A principal example is the tenured job, fully protected by modern labour law. It provides the employee with access to many facilities and allowances. Formally, a representation allowance, by way of illustration, is not income but it entitles the beneficiary to make representation costs; this improves his entitlement position.

Introducing the qualification *structural* in regard to entitlement positions signifies a need to look beyond what people can acquire on the basis of their current rights and duties. Thus, a closer analysis reveals the operation of entitlement *systems*, that is, regularized arrangements for establishing legitimate claims. It is in their positions in entitlement systems that people find socio-economic *security*.

At this point two relevant distinctions between types of entitlement systems may already be introduced. The first is *formal* as opposed to *informal* entitlement. Informal entitlement prevails in what economists call the informal or hidden economy. The latter term already indicates that the dominant *money metric approach* to measurement of welfare (Hanmer, Pyatt and White, 1996b) faces serious difficulties here. Socio-economic security cannot be assessed, however, while disregarding the informal economy. This is generally realized in regard to Africa, but it also applies to other parts of the world. In the countries of Central and Eastern Europe, for example, the hidden economy is of crucial importance (Ekes, 1994). In formal entitlement positions the legal rules tend to be much clearer. Actual acquirement, however, may be more problematic than in the informal economy whose basic characteristic lies in the lack of restriction by institutional or systemic rules.

The second distinction is between *primary* and *subsidiary* entitlement systems. Subsidiary entitlement means that titles to claim materialize only after failure to acquire on the basis of rights that are operational with immediate effect. One example is social welfare for people who fail to get earnings from labour, another one is food aid. Subsidiary entitlement may be easily affected by the sociopolitical culture as expressed in the spirit of the time (*der Zeitgeist*). Hence, people prefer primary entitlement in the sense of having access to resources and rights to goods and services on the basis of their integration into the community rather than subsidiary entitlement as compensation for their marginalization. In India, for example, the introduction of green revolution technology seriously affected the primary entitlement positions of the weaker groups in the rural areas. Subsidiary entitlement in the form of food coupons distributed by the state could not be regarded as a satisfactory compensation (Ramprasad, 1990). Illustrative, too, is a shift in government thinking about poverty in South Africa: 'Previously the emphasis was on redistribution of incomes ... closing the gap. Now the focus is on more jobs' (SA Institute of Race Relations, in Mogotlane, 1996, p. 3).

It should be clear by now that among the three paradigms within which income distribution theory has been conducted, *productivity*, *exploitation* (Marxist theorising), and *appropriation* (Samuels and Kelsey, 1991, p. 126), the entitlement systems approach relates to the latter. Appropriation theory attempts to find the 'factors actually at work which determine the distribution of income' (ibid.).

Indeed, the focus of this chapter is the problematique that lies beyond income distribution, that is, *the acquirement problem*. The latter expression has been coined by Sen, probably because the more current term 'acquisition' has obtained a different usage. Acquirement is to be understood here as the practice of getting access to the necessary resources and acquiring the goods and services needed. Sen speaks of 'legal channels of acquirement' (Sen, 1987, p. 8). 'The acquirement problem', he states, 'is often neglected not only by non-economists, but also by many economists, including some great ones' (Sen, 1986, p. 5).

Naturally, highlighting the acquirement problem does not imply that existing analyses of income distribution have become useless. Hence, any endeavour towards theoretical innovation should start with a review of the field.

Firstly, I shall assess methods of *describing* personal income distribution. Next, economic *theory* of income distribution will be examined with particular reference to issues of socio-economic security and structural acquirement. The section will be concluded with a brief examination of some relevant policy issues.

A general deficiency in 'orthodox' economics of income distribution appears to be the lack of insight in socio-economic processes at the micro-level. Entitlement systems analysis constitutes a response to the challenge of understanding the dynamics that lie behind human poverty. It is based on an effort to perceive the role of law in society in relation to institutional arrangements.

The significance of entitlement systems analysis will be demonstrated in regard to the problematique of development. Indeed, the entitlements dimension will be shown to provide crucial insight into the different implications of distinctive development strategies and policies. Finally, a concluding section will focus on the test of operationalizing entitlement systems approaches to the acquirement problem.

2 THE STATE OF THE ART

It may be a matter of political economy
as much as economics.
Atkinson, 1996

2.1 The Description of Personal Income Distribution

If orthodox economics implies a major focus on statistics and mathematics, current literature on personal income distribution notably reflects this trend. A first preoccupation is with money as a standard of measurement. There is an abundant range of inequality indices, curves and criteria which all require calculations in pecuniary values.[1] Remarkably, one author, noting that there is no 'best' measure of inequality and hence conclusions based on such concepts remain subject to doubts, then proceeds to study *axiomatic fuzzifications* of inequality measures as well as constructing *confidence intervals for the crisp conclusions of inequality indices.*

Inequality is studied in regard to regions, countries, gender, race, age, one-earner and two-earner households, the employment factor, annual as against life-time earnings, intergenerational and intra-family aspects, etcetera. Studying just the conclusions of all these descriptive and evaluative exercises, one is first struck by a notable degree of difference and disagreement in almost any section of the field. Was or wasn't income inequality increasing during the eighties, in which countries and with which exceptions to the supposed rule?[2]

For the student of development, there is, unfortunately, not much to learn.[3] However, outside the first world we find an interesting study of the distribution of wealth in three villages in Indonesia (Edmundson, 1994), conflicting studies on income distribution in the Asian Tiger countries (for example, Krongkaew, 1994), and relatively much on China.[4] Again, in terms of explanation the studies are rather poor. Indicative is Howes' tautological finding that income inequality in urban China is low compared to other developing countries because the income share of the poor is relatively large and that of the rich relatively small (1993).

A major constraint lies in the unreliability of statistics in developing countries. Moll, in his paper *Mickey Mouse Numbers and Inequality Research in Developing Countries*, stresses this point particularly in regard to research on income distributional issues. He found, for example, that much of the evidence underlying the widely held belief that the distribution of income in Taiwan equalized greatly between 1950 and 1980 is flawed. His conclusion is that economists should be far more concerned about data problems in their research (Moll, 1992). In the light of such problems it is not surprising that I found very little on personal income distribution in Africa. Statistics for SNA (Systems of National Accounting) are hardly available; household surveys are no longer carried out. One exception is an interesting study on Botswana published in two different journals, both in January 1993 (Valentine, 1993a,b). Household surveys were conducted in 1974–75 when agricultural production was at its best and in 1985–86 at a time of severe drought. Rural household real income remained constant, however. This is explained by an income-maintenance strategy made possible through *transfer entitlements* from private and public sources (drought relief). Here at least we find a notion of entitlement and a focus on distribution in kind.

Descriptive exercises are also undertaken in regard to global income inequality. A first problem in this connection is what exactly the statistics tell us. Notably, the United Nations Development Programme (UNDP) in their *Human Development Report (HDR)* of 1992 inform their readers that in global income distribution the ratio between the upper and lower quintiles (each some one billion people plus) may well be 150:1 while the 1996 HDR gives a figure of 60:1.[5] In regard to more reliable statistical studies the question is what the econometrics signify. An application of the Theil index of income inequality to data adjusted for purchasing power parity on 115 countries revealed, for example, a steadily declining worldwide level of intercountry income inequality between 1960 and 1985. A decomposition of the analysis shows, however, that aggregate inequality among regions was dominant as above intra-regional inequality (Levy and Chowdhury, 1994).

Doubtless, however, one major observation remains intact: income inequality is at its highest at the global level.

Naturally, indices and definitions have to be based on fictions and assumptions. Problematic, for example, is the relationship between wealth and income. Thus, SNA income neglects capital gains while computing fictitious income in case of 'own occupied dwellings'. But although the normativity of statistical assumptions, choices for indices and ways of bounding groups is generally acknowledged, conventional economics still shows an almost exclusive tendency towards money metric exercises. Rather typical is the computation of the Gini coefficient, taking a value of 100 per cent if all incomes are received by one person. Should that happen then some sort of distribution in kind would naturally follow, as, for instance, in the case of the patriarchs (Abraham, Isaac and Jacob).[6]

Some forty years ago Tinbergen noted a contrast between 'fairly satisfactory' description of income distribution and 'an unsatisfactory state in the area of interpretation' (Tinbergen, 1956, p. 156). In regard to the first part of this statement one is struck today by a notable decline in the marginal returns of statistical sophistication and a highly unsatisfactory state of data collection in the developing world. But we shall now turn to theory to see if in that realm there has been significant progress.

2.2 Income Distribution Theory

Of the three fields of income distribution theory – functional, categorical and personal income distribution – primary attention still goes to the former: the determinants of payments to factors of production as resulting from their productive employment. The relationship between functional distribution and personal distribution is either 'typically not spelled out' (Atkinson, 1996, pp. 1–2) or simply taken for granted.[7]

In theoretical investigations personal income distribution tends to be treated first and foremost as a macro-economic variable whose behaviour is to be studied in relation to other variables such as GDP, aggregate employment, or some index of inflation. What, for example, is the influence of wealth and income inequalities on inflation (Varoudakis, 1995)? A major concern is, indeed, with the relationship between income distribution and growth, debating Kaldor's model (1956) as against Kuznets' inverted U-shaped pattern of initial increase and subsequent decline in inequality as real incomes rise (1955). Is inequality good or harmful for growth and the other way round?; those are the questions (for example, Adelman, 1995; Beckerman, 1995; Letelier, 1995; Perotti, 1992; Persson and Tabellini, 1994; Sarmiento, 1992). In line with opposite theoretical views, empirical evidence, too, is of a rather conflicting nature. For the United States after World War II Ram found an uninverted U-curve (1991). Falkinger (1994) relates the issue to product diversity, arguing that if productivity grows proportionally to product diversity, an unequal distribution of income will have a positive effect on growth. Persson and Tabellini (1994) have brought the political factor into the analysis, stating, testing and confirming the hypothesis that inequality is harmful for growth particularly in democracies. Clarke submits empirical evidence that inequality is negatively correlated with growth in nondemocracies too (1995).

Related to this debate is the issue of the effects of redistribution through taxation. It is argued that redistribution comes at a cost in aggregate income, but also the opposite view can be found (for example, Hoff and Lyon, 1994).

Naturally, judgements of existing degrees of inequality need criteria. For positivist orthodoxy, Rawls's *Theory of Justice* (1972) with its 'non-ideal' normativity came as a gift from heaven. Thus, the difference principle[8] got its place in the justification of rising inequality. Gallaway and Vedder, for example, argue that the increase in inequality in the United States during the eighties met Rawlsian standards of 'justice as fairness' because the poor did not lose ground but the rich gained more ground than the poor (1993). What is entirely lacking in such analyses is any notion of people's own perceptions: participatory approaches fall beyond the scope of economic orthodoxy.

Of all economists with a reputation in conventional circles it is primarily Jan Tinbergen who showed great concern with inequality in income distribution. Not surprisingly therefore, Atkinson devoted his Tinbergen Lecture for the Royal Netherlands Economic Association to income distribution (1996). Indeed, Tinbergen remains an important theoretician in regard to both the explanation of positive distribution (for example, 1956) and the question of optimal distribution of income (for example, 1992). Atkinson sees his supply-demand explanation of earnings differentials based on a race between technological development and education, as a valuable starting point that needs refinement. (It seems rather illustrative that in income distribution theory refinement of a valuable starting point may have to wait for more than forty years.) In regard to optimal distribution Atkinson focuses on the idea of a basic income (see also Van Parijs, 1992). While in Tinbergen's work the link between normative (optimal) and positive distribution – through studies of mechanisms of redistribution – is not always evident, Atkinson does analyse the practicalities of the basic income, including the politics of the exercise. In that respect his Tinbergen Lecture reveals a slightly heterodox tendency.

2.3 Policy Issues

We touched already upon expressions of concern with positive income distribution. There is a certain degree of apprehension, for example, with the effects of inequality on education and training (Atkinson, 1996, p. 10).[9] Another worry regards employment. Will inequality result in less employment or is there a trade off between unemployment and wage inequality as some of the empirical evidence might seem to reveal (OECD, 1994, part II, P. 2)? In case of more than just a coaccidental correlation could such effects of increasing equality be offset by the creation of more public sector employment (Atkinson, 1996, p. 13)? The issue seems to be of rather marginal importance in relation to the employment question as such. Atkinson's investigation of the sources of the exceptionally large increase in inequality in the UK between 1975 and 1985 suggests that it 'could be decomposed arithmetically into around half due to the rise in earnings dispersion and a half due to the fall in the proportion of families with income from work from 80 per cent to under 70 per cent' (Atkinson, 1996, p. 14). Indeed, the real issue is *jobless growth* rather than just the effects of (in)equality. Not less than 30 per cent of the world's potential labour force is unemployed (ILO, 1996) and hence gets no wage earnings at all, although their acquirement depends on these.

In regard to effects of inequality another issue is social discontent, socio-political stability and its consequences for the politico-economic environment and investment (Alesina and Perotti, 1993). Such concerns encourage enquiries into the effects of certain policies on income distribution. It is rather clear, for example, that privatization correlates with increasing inequality (Alexeev and Kaganovich, 1995; Giariato, 1994; Ruhl, 1993; Szekely, 1995). Other objects of empirical research into correlations pertain to deregulation (Brenner, 1991), commercialization in agriculture (Minami, 1994), trade liberalization as against protectionism (with conflicting evidence for different parts of the world, see Fischer, 1991), the bequest, inheritance and gift structures in private law, structural adjustment programmes (Van der Hoeven and Stewart, 1993; White, 1996), inflation (Silber and Zilberfarb, 1994) and, of course, corruption.

Wong's conclusion that widespread corruption creates severe income distribution problems does not come as much of a surprise (1992). It shows, however, a certain awareness of the acquirement problem in the sense of undue enrichment. Indicative for a growing interest in this problematique is a book entitled *The winner-take-all society: How more and more Americans compete for ever fewer and bigger prizes, encouraging economic waste, income inequality, and an impoverished cultural life* (Frank and Cook, 1995), that describes the development and growth of 'winner-take-all' markets. Siegfried, with different co-authors, set himself to an analysis of 'How Did the Wealthiest Britons Get So Rich'? (Siegfried and Roberts, 1991), 'How Did the Wealthiest Americans Get So Rich?' (Blitz and Siegfried, 1992), and 'How Did the Wealthiest Australians Get So Rich?' (Siegfried and Round, 1994). Key notions are ownership of scarce essential resources, property development, exploitation of market disequilibria and the returns to scarce entrepreneurial and managerial skills.

Naturally, a major concern in terms of policy dilemmas is with the downside of processes of enrichment: exclusion and extreme *impoverishment*.

2.4 The Poverty Problematique

More important than measurement of degrees of inequality in income distribution would seem to be an assessment of poverty. Here, one has to look beyond data generated on production and income and determine their significance for human beings. There is disagreement on the suitability of Gini coefficients as indices of poverty as against Sen's measure of inequality (Chaubey, 1994), for example. The Human Development Report 1997 presents a *Human Poverty Index* (HPI), based on three variables: vulnerability to death at an early age, illiteracy, and a less-than-decent standard of living comprised of a lack of access to health services, safe water and adequate food.

Of great sensitivity is the construction of absolute and relative *income* poverty *lines*, an exercise illustrative of the problem of converting everything into pecuniary values. To enable a clear determination of the number of people deemed to be poor both income in kind and basic needs (for example, calorie needs) first have to be assessed and then transformed into pecuniary values. The measurement of poverty is of course extremely sensitive to the line chosen (Johnson, 1996). In China, for example, the World Bank first raised the poverty line from $ 0.60 to $ 1.00 a day which raised the number of Chinese poor from under 100 million to over 300 million. Next, this poverty assessment lowered estimates of Chinese GDP per person measured on purchasing-power-parity (PPP) basis from $ 2,500 to $ 1,800. 'The world of statistics can often seem faintly unreal', *The Economist* notes (12 October 1996, p. 67). 'But the estimates put out by the World Bank and others matter because they affect the real world.' This is precisely the point. Poverty assessments serve as a basis for anti-poverty policies.

In 1996 the Netherlands government asked a team of economists of the Institute of Social Studies to evaluate twenty five *Poverty Assessments* that the World Bank did on African countries (Hanmer, Pyatt and White, 1996b). The question was: 'what can we learn from these exercises?' One major conclusion of the study is rather disappointing: we can't learn much because there is something fundamentally wrong with those studies. Firstly, 'the various assessments use a bewildering array of poverty measures and it is only occasionally that two assessments use the same measure' (p. 3). But more importantly, the reports get stuck in their money metric approach, producing percentages of poor people that tell 'us more about where the poverty line is drawn than the extent of poverty' (p. 24).

The authors of this study also had to establish the contribution of the World Bank Poverty Assessments to an understanding of the dynamics of poverty in Africa. In this respect the reports had to be considered as being extremely deficient. The basic remedy envisaged is simply economic growth, requiring subsistence farmers to move into the market economy. In the light of evidence suggesting that even in the highly developed economy of the United States macroeconomic growth as such is not an effective anti-poverty tool (Blank, 1991), this is a rather remarkable creed.

To get into a position for proposing anti-poverty measures it is necessary to move beyond the money metric[10] to *socio metric* methods, using participatory approaches to grasp power relations at the household level, including the dynamics of gender, assessing the assets base of the poor and looking into ways in which their rates of return might be increased: 'We conclude that analysis of the asset base of different socio-economic groups has to be combined with an understanding of how social relations effect the returns on ownership of these assets' (Hanmer et al., 1996b, p. 25).

What matters, in other words, is not static measurement of the extent to which an individual may be regarded as poor, but the dynamics of entitlement that lie behind poverty. In terms of policies the challenge is not poverty alleviation or relief but processes of empowerment.

We shall now examine how far entitlement systems analysis might assist in trying to understand socio-economic processes at the micro level. As stated already in the introduction, our attempt will be to look beyond income distribution while assessing the acquirement problematique. It is clear now that economics does have to contribute here – and hence some of the literature reviewed will have to enter into the analyses – but our study must be of an interdisciplinary nature. It is, indeed, a matter of political economy.

3 AN INSTITUTIONAL APPROACH TO ENTITLEMENT AND ACQUIREMENT

> *For I the LORD love law.*
> *I hate robbery and wrongdoing.*
> Isaiah 61: 8a

Life, in an economic-juridical sense, is a matter of making and taking claims. Thus, we may start our working days claiming access to a bicycle or motor car (usually with a little key) or to a train (usually with a ticket). We may then claim access to a building (an office or factory), and so forth. Apart from making such claims, we also have to accept claims. Normally these are undisputed. But in case of dispute people have to show that their claims are *legitimate*, that is, based on entitlement.

Entitlement, as stated in the introduction to this chapter, is a function of both power and law. A right without power is not complete. The owner of a car, for example, becomes rather helpless once her vehicle has been stolen. Of course she may go to the police but as long as the command over her car has not been returned to her, she lacks a means of private transportation. Whether her formal right materializes in the form of realized claims depends on certain additional arrangements (for example, insurance) and the relative strength of law in that society. Illegitimate power does give the possibility to claim but it lacks acceptability within the community one lives in and with that *security*. This is the position of the car thief. One might also think here of situations in which positive law is based purely on legalization of power rather than processes of legitimation. Illustrative is the position of former rulers in the former German Democratic Republic. Living in a separate village for party leaders, their entitlements used to be above question. Six years after reunification, however, they received rather high prison sentences when the Constitutional Court in Karlsruhe ruled that the legal principle *Nulla poena sine praevia lege*[11] rests on the Rule of Law which comprises not just formal but substantial justice. Hence, a person responsible for 'extremes staatliches Unrecht'[12] could refer to the formal law on the basis of which he was acting, only as long as that type of state power actually existed (*Bundesverfassungsgericht*, 24 October 1996, pp. 48–51). Apparently there are processes that can turn legality into illegality.

Entitlements analysis received a strong impetus through the work of Amartya Sen. In his *Poverty and Famines: an Essay on Entitlement and Deprivation* Sen tackles the problem of entitlement in regard to food. He explains some specific cases of famine by pointing at *entitlement failure*, rather than a decline in food availability (Sen, 1988). His further work, too, provides many illustrations of the need to move beyond pure calculations of aggregate economic variables.

Activities focused upon increasing productivity, imply change and change produces conflict in terms of rights and obligations. Entitlements analysis is a way of getting insight into such disputes. To understand this let us first take a juridical look at the acquirement problem.

3.1 Law and Society

In the library of the Harvard Law School an inscription proclaims: *Of law no lesse can be acknowledged than that her seate is the bosom of God* (De Gaay Fortman, 1972, p. 16). Indeed, without law there would certainly be no personal security. Life would be reduced to pure robbery and protection against it, or, in the words of Thomas Hobbes, 'The condition of man ... is a condition of war of everyone against everyone (*Leviathan* I, 4). His *homo homini lupus est*[13] may be seen as a reaction to an adage from Caecilius Statius (219–166 B.C.): *Homo homine deus est si suum officium sciat.*[14] Law is, indeed, a way of making human beings realize their duties.

In situations in which there is no law, economic agents get faced with a dilemma between production and predation. It is interesting to note that even this question has been made subject to economic analysis, studying 'the appropriative interaction between a prey who tries to protect its own resources and a potential predator who tries to appropriate the resources of the prey' (Grossman and Kim, 1994b). In another paper a two-person, two-period economy is constructed in which each person can consume, plant, transfer, or steal corn (Eaton and White, 1991). Circumstances are found in which redistribution of wealth is Pareto optimal and increasing sanctions against theft are not.

Naturally, to protect regularized entitlement more is required than just sanctions on theft. In this connection, reference may be made to North, who stressed that where certain conditions for *path-dependent development* do not obtain, people tend to tune their economic activities towards (re)distribution rather than production (1990). Such redistributive activities may manifest themselves in various different forms, including illegal behaviour. Indeed, the relationship between economic welfare and economic security appears to be quite complex, already in models of a purely theoretical nature (Grossman and Kim, 1994a).

In modern days economic security requires primarily a well functioning state. At this point it may be useful to recall an important task of government in a free market economy, as conceived by Adam Smith: 'the duty of protecting, as far as possible, every member of the society from the injustice or oppression of every other member of it, or the duty of establishing an exact administration of justice' (Smith, 1776, p. 540).

Through *an exact administration of justice* the state guarantees personal security in the sense of freedom from fear of violent attack against one's person or property. It should be realized in this regard that substantive law is only part of the legal system; other elements include procedural law, decision rules, personnel organization and resources (Dror, 1970). Law-declaring, law-enforcing and dispute settlement constitute, furthermore, only part of the regularization of society. Other types of activities may result in the reconstruction or even unmaking of law. As Ghai has noted:

> Law is not self-executing. It may open up possibilities, it may even facilitate changes and trends, but it is an instrument strongly susceptible to manipulation and neutralisation by other forces. To consider that the mere passage of a law has achieved its objectives is seriously to misunderstand the nature of law (1978, p. 123).

Law is, indeed, not a product, in the sense of a given set of rules and given procedures for their enforcement and for dispute settlement, but rather a process (Falk Moore, 1978). Law is not a noun but a verb. It cannot be abstracted from its social context. The decisions people make are not only influenced by law but also by rivalry, social, religious or economic coercion, various types of inducement and collaboration. This is the perceptual background from which we shall now examine processes of implementing rights and duties.

3.2 From Rights to Realized Claims

Rights enable us, among other things, to participate in processes of production, distribution and consumption of goods and services. Economic rights represent 'the abstract acknowledgement of the legitimacy of claims to income and to participation in resource allocation' (Samuels, 1974, p. 118). But the problem with rights is their relativity. One individual's rights are limited by another person's rights. Ownership, for example, is not to be regarded today as an absolute right 'to use and abuse' property but rather as a general presumption of entitlement on the part of the owner. Whether the owner's claims, indeed, will be realized, depends also on other people's interests and the possible protection of these interests through rights.

Behind different rights there are different interests. Rights legitimize claims only in so far as there are corresponding obligations on the part of others to respect these rights. This depends on the relative strengths of the respective rights. In a society that tries to settle conflict through law, the conflicting interests are weighed against one another by some institution or person not part of the conflict, on the basis of norms.

Because of the general uncertainty as to the acceptance of a person's claims Samuels argues that rights cannot be regarded as pre-existing: 'The economic reality is that rights which are protected are rights only because they are protected; they are not protected because they are pre-existing' (Samuels, 1974, pp. 118–19). Here he confuses rights and effectuated claims as becomes further apparent in the sentence: 'Each present right is only one successful claim or expectation among others which did not materialize ...' If, however, a claim does not materialize it does not mean that the person (A) had no (pre-existing) right. There was just something lacking in the conditions necessary for the materialization of his claim. The problem may have been the existence of a conflicting claim by another individual (B) whose right had to take precedence. To say 'that for Alpha to have a right is for Beta to have a nonright, when both are in the same field of action' (Samuels and Kelsey, 1991, p. 134) is a misunderstanding following from American legal positivism.[15]

> Law, as we saw, is a process of continuous change in the way in which human behaviour is ordered through making and applying rules and settling disputes. Inevitably, legal rules are imprecise, requiring a non-mechanical application. This makes it impossible to determine in a normative and predictable manner which types of loss or injury to private persons should be compensated. The compensation problem, in other words, is theoretically insoluble (Samuels, 1974, 1978, 1980).

Legal anthropologists have taken great trouble in trying to describe real types of legal order in terms of different distributions of rights and duties among individuals and groups. Such attempts are, however, bound to be frustrated by the radical indeterminacy of any type of legal order. The actuality of pre-existing rights does not imply a pre-existing legality since, as was pointed out above, one person's rights may collide with another person's rights or with public interests. Hence, Sally Falk Moore has proposed a conceptual framework that takes indeterminacy as the theoretical basis of social, cultural and legal relationships, an indeterminacy which individuals either try to exploit through 'processes of situational adjustment' or try to combat through 'processes of regularization' (Falk Moore, 1983, ch. 7).

Certainly, to have a title by no means implies to get one's rights actually realized. Rights are just *images* of power; to get a concrete claim realized certain action must be taken. Subjective rights, in other words, are generally *action*-oriented. This applies even more to rights of a subsidiary nature. Thus, there are many examples of people in destitute conditions who do not succeed in acquiring the benefits intended for their welfare. Indeed, the problem of non-take-up of benefits is well known in the literature on social welfare.[16]

It is in these dialectics of law and power that people's entitlements get actually determined. We shall now examine various sources of structural possibilities to acquire.

4 ENTITLEMENT SYSTEMS

> *There is no system in which each and every*
> *person decides his or her own wage/income.*
> Samuels and Kelsey, 1991, p. 128.

Sen's approach to the acquirement problem is based on individual entitlement while focusing on ownership:

> In an economy with private ownership and exchange in the form of trade (exchange with others) and production (exchange with nature), E_i [the entitlement set of person i in a given society, in a given situation] can be characterised as depending on two parameters, viz. the *endowment* of the person (the ownership bundle) and the *exchange entitlement mapping* (the function that specifies the set of alternative commodity bundles that the person can command respectively for each endowment bundle). For example, a peasant has his land, labour power, and a few other resources, which together make up his endowment. Starting from that endowment he can produce a bundle of food that will be his. Or, by selling his labour power, he can get a wage and with that buy commodities, including food. Or he can grow some cash crops and sell them to buy food and other commodities. There are many possibilities ... (Sen, 1988, pp. 45–6).

What Sen describes here is the whole field of socioeconomic relations governed by private state law (principally property and contract). He disregards, however, the extent to which social order in society is based on interaction in and among organizations (Falk Moore, 1983, p. 23). Indeed, the acquirement problem cannot be studied satisfactorily without a corporate focus. Individuals are members of various corporate groups. A corporate analysis is necessary to escape 'from the conventional Western juristic categories, which though very useful for some purposes, are more often than not narrowly addressed to a particular kind of property, a particular category of transaction, or a particular category of relationship, rather than to a social milieu in the round' (Falk Moore, 1983, p. 25). A focus on the whole social environment reveals, moreover, that people have not only rights but obligations as well, not only freedom but responsibility.

I discern four different entitlement systems:

1. Direct access to resources
2. Affiliation to institutions
3. Arrangements by the State
4. The international legal order

4.1 Direct Resource-Connected Entitlement

The key-word in entitlement positions which are based on direct access to
resources is the adjective *own*: his own land, her own labour, his own shop,
her own knowledge, etc. Such ownership enables people to engage in
transactions with others on the basis of rights and obligations. Indeed,
property and contract constitute the juridical basis of such entitlement
positions.

Here it is private law, as guaranteed by the state that is to provide security
in the sense of 'the predictive states of mind, the *expectations*, that result
from assurances given by the law of property and contracts' (Karst and
Rosenn, 1975, p. 637). Thus a person who owns a piece of land may expect
to be able to use its produce because society protects property, and a person
who sells something under contract may expect payment because organized
society has provided a regularized means of enforcing contracts. It is the law
that enables individuals to make legitimate claims.

Unlike institutions with a 'real' existence, that is, forming part of reality
whatever their legal status may be, property and contract are not real things
but legal constructions, conceptions created by law. As Bentham has put it:
'Property and law are born together and die together. Before laws were made
there was no property; take away laws and property ceases' (De Gaay
Fortman, 1982b, p. 79).

Private law is based on individual freedom coupled with individual
responsibility. It has developed mechanisms for weighing different interests
against one another on the basis of universal rules which ought to be applied
equally in equal cases. Thus it constructed a law of torts. Where other
people's interests are harmed even an owner may act unlawfully and hence
be condemned to restoration or at least compensation. Yet there remain many
cases of damages without compensation because the action concerned was
not considered to be unlawful (*damnum absque injuria*).

Direct resource-connected entitlement typically relates to a market
economy based on freedom of enterprise and consumption and free exchange
through a system of prices and markets. In such an economy there tends to be
continuous change of which individual A, through the use of his rights, may

benefit more than individual B. Thus, some people may see their wealth growing while others get into a state of poverty. It is not the primary function of private law to correct this. Beside freedom, though, it does accept equality as a legal principle. This takes, first of all, a formal character (both partners in a contract are 'equal' before the law).

Through concepts like 'abuse of law' and 'undue influence' there has also been a growing attention for material inequality in the sense of inequality following from an unequal distribution of power. Principally, however, private law is not particularly well equipped to prevent substantial socioeconomic inequality from arising, nor to tackle the relative poverty resulting from such conditions (Langemeijer, 1970, p. 41). It is, as Anatole France cynically remarked, the majestic equality of all before the law that prohibits the rich and the poor alike to sleep under bridges and to beg on the streets.

The debate in the British parliament in the early nineteenth century on the abolition of slavery presents an interesting example on the dichotomy between private law and public justice. While some members maintained that the masters must be compensated for the loss of their slaves Benjamin Pearson argued that 'he had thought it was the slaves who should have been compensated'. Samuels, who discusses this example in the framework of his analysis of the compensation principle, sees it as an indication 'of the need, in advocating public policy, of an ethical system, of a concept of justice' (Samuels, 1974, p. 126, note 29). Although to some extent a 'socialization' of private law may well take place this type of law remains rather unrelated to social justice (De Gaay Fortman, 1982a, pp. 477–8). Its essence lies in the old Justinian precept *suum cuique tribuere* (giving everyone her due) in the sense of respecting existing rights rather than guaranteeing to people the entitlement that morally should be theirs. Modern systems of private law are of a 'universalist' rather than 'particularistic' nature. It is the market with its impersonal relationships, which calls for rules formulated in such a manner that they can be applied to everybody in a more or less predictable way. In case of dispute the idea is primarily to apply the rules pertaining to the case rather than restoring harmony. It is not so much the two individuals A and B (plaintiff and defendant respectively) but society as a whole that should be able to live with the decision in the case between A and B. Essential is a certain degree of legal security in the sense of predictability of legal decisions. For this purpose disputes are brought to a judiciary whose independence, impartiality and professional competence are considered to be essential. It is one of the tasks of lawyers to assist their clients in such a way that economic relations are embedded in a proper juridical setting. Thus, an adequate functioning of direct resource-connected entitlement in society requires much more than just a set of laws with jurisprudence.

4.2 Institutional Entitlement

As sources of entitlement, institutions may be seen as 'semi-autonomous social fields'. An institution is autonomous in the sense that it possesses its own rule-making capacities, and the means to induce or coerce compliance. It is only *semi*-autonomous as it is part of a larger social matrix which may invade into its autonomy (Falk Moore, 1983, pp. 55–6).

An obvious example of such a *semi-autonomous social field* is the tribe which allocates access to the land together with entitlement to the fruits of its exploitation – usually under the chief's authority – at the same time expecting the fulfilment of various obligations. The (extended) family, too, is an important institution that regulates entitlement. But modern society is full of such institutions as well, taking the form of associations rather than (primordial) communities.

Other institutions in which entitlement may be rooted are political parties, trade unions, schools, universities, sports clubs, churches and other religious organizations. Business organizations, too, tend to function as entitlement subsystems. As was shown already, a job usually means much more than just a transaction in which labour is hired for a certain price (*locatio/conductio operum*). Within enterprises people are likely to acquire substantial and complicated entitlement positions. Socio-economic security – the feeling of being protected against economic threats and risks – is derived from the relationship to such institutions.

While attempts may be made to rule modern institutions as Weberian bureaucracies, dispute settlement within such organizations tends to be of a more *particularistic* nature, that is, it considers an individual's place in the system not so much on the basis of general rules, but according to her own relative authority within the association and the particular nature of the relationships in which she finds herself.

For different categories of people, peasants for example, in a certain area, or workers in a certain industry or people in the informal sector in a certain town, analyses might be made of their entitlement basis. This is, to a large extent, a matter of organizations, their relative power and their external and internal arrangements. In her paper on *Law and social change: the semi-autonomous social field as an appropriate subject of study* Falk Moore presents such an analysis of the production of expensive ready made women's dresses in New York:

The key figures in this part of the dress industry are the allocators of scarce resources, whether these resources are capital, labor, or the opportunity to make money. To all of those in a position to allocate the resources there is a flow of prestations, favors, and contacts, producing secondary gains for individuals in key positions. A whole series of binding customary rules surrounds the giving and exchange of these favors. The industry can be analyzed as a densely interconnected social nexus having many interdependent relationships and exchanges, governed by rules, some of them legal rules, and others not. The essential difference between the legal rules and the others is not in their effectiveness. Both sets are effective. The difference lies in the agency through which ultimate sanctions might be applied. Both the legal and the non-legal rules have similar immediately effective sanctions for violation attached. Business failures can be brought about without the interventions of legal institutions. Clearly, neither effective sanctions nor the capacity to generate binding rules are the monopoly of the state (Falk Moore, 1983, p. 79).

Thus, an analysis of institutions as bases of entitlement and commitment should focus not so much on rules *per se* but rather on the sources of the rules and the sources of effective inducement, coercion and claiming. This appears to be largely a matter of networks and people's position within these. In this respect, *marginalization* may be regarded as a process of outplacing people in the sense of disconnecting them from effective networks.

One institution that does get an increasing attention among economists concerned with income distribution, is the family. Often, the standard of living of individuals does not depend so much on the income they themselves earn as on the total income of the household to which they belong and how the household organizes the use of its income. In the light of intra-household gender relations the term 'organizes' might be seen as a euphemism here. It is, indeed, through gender analysis that the public/ private divide in economic analysis is gradually being broken.

4.3 State-arranged Entitlement

Today, access to health-care, education, police protection and other collective goods is largely regulated by the state. State law produced for this purpose tends to be of an instrumental character in the sense that it is supposed to support and promote policies for collective action. Processes of socio-economic collectivization are based on interdependence within modern economies (De Swaan, 1988, p. 13).

The state not only gives, it also takes, through various forms of taxation. Thus, it rearranges entitlement. Policies for this purpose are, however, not always easily accepted. People may try to circumvent laws by changing the situation on which their treatment by the state was supposed to be based. In reaction to increased taxation, for example, they may attempt lifting up the level of their deductible costs. One might call this *fiscalization* of behaviour. It results in side law (*ius obliquum*) in the sense that not the intended effects of instrumental law but rather *unintended effects* predominate. A similar situation may arise in cases of subsidization. People may try to fall into the category that would entitle them to a subsidy although clearly this subsidy was not intended for the likes of them. As an example we may mention subsidized housing of which persons in higher income categories manage to benefit. The opposite occurs when people in the lower income categories do not succeed in acquiring subsidies intended for their benefit (see note 16).

Indeed the modern state does not restrict itself to provision of collective goods; it also tries to implement policies on income distribution. To this end citizens are classified into different categories entitled to receive support, such as 'minimum incomes' or 'people living below the poverty line'. For administrative purposes such classifications have to be translated into legal categories. For reasons of distributive justice the definition of one social category leads to definitions of other categories that would otherwise get into an unfair position. Thus in the Netherlands in the 1980s thirteen different categories of 'social minima' had been defined. Schaffer speaks in this regard of 'the irony of equity' (Schaffer and Lamb, 1981). A bureaucratic measure in order to achieve equity results itself in new inequity that is corrected with a new bureaucratic measure, etc. Apart from financial problems – a high degree of taxation requires strong government and even then there will be increasing attempts at circumvention – bureaucratization constitutes a major constraint to state-arranged entitlement. There appear to be clear limits to the effectiveness of central administration.

Instrumentalist policies tend to be faced with not just side-effects and attempts to 'circumvent' intended entitlement reductions but also with a simple reluctance to obey the law. Thus, apart from a formal (official) sector and an informal ('circumventing') sector, an evading sector (black market) comes into existence. As a result it becomes rather difficult to analyse, let alone direct, processes of entitlement.

A general problem with state-arranged entitlement is its *subsidiary* nature. Subsidiary entitlement may easily be interpreted as charity. Actually, in practice there are no 'acquired rights' in the sense of a permanent and standing guarantee of entitlement by the state. New notions such as 'deregulation', 'privatization' and 'no nonsense' may result in new policies with direct effects on the entitlement situation of certain categories of people. Indeed, state-arranged entitlement makes people dependent on those who are in a position to use (or manipulate) state-power. This becomes particularly problematical in situations of a *corruptive* nature in the sense that the whole process of declaring and enforcing state-law and settling disputes is misused for purposes other than their public-political aims. Where the distribution and organization of power is of a highly personal nature – networks of patron-client relationships – the introduction of new authority for public officials might merely promote corruption. Corruption, in a general way, may be defined as the misuse of office. In terms of legal sociology it may be regarded as the combination of universalism in theory with particularism in practice. This way of putting things makes clear that some degree of corruption is bound to exist everywhere.

Obviously, state power may be used not merely to establish separate *state-arranged* entitlement systems but also to intervene in entitlement positions in general. To prevent undue intervention in private and corporate entitlement relations, corruption or, worse, tyranny, state power has to be depersonalized. The binding of all power, including that of the state, to law – 'not might but right' – is a first principle of the *Rechtsstaat* (a state ruled by law). Other such principles are democracy in the sense of accountability and substitutability of those executing state power, and a judiciary independent from the executive.

In a *Rechtsstaat* administrative law takes three different forms: law legitimizing the execution of state power, instrumental law aiming at certain policy effects and law guaranteeing the rights of citizens in processes of collective action. Often these three different aspects can be found in the same Statute. As an example we may mention the field of environmental protection. The state should have power in this field, that power ought to be used for certain specified purposes and where it is used there should be guarantees for residents whose entitlement in terms of rights to health and well-being would be affected. Generally, in such an area of public policy, entitlement is arranged through a specification of duties including certain obligations on the part of the state. In a state ruled by law citizens may demand that these be maintained.

4.4 The International Legal Order

National economies get increasingly affected by international economic integration. There are regional as well as global *supra-state* trade arrangements.[17] These have the character of structured interventions in people's entitlement positions – affecting prices, for example – rather than assuming the nature of entitlement systems in their own right.

There still exists a striking dichotomy between economic globalization and the lack of global political control. What *The Economist* noted in 1930 is still true today: 'our achievements on the economic plane of life have outstripped our progress on the political plane to such an extent that our economics and our politics are perpetually falling out of gear with one another' (11 October 1930, p. 652). Conceptually, the foundation of a universal intergovernmental organization for peace and development may, indeed, be characterized as one of the few 'breakthroughs in twentieth century politics, regardless of how successful it has been in practice' (Bassin, 1994, p. 1), but world government remains an illusion. While in a national context processes of social development could correct economic inequality and social imbalance, globally we lack such mechanisms. To global processes of *jobless growth*, for example, there are no global socio-political answers.

Yet, in one respect the international legal order directly affects entitlement positions: *Human Rights*. Human rights constitute a fundamental rights-based protection of human dignity. In a moral sense they are founded upon the general principles of freedom, equality and solidarity (brotherhood). Their specification in the *Universal Declaration of Human Rights* – generally considered as part of international customary law and hence globally binding – as well as various covenants, protocols and conventions of the United Nations may be seen as an attempt to bind power, including the power of the national state, to certain legally defined norms. Both civil and political rights – the 'basic freedoms' – and social and economic rights imply subjective rights and corresponding duties.

A supranational process to guarantee human rights to individuals effectively exists only in Europe. It is true that states are under a general obligation to respect and promote human rights but procedures to enforce their realization by unwilling governments are of a political rather than judicial nature. In terms of individual entitlement people are dependent primarily on specification (particularization) and positivization (transformation into positive law) by the legislative, the executive and the judiciary as institutions of their national state. In that way, as an entitlement system human rights are of another character than the three types of entitlement systems mentioned above: they ought to get their proper place within national state-law.

The dependence on national states in regard to implementation puts those who lack citizenship – refugees, for example, or stateless people – in a particularly weak position to enforce realization of their human rights.

This is not to say that as a source of entitlement human rights are insignificant. Notably, it is not only the state but other institutions as well which may threaten as well as implement human rights. Binding the execution of power to a common (universal) morality of basic human dignity, translated into subjective rights and freedoms that should trump other rights, constitutes the essence of the human rights idea. Wherever power is executed and disputes arise, human rights may influence such processes as well as their outcome. 'The language of human rights', Justice Bhagwati has observed, 'carries great rhetorical force ... At the level of rhetoric, human rights have an image which is both morally compelling and attractively uncompromising' (Bhagwati, 1989, p. 1). It is, particularly, the judiciary which may play an important part in translating this rhetoric into normative decisions. Judges tend to reason in an *evaluative* manner, not so much oriented towards goals but rather towards norms (Graver, 1989, p. 60). They judge facts in the light of set norms while balancing various values against one another (for example, social justice versus economic effectiveness, equity versus legal security). In processes of evaluating different interests in the light of norms human rights may play an important part. In his speech to a human rights seminar in the Caribbean in 1989 Justice Bhagwati cited several cases in which human rights have been positivized by the Indian judiciary (for example, free legal aid for criminal defendants, as a result of interpreting Articles 2 (3)(a) juncto 14 (3)(d) of the International Covenant on Civil and Political Rights).

Judicial activism in the positivization of human rights is possible only where the judiciary is independent, creative and committed to human rights. But even then these rights will not lead to actual entitlement if law does not rule. It appeared to be difficult, for example, to implement the Indian Supreme Court's condemnations of bondage in outlying areas in which feudal landlords rather than the law were in control.

It is indeed in the institutions of society that human rights find their protection. In the area of civil and political rights it is now widely acknowledged that one should not expect their realization in political structures of a dictatorial, let alone tyrannical, nature. But economic and social rights, too, are more than just 'instructions' – whatever, in a juridical way, that may mean – to national states. These rights are not simply a matter of subsidiary arrangements by the state; they may play their part in all processes of entitlement. What is the meaning of a right to food or a right to housing, for example, in relation to property rights? In his *Poverty and Famines* Sen relates how during a famine in Bengal people were starving on the pavement of well-stocked food shops (Sen, 1988, p. 63). Police protection was used here to prevent rather than promote a realization of the right to food.

The meaning of human rights is not just in a vertical relationship between legal subjects and the state; they also have a horizontal significance in the relations between people. What strikes in Sen's example is the apparent passivity, not just of those suffering from entitlement failure but also of government actors and other economic agents concerned. Notably, the human rights idea is more duty-oriented than is often realized; what matters is not just one's own rights but the rights of all these other human beings. This gives these rights a substantial role in processes of entitlement despite their dependence on the state when it comes to particularization and positivization. Through their influence on entitlement human rights necessarily enter even the realm of economics.

Finally, before concluding this section, I wish to emphasize that naturally, these entitlement systems never operate in any pure form. In reality economic agents are faced with mixtures of entitlement subsystems. In our efforts to analyse what is happening to people's entitlement positions in processes of change, it may help, however, to disentangle such subsystems while interpreting each of these in the light of our understanding of the entitlement system to which it shows resemblance. In the next section this will be illustrated in regard to development.

5   ENTITLEMENT AND DEVELOPMENT

> *Do not attempt to do us any more good.*
> *Your good has done us too much harm already!*
> Sheikh Mohammed Abduh (1890)

It is, particularly, in regard to *development* that the relevance of an entitlement systems approach to the acquirement problem manifests itself. This term has the connotation of improvement of a *structural* nature. But what should be structurally improved? We discern three different meanings:

(1)   The development problematique is of an economic nature. Development implies improvement of the *economic structure*, restructuring the economy in such a way that with available resources at least people's basic needs can be satisfied. The challenge is *to increase productivity*.

(2)   The development problematique is of a *macro-political* nature. What should be improved is the *economic order*, that is, the distribution and way of control of economic power. The challenge is *to reduce dependency*, both internationally and within the national economy (a dominant private sector).

(3)   The development problematique is of a *socio-cultural* nature. What should be improved is the *social order*, particularly the opportunities for people to achieve better living conditions through their own

decisions and their own efforts. The challenge is *individual and collective empowerment.*

Clearly, we here have three different interpretations of the acquirement problem under conditions of structural deficiency. Each of these three notions of development will now be reviewed while paying special attention to questions of entitlement.

5.1 Development as Increasing Productivity

In the industrialized countries productivity has increased greatly through division of labour and specialization with technological advancement based on the exploitation of economies of scale. A process of intensification of agriculture, industrialization and urbanization has resulted in significant increases in average living standards. Even when it is conceded that there is no automatic trickling down process ensuring the elimination of poverty, the first challenge in this view remains to increase the cake before trying to share it fairly.

In the Western world this has resulted in a development strategy based on free enterprise, open competition and a market economy. It implies, as was shown above, direct resource-connected entitlement within the framework of a universalist legal system.

In their case book on *Law and Development in Latin America*, Karst and Rosenn show the problems arising with the introduction of a universalist legal system in a society with a predominantly particularistic legal culture (Karst and Rosenn, 1975, pp. 638–9). In Latin America it appears to be difficult for the universalist system to find any proper place at all, since personal connections still tend to triumph over a system of rules. This situation has its roots in the way the rules were introduced and applied in the colonial period. In a study of the colonial heritage of Latin America, Stein and Stein conclude that 'To the elite law became a norm honoured in the breach. To the unprivileged, law was arbitrary and alien, therefore without moral force' (Karst and Rosenn, 1975, p. 701).

The institutional requirements of a market-oriented development strategy should not be underestimated. It implies a general transition from production-based to exchange-based entitlement. This requires a stable currency so that both in calculation and in actual exchange entrepreneurs stand on firm ground. For that purpose a high degree of independency on the part of the Central Bank should be assured. Furthermore, there should be a properly trained and independent judiciary making sure that disputes likely to increase with a transition from a subsistence to an exchange economy are settled in such a way that society can live with it. Of course, the freedom of the market economy cannot be a freedom to reap another person's harvest or to transfer another person's harvest to one's own stores. It is a freedom within the boundaries of the law. In implementing this law, society is more reliant on general respect for law and order than on the establishment of courts and bailiffs. Indeed even the market economy requires much more than just a set of laws; there has to be a mentality of professional honesty and integrity. This applies particularly to book keepers, auditors and managers, who constitute an especially significant group in the market economy.

In terms of entitlement some more problems are likely to arise. Specific attempts to modernize the economy often fail because traditional structures of entitlement have been neglected (Schott, 1981). Where the entitlement structure changes from institution-based to direct resource-based entitlement, processes of marginalization of the weaker members of the community are likely to take place. Generally, as we saw, processes of direct entitlement may result in structurally increasing inequality. People may easily lose their access to land and/or capital goods while getting into the position of 'the unprotected worker' (Harrod, 1987). In Latin America this has been the fate of the indigenous population in processes of agricultural commercialization: from subsistence peasants to subsistence workers. In India the introduction of green revolution technology has seriously affected the entitlement positions of the weaker groups in rural society.

In terms of productivity the subsistence economy suffers from a serious flaw: lack of productivity. Hence, 'to bring subsistence farmers into the market economy' as the World Bank sees it, seems to be a natural development strategy. But subsistence production does mean production-based entitlement, and that eliminates the problem of distribution. It is, indeed, generally accepted today that in reality automatic 'trickling-down processes' do not operate. Seers, for example, has thoroughly explained why GNP can grow rapidly without resulting in any reduction of poverty, unemployment, and inequality, while certain types of growth may actually cause social crises and political upheavals (Seers, 1972, p. 22). In his study of development strategies and the rural poor Saith came to the conclusion that 'if the required employment and food balances are violated, the process of growth in any egalitarian institutional environment is likely to have regressive distributional consequences' (Saith, 1989, p. 43).

With its money metric approach orthodox economics already faces difficulties in just measuring the value of subsistence production and hence subsistence income (Van Heemst, 1984). Consider Usher's shock when he visited Thailand and noticed a major contrast 'between what I saw and what I measured'. He had computed statistics of real national income 'showing people in Thailand to be desperately if not impossibly poor'. What he saw, however, was a people 'obviously enjoying a standard of living well above the bare requirements of subsistence'. He decided to believe his eyes rather than his figures: '... there must be some large and fundamental bias in the way income statistics are compiled ... Something is very wrong with these statistics' (Usher, 1968). Other observations confirm this point (De Gaay Fortman, 1980, pp. 112–13).

It is not just the value of subsistence production that tends to be underestimated but the legal systems in which it is embedded as well. In his paper with the appealing title *Why the 'haves' come out ahead* Galanter has pointed to four factors explaining practical inequality in a society based on the principle of legal equality: the different strategical positions of parties, the role of lawyers, institutional facilities and characteristics of the legal rules themselves. In developing countries those who lost their traditional access to the law while not knowing how to manipulate the legal system will be particularly active in 'lumping' (skipping) the law (Nader and Todd, 1978, p. 8). 'This is done all the time by "claimants" who lack information or access or who knowingly decide gain is too low, cost too high (including psychic cost of litigating where such activity is repugnant)' (Galanter, 1974, pp. 124–5).

Although in a state of continuous marginalization, traditional institution-based entitlement is not always irrelevant. Schott, for one, has given a number of examples of failures in development projects in Ghana due to ignorance of traditional entitlement structures (Schott, 1981). It is important to regard customary sources of law not so much as possible constraints to processes of modernization but rather as guarantees against growing inequality and marginalization. If traditional institutions really have to go, then they should be replaced by new entitlement processes, also rooted in firmly built institutions. Indeed, there appear to be substantially negative consequences of a process of continuous marginalization of traditional (customary) law. On the other hand we do come across situations of what may be called a small capitalistic nature in which peasants use new market opportunities while their entitlement basically remains within the sphere of traditional law (De Gaay Fortman, 1990, p. 240).

With a change in the entitlement structure people have to be made aware of their new rights. (The loss of old rights will be evidently noticed.) A second problem is their access to a new system of settling disputes. Those who often profit from the imposition of centralized universalist law are the legal and paralegal professionals. 'Those who often suffer are the preliterate, the illiterate, the common people closest to urban centres – people whose indigenous systems of law are sabotaged under pressures of modernization' (Nader and Todd, 1978, p. 2).

In developing countries the marginalization of traditional institutions has generally resulted in a vacuum in the sphere of 'meso-structures' or to use a revived expression, 'civil society'. There is a lack of strong, properly functioning institutions in between the macro-bureaucracies of states and giant corporations and the micro-structures of more or less extended families. In development processes in the sense of attempts to increase a country's productive potential, the transition is often from institution-based entitlement to direct resource-based entitlement. To prevent a growing inequality and resulting patterns of poverty, development policy might rather attempt to find transitions from traditional institution-based entitlement to entitlement processes rooted in new institutions. Since institutions cannot be satisfactorily imposed upon people from above; this implies more *participatory* types of development, as will be discussed below (5.3).

5.2 Development as Reducing Dependency

Dependency is viewed primarily in an international context, as 'a situation in which the economy of certain countries is conditioned by the development and expansion of another economy to which the former is subjected' (Dos Santos, 1971, p. 271). Efforts in the seventies to correct this situation by creating a New International Economic Order (NIEO) have not met with much success. Significant changes in the distribution of power are rarely achieved at the conference table. Within the national economies of the newly independent countries a remedy was sometimes sought in control of the dominant sectors (the export oriented enclaves) by the state. Such state-oriented development strategies were regarded as necessary in the struggle against 'neo-colonialism' and 'neo-imperialism'.

In attacking the power of the Transnational Corporations (TNCs) these strategies have not been very successful. Usually, the TNCs could maintain their power (including the possibility of expatriating profits) through management contracts. The creation of state corporations and parastatals did, however, affect processes of entitlement. A new type of institution-based entitlement came into being: membership of the ruling political party or other forms of affiliation to the institutions of the state that entailed special forms of access to collective goods and services and state-connected sources of income.

A state-oriented development strategy may not only transfer a major part of the economy to the collective sector, it may also manifest itself in price manipulation through taxation, subsidies, incomes policies and price control.

For agricultural commodities, prices may be set directly, using monopoly marketing boards. Of course these policies directly affect entitlement. Those who generally benefited from such development policies were mostly the urban consumers; those who suffered tended to be the rural producers. The latter could react by avoiding the law or by 'lumping it'. Where producer prices are subeconomic a lot of produce will tend to be sold in black markets.

Tanzanian land reform after independence presents an interesting example of avoidance of new laws rearranging entitlement. As early as 1962 President Nyerere expressed his concern with freehold tenure:

> The government of the one-party state must go back to the traditional African custom of land-holding. That is to say a member of society will be entitled to a piece of land on condition that he uses it. Unconditional or 'freehold' ownership of land [which leads to speculation and parasitism] must be abolished (in Rosen, 1978, p. 19).

The new policy resulted in a new land law in which title was dependent on appropriate land use, defined to mean cultivation by the fifth year of occupancy of five-eights of the land leased. In order to avoid losing their titles, absentee land-owners now planted long-term crops such as coffee and citrus but then left them untended, thus failing to increase local food production. Under the new law land could still be sold, but with the consent of the government, and Valuation Officers had to establish the value of the improvements. Those officials were, however, also responsible for the collection of transfer taxes. Since these taxes increased with the value of the land, there was a constant tendency to upgrade that value with little regard for actual improvements. Rosen analyses this situation in his review of law as an instrument of development and concludes that:

> ... despite the claim that private ownership would be brought to an end, the rights of Tanzanian landholders probably remain as great after the passage of the new land laws as before. Landholders still have the right to develop their land through the use of wage labor and to sell that land for profit. The new laws may have decreased the farmers' security in the land but their ability to transfer land has changed less than have the procedures for alienating it (Rosen, 1978, pp. 20–1).

The reason for this legal reform was the fear that the continuation of freehold after independence would result in the formation of a class of African landlords. Instead, another elite has emerged: the new bureaucrats (Ergas, 1979).

The problem with public officials in Africa is that their attachment to their office is often in terms of personal entitlement rather than legal and moral obligations. The term 'personal' should not be understood as 'individual' here. These civil servants live in constant awareness of their communal obligations but those are not the same as civil duties (Jackson and Rosberg, 1985, p. 52).

Unfortunately, most African states can be described as marginal in the sense of lacking internal legitimacy. 'The national realm of open, public politics that usually existed for a brief and somewhat artificial period before and immediately after independence has withered and been supplanted by personal power, influence, and intrigue in most sub-Saharan countries' (Jackson and Rosberg, 1985, p. 52). The problem is not just the 'softness' of state institutions but their total lack of relevance except in regard to entitlement for those instrumentally attached to them. Indeed, in societies in which knowing one's rights matters less than knowing one's friends state-oriented strategies for development are bound to fail in terms of both productivity and equity. State power becomes the *dominant social good* in the sense that those who have it 'can command a wide range of other goods' (Walzer, 1983, p. 10). Under such conditions economic development gets seriously hampered while politics takes the form of a fierce fight for state-arranged entitlement positions.

In modern society state-arranged entitlement is, of course, inevitable. A general problem in socio-economic processes involving state-arranged entitlement is, however, that rights and obligations are not as closely connected within the same structures as is usually the case in other entitlement systems. Particularly in the provision of social services a separation of benefits and contributions cannot be avoided. This drawback is likely to be of lesser significance when the supply of collective goods is a result of genuine processes of collective action based on a general awareness among the citizenry that protection against the risks in question is in the public interest (De Swaan, 1988). In developing countries, however, such goods are often imported in the same way in which individual goods get to the local market. While colonial rule meant rather thinly spread administration (Killingray, 1986, p. 413), the marginal state inherited at independence has now got overburdened with tasks for which it never received the proper political, legal, economic, social and cultural equipment. In Africa, this constitutes a major constraint to development.

Where development policies result in undesirable effects on primary entitlement often the reaction is not to rethink development but rather to look for compensation in state-arranged schemes of subsidiary entitlement. With a relatively strong state such schemes may meet with some degree of success (see, for example, Kohli, 1989, on a 'Food for Work Programme' in West

Bengal) but marginal states are bound to fail in achieving both efficiency and equity in this way.

In reaction to the marginality of some states in developing countries two different tendencies may be observed. The first is a 'structural adjustment programme' as requested by international financial institutions such as the World Bank and the International Monetary Fund. Deregulation and privatization, however, require not a soft but a strong state, as experience in Western industrialized countries has demonstrated. This is less paradoxical than at first sight it might seem to be since, as was already observed, a market-oriented development strategy implies a number of important institutional demands. If deregulation is simply regarded as a return to nineteenth century capitalist *Gesellschaft*-types of law it would merely 'help to legitimate a legal order based on social and economic inequality' (Hepple, 1988, p. 165).

A second type of reaction to the paradox of the overburdened marginal state has been the replacement of state-arranged entitlement by new frameworks administered by non-governmental development organizations. The snag here has been noticed by Saith, in relation to rural poverty:

> Arising from an increasing awareness of the inability of the official delivery systems to reach the poor, who have virtually no representation in them, there has been a general drift towards reliance on the institutional form of the non-governmental development organisation as a device for affecting this transfer of official or other resources. Bootstrap operations and self-help schemes abound and are intended to provide an appropriate institutional framework for generating a reoriented pattern of development. However, these schemes even collectively constitute a very minor change ... In addition, virtually all such NGDOs carefully circumvent most structural issues to do with the organisation of labour as a collective countervailing force, or to do with access to laws (Saith, 1989, p. 53).

Although the last observation might be regarded as an exaggeration, Saith certainly has a point here. Where processes of entitlement require collective action for the provision of collective goods, NGDOs tend to be poor substitutes for state institutions. Often the sphere in which they operate is one of particularism, with power rooted in relations to foreign donors rather than in social relations directly involving the 'target groups'. The typical role for NGDOs is in the construction of civil society (the 'meso-structures') in an economy in which division of labour, specialization and exchange gradually take the place of subsistence production. Thus they would, indeed, contribute to institution-building albeit of a different nature than in the provision of collective goods and services.

Non-governmental organizations cannot solve the problem of dependency where national states are weak, nor can they replace the state in its function as guardian of personal security (Rothschild, 1995, p. 80). Effective supranational authorities based on processes of not only economic but also political integration could. But for most developing countries such institutions have not yet been formed. Hence, the decline and fall of marginal states remains a cause for concern.

5.3 Development as Empowerment

In socio-economic policies three different notions of poverty may be discerned. First, poverty is regarded as *abnormality*, as a deviation from the 'normal' pattern, as a disturbance of law and order. Hence, poverty would have to be isolated from the rest of society. The poor are the rebels, actual or at least potential. In former ages this view resulted in the construction of 'poor-houses' or 'work-houses', where the poor were being forced to work. Today we may think of certain suburbs or shanty-towns that have got the character of ghettos. Because these places cannot be completely cut off, the rich feel they also have to isolate their wealth from the poor by big walls, dogs and guards. On an international level this is done by a rigorous visa policy combined with a thorough protection of the borders ('fortress Europe').

A second way of looking at poverty is to regard it as *need*. The poor are the needy, the destitute. They should be helped. Of course, they should themselves cooperate in the process of 'aid to the poor'. Thus, poor people should concentrate on their basic family needs. In the thirties, in England for example, this view led to quite some discussion on the question of what poor people really needed. Naturally, the first change in their own consumption pattern should be to avoid pubs. Beer is not good, but also newspapers are not really necessary, and what about birthday presents? Some relief workers felt these should also be avoided, others regarded birthday celebrations as part of basic needs.

The point is that in this second view poverty is regarded as a phenomenon of an absolute nature. Why do we sometimes see television antennae in slum areas with undernourished children? Because television is part of modern society and needs are of a social rather than individual nature. This insight results in a third way of viewing poverty: as *social injustice*, as a consequence of socio-economic exploitation and, in a modern context, *exclusion*. Indeed, processes of exclusion of some groups of people – as manifesting themselves at practically all levels: the labour market, education, health etc. – are not unrelated to processes of advancement. As Elliott has argued, 'both exclusion and downward mobility, which are no more than the processes of relative and absolute impoverishment, are most frequently the reverse image of the enrichment of another group' (quoted by Gore, 1994, p. 14).

Thus, poverty is primarily relative, rather than absolute. The poor are victims of unequal patterns of distribution of power. Poverty, basically, is a matter of inadequate positions in entitlement systems. An unequal distribution of power is rarely corrected from above, as a kind of favour. It can be rectified only through *emancipation* of the poor themselves or, in other words, 'development from below'.

Indeed, law often has to be seen as a constraint to efforts towards *inclusion* rather than as a resource for the poor. *Laws grind the poor and rich men make the law*, goes a 17th century song quoted by Hill (1995). Indeed, Sen concludes from his analysis of famine that 'The law stands between food availability and food entitlement'. It has led him to work on *strategies of entitlement protection* (Drèze and Sen, 1989). The question is, indeed, whether, in the words of Keynes, men should always die quietly? He believed not: 'For starvation, which brings to some lethargy and helpless despair, drives other temperaments to the nervous instability of hysteria and to a mad despair' (Keynes, 1920, p. 213). Illustrative in this connection is the old Dutch parable of the 'beggarman' and the 'nobleman'.[18]

Entitlement, it may be recalled, is a matter of both power and rights. Since power is unlikely to be properly distributed from above, it has to be acquired from below, through cooperative action by those who lack entitlement. Karst and Rosenn's discussion of Bolivian land reform in 1952–53 is entitled *Land Reform First, Then Law*. 'Effective land reform in Bolivia occurred when the *campesinos* occupied the great estates, ejecting both owners and administrative foremen' (Karst and Rosenn, 1975, p. 650). This land reform was followed by a great deal of legal activity arising out of the peasants' desire to stabilize the situation by acquiring proper titles. In Latin America this is still a prevailing 'development' strategy among the poor. Thus, in 1996 some hundreds of people illegally occupied land as squatters in São Paulo and started an (in the end successful) struggle to get their titles recognized.

Thus, emancipation-oriented strategies for development primarily aim at social rather than legal change. For those involved in 'self-help' action against positive law it is important that they can base themselves upon a universally accepted morality. It is here that human rights may play an important part, especially social and economic rights such as the rights to work, food, health, education, clothing and housing.

In Roman law we find a specification of an economic right in the rule 'Nemo de domo sua extrahi debet' (Nobody should be ejected from his own house). Acceptance of the right of squatters to occupy a building kept empty for purposes of speculation, such as has become legal practice in the Netherlands, goes a great deal further in positivization of a right to housing. Thus, economic and social rights may have an impact beyond the policies of the state while influencing social and economic relations among people. This is termed their 'horizontal operation'.[19]

A first step in any entitlement-oriented development strategy remains *conscientization* in the sense of promoting people's awareness of their human rights. But the real challenge is to build institutions in which realization of these rights finds its guarantees, in the first place through unionization of the poor. Empowerment requires a thorough grounding of entitlement in well-functioning institutions. Development appears to be indeed, first and foremost, a matter of institution-building and institution-strengthening. In the first period of development cooperation – the fifties and sixties – this view used to have a certain influence on policies of international agencies such as the World Bank. During the later seventies and the eighties 'no-nonsense politics', 'the new realism' and 'supply-side economics' resulted in significant changes in development policies. Entitlement analysis may support a return of development policy to its core: *institution-building*.

6 THE CHALLENGE OF OPERATIONALIZATION

> *What we cannot formalize,*
> *we simply do not see.*
> P. Krugman (1996)

In development policy the three different views on development as described above are found in various mixtures, although development as empowerment of people ('alternative development') has never been at the forefront. But since the eighties, the major focus is clearly on productivity. Etatist development collapsed in 1989 together with the Berlin wall. It has also increasingly been realized that plan and market cannot be mixed in the same way in which a woman, in Marx's metaphor, cannot be a bit pregnant. Thus, we also saw a collapse of confidence in the parastatal enterprise. While naturally a market sector of the economy can coexist with a state sector – the so-called *mixed economy* which is the prevailing type of economic order everywhere – it is not very helpful to attempt integrating market elements into the planning system or vice-versa.

Yet, evidence such as brought forward in this chapter also suggests that growth, even if structural, is not the right instrument to attack and prevent poverty. It is particularly in two major areas of policy that we notice fundamental deficiencies of a purely productivity oriented development strategy: structural adjustment and transition.

The first, then, is structural adjustment. Its effects in regard to poverty were already mentioned above. Elson examined structural adjustment models theoretically from one particular entitlements perspective, *viz.* gender. She concludes that these models, besides having closed their eyes to gender, are also blind to everything else beyond their macroeconomic perspective (1995). Hence, not without reason UNICEF has advocated qualifying structural adjustment programmes *with a human face*. In practice this leads merely to policies of a remedying nature, rather than a fundamental change of the model itself.

The second area in which pure growth-oriented strategy meets with obvious drawbacks is transition. A radical transition from centralist socialism to a market-oriented economy was in itself inevitable. But, while there is no workable substitute for *markets* as a system for coordinating production, distribution and consumption of goods and services, one should realize that it is not markets which are delivering output; markets just set the rewards for productive activities (Maital and Milner, 1993). Taking the transition process in Russia as an example here, neither Yeltsin nor Gorbachev, seemed 'to appreciate that increasing economic efficiency is merely a means to an end, and that end should be an improved standard of living for the average Russian citizen. Successful economic reform requires more than closing down unproductive factories' (Lapidus, Zaslavsky, Goldman, 1992, p. 76).

The first three years of reforms in Russia resulted in a process of mass impoverishment that brought the share of the population with an aggregate per capita income below the officially set subsistence minimum to about 30 per cent, of which 5 per cent starving (Tchernina, 1995, p. 131). This frightful trend of *reverse development* still persists. What went wrong? 'It was a mistake to plunge head down into the water, as we did in January 1992', commented Prime Minister Chernomirdyn on the preference for authoritarianism expressed by the Russian voters in the parliamentary elections of December 1993. 'Where in the reform programme do we find the human being?', wondered Tatiana Zaslavskaya, a sociologist who criticized the Soviet economic system in a famous report of 1983. Reforms in Russia have failed so far because people were unprepared for them, because they were imposed from above, because there was no integrated approach to the economic, political, legal, social, cultural and psychological aspects of transition and because they lacked subtility and graduality (De Gaay Fortman and Tarifa, 1995).

It is held here that an entitlement systems approach to the challenges of transition would have prevented two major mistakes. The first difference is that its focus on the human being would have resulted in a more gradual implementation of reforms. The point is that liberalization not just sets the stage for the market but also causes a major shock to the operation of entitlement systems: from state-arranged to direct resource-connected. The second error is a failure to properly assess the nature of institutions. The state under centralized socialism is entirely different from the capitalist state. Here we touch upon a basic mistake in transition processes from a centralized command economy to a free market system. In real existing socialism, the idea is that there is already a state, but it is just too big. What is needed beyond liberalization of trade and finance is deregulation and privatization. But even in the already functioning market economies deregulation means in effect re-regulation. As Hepple has observed:

> The common future of the modern trends to deregulation is not that state intervention is made to disappear so as to revive a lost ideal of the 'pre-intervention' state. It is rather that the priorities of an interventionist state, and its methods have been changed. Instead of giving priority to state policies such as the protection of tenants or of individual employees, the overall objective of the state has been redefined as being the *revitalisation* of the profit-based market economy. Business men and others are being freed from legal responsibilities which might prevent them from responding effectively to changes in the market. The return to markets of freely contracting individuals responding to the price mechanism (generally on the basis of private ownership) does not mean an absence of legal intervention. On the contrary, it means an unprecedented increase in the regulation of society by the mechanisms of private law (1988, pp. 165-6).

In fact, deregulation without re-regulation and privatization without ensuring competition just meant enrichment of a very small number of people and impoverishment for the rest.

So the challenge remains to put the entitlement systems approach in practice. Operationalization appears to be rather problematical, however, as becomes apparent in failures to implement combined strategies of growth (of productivity) *and* redistribution. It should be noted here that redistribution is usually regarded as a matter of correcting the outcome of the economic process as it would have taken place without intervention. It is, in other words, seen as a matter of justice in the sense that an intolerable outcome of the economic process should be accommodated through corrective mechanisms. In practice, however, this appears not to be easy. In Brazil, for example, a development strategy based on three stages – first *productivismo*, then *redistributivismo*, and finally *desenvolvimento social* – always kept stuck in the first phase (De Gaay Fortman, 1981, p. 106). The 'relative and absolute impoverishment induced by the increase in productivity', as she saw it, provoked Irma Adelman to a strategy of *redistribution before growth* (Adelman, 1979). But politically a programme of land reform, for example, before any major development in the agricultural sector appears not to be easy. The same applies to *redistribution with growth*, as advocated by Jolly (1975).

The point is that any focus on the acquirement problem implies a *qualification* of growth. Policies for increasing productivity have to be checked right from the start on their entitlement effects. But how to convince economists, and with them politicians, that an entitlement systems approach has to become operational?

Orthodox economics, as we know, understands only one language: mathematics. Krugman, for example, recognized the need for a translation of his theory on economies of scale through construction of mathematical models based on all sorts of bold assumptions. This has been successful in the sense that it is now widely realized that 'the production of goods and services tends to take place under conditions of economies of scale' (Hilhorst, 1996, p. 1). Sen's effort to start similar exercises for entitlements analysis (F_j, as maximum food entitlement of group j, given by q_jp_j/p_f, etc., Sen, 1988, p. 50) may have helped to legitimize entitlement among our orthodox colleagues. However, Gasper is right when he observes that entitlements theory is not a causal model (1993, p. 709), and hence it should not be presented as such.

Although we may make progress in a further systematization of entitlements analysis, we should realize that the approach will have to remain, in essence, qualitative. (As is true for ecological approaches, no matter how much advance is made in exercises like green accounting.) Entitlements analysis requires a sociometric approach based on participatory methods of finding out what is happening in the life of human beings.

Such analysis is, however, not something new. In development policies gender effects, for example, are checked more and more in advance, and the same applies to environmental effects. More generally oriented entitlements analysis could learn here.

Thus, the challenge remains to move forward towards analyses that look beyond money values and even income distribution, interpreting costs and benefits in a wider normative sense as affecting the full human being and the communities in which she lives.

NOTES

1. In my perusal of publications between 1991 and 1996 I touched upon E- or S-Gini indices, second degree stochastic dominance in comparing income distributions (the Lorenz criterion) or, as a 'Rawlsian extension' of that normative criterion, third degree stochastic dominance (Davies and Hoy, 1994), Lorenz and Engel curves, Theil decomposable indices for inter-country comparisons, transfigurations from nominal to real income inequality by using Laspeyres type price indices (Ruiz-Castillo, 1994), lognormal extrapolations and income estimations (Cloutier, 1995), different views on grouping bounds, notes on intra-quintile and intra-decile inequality, Atkinson indices of racial income inequality (Conrad, 1993), a Lorenz ordering of Singh-Maddala income distributions (Wilfling and Kramer, 1993) and so on and so forth.

2. Typical is an exploration of the following question concerning income distribution in the United States: 'How much of the increase in income inequality between 1992 and 1993 was due to changes in the economy and how much was due to technical changes in the Current Population Survey?' (Ryscavage, 1995). The real question is of course: what happened to the personal distribution of income, by what causes and with which effects? The studies incline, however, towards pure descriptions and even then conclusions are rarely firm and doubts persist. One pretty strong piece of evidence is on sharply increasing household wealth inequality in the United States between 1983 and 1989 (Wolff, 1994). Naturally, the years of such an analysis are determined by household surveys.

3. Illustrative is a paper in the *Journal of Economics* which, based on consumption models with a permanent income hypothesis, finds a positive effect of increasing inequality on the consumption of motor vehicles and parts and services but a very small negative effect on the consumption of other goods (Fitzsimmons and German, 1995).

4. After an initial movement towards more equality in the first stage of the Chinese economic reform programme, apparently inequality in the distribution of rural income in China was later rising (Chai and Chai, 1994). By 1988 it was about as unequal as in India (Khan, 1993) while in housing asset holdings the wealthiest rural quintile owned 6.5 times as much as as the bottom quintile (McKinley and Wang, 1992).

5. The figure in the 1992 HDR is an estimate based on correction of a figure that places the richest 20 per cent in the richest countries and the poorest 20 per cent in the poorest countries (34–36). The computations in the 1996 HDR are based on uncorrected data (13). The report emphasizes the *rise* in global inequality:

    > Between 1960 and 1991 the share of the world's richest 20 per cent rose from 70 per cent of global income to 85 per cent – while that of the poorest declined from 2.3 per cent to 1.4 per cent. So, the ratio of the shares of the richest and the poorest increased from 30:1 to 61:1. All but the richest quintile saw their income share fall, so that by 1991 more than 85 per cent of the world's population received only 15 per cent of its income – yet another indication of an even more polarized world.

    The 1997 HDR gives a figure of 78:1, calculated upon the same basis as the 61:1 in 1996. It should be noted that all figures mentioned in this note are based on uncorrected US$. Corrections for PPP (Purchasing Power Parity) would probably lead to reductions in statistical disparities.

6. Exceptions to the money metric approach can be found in the *Journal of Income Distribution* and the *Review of Income and Wealth*. Highly interesting, for example, is a paper entitled *Is Money the Measure of Welfare in Russia?* that stresses the role of non-monetized resources under real existing socialism as opposed to a market economy (Rose and McAllister, 1996).

7. 'Once prices and quantities are known, one's personal income is the product of the price vector and one's vector of factor services' (Odink, 1992, p. 141).

8. The 'difference principle' stipulates that inequalities can be tolerated only if they are to the greatest benefit of the least advantaged members of society.

9. Reflecting the situation in the author's homeland Argentina, a theoretical model has been constructed to show that 'poor' people do not go to school, 'middle income' people attend public educational institutions and 'rich' people opt for private schools (Gasparini, 1994).

10. Critics of the money metric approach to poverty sometimes refer to the 'golden triangle' of field research of this nature, with the three lines running between the Office of the UN Resident Representative, the Ministry of Finance and the Intercontinental hotel.

11. No punishment without previous legislation.

12. Extreme injustice committed under state authority.

13. Man is to man a wolf.

14. Man is to man a god when he recognizes his duty.

15. Samuels' view comes down to the belief that all subjective rights are merely fictions. This view was taken by Bentham who stated:

> The word right is the name of a fictitious entity: one of those objects, the existence of which is feigned for the purpose of discourse, by a fiction so necessary that without it human discourse could not be carried on. A man is said to have it, to hold it, to possess it, to acquire it, to lose it. It is thus spoken of as if it were a portion of matter such as a man may take into his hand, keep it for a time and let it go again (as quoted in Olivier, 1973, p. 50).

Today this view is taken by legal positivists, who refuse to discuss law in normative terms.

16. A citizen who wishes to make use of her rights to a subsidy or welfare allowance has to cross at least five different barriers:

1. She should know that there is such a scheme.
2. She should know where to get information about that scheme.
3. She should overcome any embarrassment in collecting the information.
4. She should be able to understand the information (the brochure) and to apply that to her own situation.
5. She should fill in the forms while going through the whole bureaucratic procedure.

One particular cause of trouble arises during the moment of applying. In an investigation into take-up of benefits in the Netherlands, Filet found that no less than 30 per cent of the respondents were of the opinion that they had submitted a formal request for social welfare while the civil servants concerned felt they had just supplied information (quoted in Van Oorschot, 1989, p. 9).

17. In a previous working paper (De Gaay Fortman, 1990) I confined this discussion to global human rights. It was Chris Kortekaas who drew my attention to *supra-state* arrangements affecting entitlements (see De Gaay Fortman and Kortekaas, 1996).

18. While passing the nobleman's land the beggarman asks him: 'Whose is this land?' 'It is mine', is the answer. 'And how did you get it?', the beggarman continues to ask. 'Well, I inherited it from my father'. 'And how did he get it?' 'Well, he inherited it from my grandfather'. 'And he?' 'From my great-grandfather', is the answer. 'And he?' So they go on and on until they come to a great-great-....-great-grandfather who lived in the middle ages. Here the nobleman has to reply: 'He fought for it!' 'Ah', says the beggarman, 'shall we fight for it again?'

19. For a horizontal functioning of social and economic rights, those who claim on the basis of these rights clearly have to take action. Through action first, and acquiescence to the new situation later, a pre-existing illegality may be turned into legality.

REFERENCES

Abduh, Sheikh Mohammed (1890), *An Egyptian in London*, London.

Adelman, I. (1979), 'Redistribution before Growth – a Strategy for Developing Countries', in *Development of Societies: The Next Twenty Five Years. Proceedings of the ISS 25th Anniversary Conference*, The Hague: Martinus Nijhoff.

Adelman, I. (1995), 'Dynamics and Income distribution: The selected essays of Irma Adelman. Volume 2', in *Economists of the Twentieth Century Series,* Aldershot: Elgar.

Alesina, A. and R. Perotti (1993), 'Income Distribution, Political Instability, and Investment', *NBER*, Working Paper no. 4486, Harvard University.

Alexeev, M. and M. Kaganovich (1995), 'Distributional Constraints on the Speed of Privatization', in *Economic Letters*, **48**(2), 212–219.

Almond, G.A. and S. Verba (eds) (1989), *The Civic Culture Revisited,* London: Sage.

Altimir, O. (1994), 'Income Distribution and Poverty through Crisis and Adjustment', in *Cepal Review*, (52), 7–31.

Atkinson, A.B. (1996), 'The Distribution of Income: Evidence, theories and Policy', in *De Economist*, **144**(1), 1–21.

Barret, G. and K. Pendakur (1995), 'The Asymptotic Distribution of the Generalized Gini Indices of Inequality', in *Canadian Journal of Economics*, **28**(4b), 1042–55.

Bassin, B. (1994), 'What Role for the United Nations in World Economic and Social Development?', in *Paper for UNDP Stockholm Roundtable on Global Change* (22–24 July).

Beckerman, W. (1995), 'Growth, the environment and the distribution of incomes: Essays by a sceptical optimist', in *Economists of the Twentieth Century Series*, Aldershot: Elgar.

Bernhardt, R. and J.A. Jolowicz (1987), *International Enforcement of Human Rights*. Berlin: Springer Verlag.

Berry, A., F. Bourguignon and M. Francois (1991), 'Global Economic Inequality and Its Trend since 1950', in Osberg's (ed.), *Economic inequality and poverty: International perpectives*, Armonk: Sharpe, pp. 60–91.

Beukes, E.P. and F.C.v.N. Fourie (1988), 'Economic Rights in a Charter of Human Rights in South Africa?', in *The South African Journal of Economics*, **56**(4), 298–316.

Bhagwati, P.N. (1989), 'Address to the Caribbean, Human Rights Seminar', Jamaica, September 1989 (not published).

Biesheuvel, M.B.W. and C. Flinterman (eds) (1983), *De rechten van de mens*, Amsterdam: Meulenhoff Informatief.

Blank, R. (1991), 'Why were Poverty Rates so High in the 1980s?', *National Bureau of Economic Research*, Working Paper: 3878, October.

Blitz, R. and J. Siegfried (1992), 'How Did the Wealthiest Americans Get So Rich?', in *Quarterly Review of Economics and Finance*, **32**(1), 5–26.

Brenner, J.S. and J.P.G. Reijnders (1991), 'Income Distribution and Economic Theory. A Comment on Samuels and Kelsey', in W.L.M. Adriaansen and J.T.J.M. van der Linden (eds), *Post-Keynesian Thought In Perspective*, Groningen: Wolters Noordhoff, pp. 147–52.

Brenner, Y. (1991), 'Deregulation and the Principle of Distribution', in *Journal of Income Distribution*, **1**(1), 4–45.

Burkens, M.C. (1989), *Algemene leerstukken van grondrechten naar Nederlands Constitutioneel recht*, Zwolle: Tjeenk Willink.

Chai, J. and K. Chai (1994), 'Economic Reforms and Inequality in China', in *Rivista Internazionale di Scienze Economiche Commerciali*, **41**(8), 675–96.

Chan, K. (1996), 'The Voluntary Provision of Public Goods under Varying Income Distributions', in *Canadian Journal of Economics*, **29**(1), 54–69.

Chaubey, P.K. (1994), 'Measurement of Poverty: Takayama Index Reconsidered', in *Journal of Quantitative Economics*, **10**(1), 191–8.

Clarke, G. (1995), 'More Evidence in Income Distribution and Growth', in *Journal of Development Economics*, **47**(2), 403–27.

Cloutier, N. (1995), 'Lognormal Extrapolation and Income Estimation for Poor Black Families', in *Journal of Regional Science*, **35**(1), 165–71.

Conrad, C. (1993), 'A Different Approach to the Measurement of Income Inequality', in *Review of the Black Political Economy*, **22**(1), 19–31.

Cowell, F. and S. Jenkins (1995), 'How Much Inequality Can We Explain? A Methodology and an Application to the United States', in *Economic Journal*, **105**(429), 421–30.

Davies, J. and M. Hoy (1994), 'The Normative Significance of Using Third-Degree Stochastic Dominance in Comparing Income Distributions', in *Journal of Economic Theory*, **64**(2), 520–30.

Davies, J. and M. Hoy (1995), 'Making Inequality Comparisons When Lorenz Curves Intersect', in *American Economic Review*, **85**(4), 950–86.

Drèze, J. and A. Sen (1989), *Hunger and Public Action*, Oxford: Clarendon Press.

Dror, Y. (1970), *Law as a Tool of Directed Social Change*, Rand Corporation: Santa Monica (January).

Dworkin, R. (1977), *Taking Rights Seriously* , London: Duckworth.

Dworkin, R. (1986), *Law's Empire*, London: Fontana.

Eaton, B. and W. White (1991), 'The Distribution of Wealth and the Efficiency of Institutions', in *Economic Inquiry*, **29**(2), 336–50.

Edmundson, W. (1994), 'Do the Rich Get Richer, Do the Poor Get Poorer? East Java, Two Decades, Three Villages, 46 People', in *Bulletin of Indonesian Economic Studies*, **30**(2), 133–48.

Ekes, I. (1994), 'The Hidden Economy and Income: The Hungarian Experience', in *Economic Systems*, **18**(4), 309–334.

Elson, D. (1995), 'Gender Awareness in Modeling Structural Adjustment', in *World Development*, 23(11), 1851–68.

Engels, J.W.M. et al. (eds) (1989), *De rechtsstaat herdacht*, Zwolle: Tjeenk Willink.

Ergas, Z. (1979), 'La politique des villages Ujamaa en Tanzania: la fin d'un mythe', in *Revue Tiers Monde* (Jan–March), 169–86.

Falk Moore, S. (1983), *'Law as Process' an Anthropological Approach*, London: Routledge & Kegan Paul.

Falkinger, J. (1994), 'An Engelian Model of Growth and Innovation with Hierarchic Consumer Demand and Unequal Incomes', in *Ricerche Economiche*, **48**(2), 123–39.

Fisher, R. (1991), 'Efoctos de una aperatura comercial sobre la distribucion del ingreso: Teoria y evidencia', *Coleccion Estudios CIEPLAN*, (33), 95–121.

Fitzpatrick, P. and A. Hunt (eds) (1987), *Critical Legal Studies*,Oxford: Blackwell.

Fitzsimmons, E. and H. German (1995), 'The Personal Distribution of Income and the Compostition of Consumption Expenditure', in *Journal of Economics (MVEA)*, **21**(2), 31–8.

Frank, R. and P. Cook (1995), *The winner-take-all Society: How more and more Americans compete for ever fewer and bigger prizes, encouraging economic waste, income inequality, and an impoverished cultural life*, New York: Simon and Schuster.

Gaay Fortman, B. de (1980), 'Between Underdevelopment and Overdevelopment', in B. de Gaay Fortman (ed.), *The Development Deadlock. A series of public lectures*, The Hague: Institute of Social Studies.

Gaay Fortman, B. de (1981), 'Ideology and Development', in B. de Gaay Fortman (ed.), *Different Dimensions of Development in the 1980s. A series of public lectures*, The Hague: Institute of Social Studies.

Gaay Fortman, B. de (1982a), 'Parlement en hercodificatie', in *Weekblad voor Privaatrecht, Notariaat en Registratie*, no. 5617, 474–8.

Gaay Fortman, B. de (1982b), 'You Cannot Develop by Act of Parliament: Rethinking Development from the Legal Viewpoint', in B. de Gaay Fortman (ed.), *Rethinking Development*, The Hague: ISS.

Gaay Fortman, B. de (1989), 'La obtención de los derechos indios', in M. Jansen (ed.), *La Visión India: Tierra, Culture, Lengua X Derechos Humanos*, Leiden: Musiro.

Gaay Fortman, B. de (1990), 'The Dialectics of Western Law in a on-Western World', in J. Berting et al. (eds), *Human Rights in a Pluralist World – Individuals and Collectivities*, Westport: Meckler.

Gaay Fortman, B. de and C. Kortekaas (1996), *Collective Violence within States. Towards a Political Economy of Entitlement, Distates, Anxiety and Human Security*, Paper for Research Seminar State-society, Institute of Social Studies, The Hague, February.

Gaay Fortman, B. de and F. Tarifa (1994), *Political Legitimacy in Communist and Post-Communist States*, Paper for CERES research day on Governance and Reconstruction, The Hague, June 1994.

Gaay Fortman, W.F. de (1972), *Recht doen. Geschriften*, Alphen aan den Rijn.

Galanter, M. (1974), 'Why the "haves" come out ahead: Speculations on the limits of legal change', in *Law & Society Review*, **9**(1), 95–160.

Gallaway, L. and R. Vedder (1993), 'The Distributional Impact of the Eighties: Myth vs. Reality', in *Critical Review*, **7**(1), 61–79.

Gasparini, L. (1994), 'Un modelo teorico sobre educacion publicia y distribucion del ingreso', in *Economica (National University of La Plata)*, **40**(2), 65–107.

Gasper, D. (1993), 'Entitlements Analysis: Relating Concepts and Contexts', in *Development and change*, **24**(4), 679–718.

Ghai, Y. (1978), 'Law and Another Development', in *Development Dialogue*, 110–31.

Giariato, L. (1994), 'Mutamenti di sistema e riforme: un' analisi dagli aspetti distributivi della transizione', in *Economis Politica*, **11**(3), 379–404.

Gore, C. (1993), 'Entitlement relations and "unruly" social practices: A comment on the work of Amartya Sen', in *Journal of Development Studies*, **29**(3), 429–60.

Gore, Ch. (1994), *Social Exclusion and Africa South of the Sahara: A review of the literature*, International Institute for Labour Studies Discussion Papers, Geneva, DP/62/1994.

Graver, H.P. (1988), 'Norms and Decisions', *Scandinavian Studies in Law*, **4**(32), 49–67.

Griffiths, J. (1989), 'Bestaat de Rechtsstaat?', in J.W.M. Engels et al., *De Rechtsstaat herdacht*, Zwolle: Tjeenk Willink.

Grossman, H.I. and M. Kim (1994a), *Swords or Plowshares: A Theory of the Security of Claims to Property*, Brown University, Dept of Economics Working Paper 94–12.

Grossman, H.I. and M. Kim (1994a), *Predation and Production*, Brown University, Dept of Economics Working Paper 94–27.

Hanmer, L., G. Pyatt and H. White (1996a), *Poverty in sub-Saharan Africa. What can we learn from the World Bank's Poverty Assessments?*, The Hague: Institute of Social Studies Advisory Studies

Hanmer, L., G. Pyatt and H. White (1996b), *Understanding Poverty in Africa: What can we learn from the World Bank's Poverty Asdessments?*, The Hague: Institute of Social Studies, 17 Nov.

Harrod, J. (1987), *Power, Production and the Unprotected Worker*, New York: Columbia University Press.

Heemst, J.J.P. van (1984), *National Accounting and Subsistence Production in Developing Countries. Some Major Issues*, The Hague: Institute of Social Studies.

Hepple, B.A. (1987), 'Deregulation and the rule of law: an English view', in M.A.P Bovens, W. Derksen en W.J. Witteveen (eds) *Rechtsstaat en Sturing*, Zwolle: Tjeenk Willink.

Heijde, L., J. Leijken, Th. Mertens and B.P. Vermeulen (eds) (1989), *Begrensde vrijheid*, Zwolle: Tjeenk Willink.

Hill, C. (1995), *Liberty Against the Law: Some 17th century Controversies*, Allen Lane.

Hilhorst, J.G.M. (1996), *Local/regional Development and Industrialization*, The Hague: Institute of Social Studies.

Hoeven, R. van der and F. Stewart (1993), *Social Development During Periods of Structural Adjustment in Latin America*, International Labour Office, Geneva, Occasional Paper no. 18.

Hoff, K. and A. Lyon (1994), 'Non Leaky Buckets: Optimal Redistributive Taxation and Agency Costs', in *NBER*, Woking paper no. 4653, 33.

Hopking, M. and R. van der Hoeven (1983), *Basic Needs in Development Planning*, Aldershot: Gower.

Howes, S. (1993), 'Income Inequality in Urban China in the 1980s: Level, Trends and Determinants', in *London School of Economics Suntory-Toyota Inter-national Centre for Economics and Related Disciplines Working Paper*. EF/3, July.

ILO (1996), *The World Employment Report*, Geneva: International Labour Office.

Jackson, R.H. and C.G. Rosberg (1985), 'The Marginality of African States', in G.M. Carter and P. O'Meara (eds), *African Independence: The First Twenty-Five Years*, London: Indiana University Press.

Jhabvala, F. (1984), 'On Human Rights and the Socio-Economic Context', in *Netherland International Law Review*, **31**(2), 149–82.

Johnson, P. (1996), 'The Assessment: Inequality', in *Oxford Review of Economic Policy*, **12**(1), 1–14.

Jolly, R. (1975), 'Redistribution with Growth?', in *Bulletin of the Institute of Development Studies*, 1–28.

Jong, L. de and J. Olivares (1989), *Het gevecht om water in Lirima*, The Hague: Solidaridad.

Karst, K.L. and K.S. Rosenn (1975), *Law and Development in Latin America*, Berkeley: University of California Press.

Keynes, J.M. (1920), *Economic Consequences of the Peace*, New York: Viking Penguin Inc.

Khan, A. (1993), 'Sources of Income Inequality in Post-reform China', in *China Economic Review*, **4**(1), 19–25.

Killingray, D. (1986), 'The Maintenance of Law and Order in British Colonial Africa', *African Affairs*, July, 411–37.

Kohli, A. (1989), *The State and Poverty in India*, Cambridge: Cambridge University Press.

Krongkaew, M. (1994), 'Income Distribution in East Asian Developing Countries: An Update', in *Asian Pacific Economic Literature*, **8**(2), 58–73.

Krugman, P. (1996), *Interview*, in *de Volkskrant*, December 7.

Langemeijer, G. (1970), *De Gerechtigheid in ons burgerlijk vermogensrecht*, Zwolle: Tjeenk Willink.

Lapidus, G.W., V. Zaslavsky, Ph. Goldman (1992), *From union tot commonwealth: Nationalism and separatism in the Soviet republics*, Cambridge: Cambridge University Press.

Letelier, L. (1995), 'Income Distribution versus Growth. Theory and Empirical Evidence', in *Estudios de Economica*, **22**(2), 389–424.

Levy, A. and K. Chowdhury (1994), 'Intercountry Income Inequality: World Levels and Decomposition between and within Developmental Clusters and Regions', in *Comperative Economic Studies*, **36**(3), 33–50.

Lindbeck, A. (1975), 'The Changing Role of the National State', in *Kyklos*, **28**(1975), 23–46.

Maital, S. and B.Z. Milner (1993), 'Russia and Poland: the Anatomy of Transition', in *Challenge*, **36**(5), 40–7.

McKinley, T. and L. Wang (1992), 'Housing and Wealth in Rural China', in *China Economic Review*, **3**(2), 195–211.

Melj-van Bruggen, R. (1989), *Grondrechten als dilemma van overheidsoptreden,* HRWB Report, The Hague, October.

Minami, R. (1994), 'Income Distribution in Prewar Japan: Estimation and Analysis', in *Economic Review (Keizai-Kenkyu)*, **45**(3), 193–202.

Mogotlane, R. (1996), *Developing South Africa in Peace: Migration in Perspective ,* Paper for Pugwash Meeting no. 218.

Moll, T. (1992), 'Mickey Mouse Numbers and Inequality Research in Developing Countries', in *Journal of Development Studies*, **28**(4), 689–704.

Monchy, S.J.R. de (1905), *De Nederlandsche Wetgever tegenover de armoede,* Doct. Diss., The Hague: Nijhoff.

Munro, R.D. and J.G. Lammers (eds) (1986), *Environmental Protection and Sustainable Development: Legal Principles and Recommendations,* London: Graham & Trotham.

Nader, L. And H.F. Todd Jr. (eds) (1978), *The disputing process: law in ten societies,* New York: Columbia University Press.

North, D. (1990), *Institutions, Institutional Change and Economic Performance,* Cambridge: Cambridge University Press.

Odink, J.G. (1991), 'Some Post-Keynesian Neoclassical Thoughts about Income Distribution. A Comment on Samuels and Kelsey', in W.L.M. Adriaansen and J.T.J.M. van der Linden (eds), *Post-Keynesian Thought In Perspective,* Groningen: Wolters Noordhoff, pp. 139–146.

OECD (1994), *The OECD Jobs Study. Facts, Analysis, Strategies,* Paris: OECD.

Ok, E. (1995), 'Fuzzy Measurement of Income Inequality: A Class of Fuzzy Inequality Measures', in *Social Choice and Welfare*, **12**(2), 111–36.

Olivier, P.J.J. (1973), *Legal Fictions: An Analysis and Evaluation,* Doct. Diss., Leyden: Beugelsdijk.

Oorschot, W. van and P. Kolkhuis Tanke (1989), *Niet gebruik van sociale zekerbeid: Feiten, Theorieën. Onderzoeksmethoden,* Rapport voor Ministerie van Sociale Zaken en Werkgelegenheid, Commissie Onderzoek Sociale Zekerheid, No.16A, The Hague, March.

Parijs, P. van (1992), 'Competing Justifications of Basic Income', in P. Van Parijs (ed.), *Arguing for Basic Income: Ethical foundations for a radical reform,* London: New Left Books, pp. 3–43.

Pearse, A. (1980), *Seeds of Plenty, Seeds of Want: Social and Economic Implications of the Green Revolution,* Oxford: Clarendon Press.

Perotti, R. (1992), 'Political Equilibrium, Income Distribution, and Growth', in *Colombia University Department of Economics,* Discussion Paper no. 595: 21.

Persson, T. and G. Tabellini (1994), 'Is Inequality Harmful for Growth?', in *American Economic Review*, **84**(3), 600–21.

Ram, R. (1991), 'Kuznes's Inverted U Hypothesis: Evidence from a Highly Developed Country', in *Southern Economic Journal*, **57**(4), 1112–23.

Ramprasad, V. (1990), *The Hidden Hunger – Food Policy in India and its Impact on Entitlement,* Penang, Malaysia: Third World Network.

Rawls, J. (1972), *A Theory of Justice,* Oxford: Oxford University Press.

Rose, R. and I. McAllister (1996), 'Is Money the Measure of Welfare in Russia?', in *Review of Income and Wealth*, **42**(1), 75–90.

Rosen, L. (1978), 'Law and Social Change in the New Nations', in *Comparative Studies in Society and History*, **20**, 3–28.

Rothschild, E. (1995), 'What is security?', in *Daedalus*, **124**(3), 53–98.

Ruiz-Castillo, J. (1994), 'The Anatomy of Money and Real Income Inequality in Spain, 1973–1974 to 1980–1981', in *Journal of Income Distribution*, **4**(2), 265–81.

Ryscavage, P. (1995), 'A Surge in Growing Income Inequality?', in *Monthly Labor Review*, **118**(8), 51–61.

Sachs, J.D. (1989), 'Social Conflict and Popular Policies in Latin America', *NBER*, paper no. 2897, Washington DC.

Saith, A. (1989), 'Development Strategies and the Rural Poor', Working Paper Series No. 66, The Hague: ISS, November.

Samuels, W. (1974), 'An Economic Perspective on the Compensation Problem', in *Wayne Law Review*, (21), 113–34.

Samuels, W.J. and T.W. Kelsey (1991), 'Some Fundamental Considerations on the Positive Theory of Income Distribution', in J.T.J.M. van der Linden and W.L.M. Adriaansen (eds), *Post-Keynesian Thought In Perspective*, Groningen: Wolters Noordhoff, pp. 119–38.

Samuels, W. and N. Mercuro (1977), 'The Role of the Compensation Principle in Society', in *Research in Law and Economics* I, 210–45.

Samuels, W.J. and N. Mercuro (1980), 'The Role and Resolution of the Compensation Principle in Society: Part Two – The Resolution', in *Research in Law and Economics*, **2**, 103–28.

Santos, Th. dos (1971), 'The Structure of Dependence', in K.T. Fann and D.C. Hodges (eds), *Readings in U.S. Imperialism*, Boston: Porter Sargent Publisher.

Sarmiento, E. (1992), 'Growth and Income Distribution in Countries at Intermediate Stages of Development', in *Cepal Review*, (48), 141–55.

Schaffer, B.B. and G.S. Lamb (1981), *Can Equity be Organized? Equity, Development Analysis and Planning*, Farnborough: Gower.

Schott, R. (1981), 'Law and development in Africa', in *Law and state. A Biannual Collection of Recent German Contributions to These Fields*, **24**, 30–41.

Seers, D. (1972), 'What are we trying to measure?', in Nancy Baster (ed.), *Measuring Development: the Role and Adequacy of Development Indicators*, London: Frank Cass.

Sen, A. (1986), *Food, Economics and Entitlements*, World Institute for Development Economics Research of the United Nations University, February.

Sen, A. (1987), *Hunger and Entitlements*, World Institute for Development Economics Research of the United Nations University, Helsinki.

Sen, A. (1988), *Poverty and Famines. An Essay on Entitlement and Deprivation*, Oxford: Oxford University Press.

Siegfried, J. and A. Roberts (1991), 'How Did the Wealthiest Britons Get So Rich?', in *Review of Industrial Organisation*, **6**(1), 19–32.

Siegfried, J. and D. Round (1994), 'How Did the Wealthiest Australians Get So Rich?', in *Review of Income and Wealth*, **40**(2), 191–204.

Silber, J. and B.Z. Zilberfarb (1994), 'The Effect of Anticipated and Unanticipated Inflation on Income Distribution: The Israeli Case', in *Journal of Income Distribution*, **4**(1), 41–9.

Swaan, A. de (1988), *In Care of the State: Health Care, Education and Welfare in Europe and the USA in the Modern Era*, Cambridge: Polity Press.

Szekely, M. (1995), 'Aspectos de la desigualdad en Mexico', in *El Trimestre Economico*, **62**(2), 201–42.

Tchernina, N. (1995), 'Patterns and Processes of Social Exclusion in Russia', in G. Rodgers, Ch. Gore and J.B. Figueiredo (eds), *Social Exclusion: Rhetoric, Reality, Responses*, Geneva: IILS/UNDP.

Tinbergen, J. (1956), 'On the Theory of Income Distribution', in *Weltwirtschaftliches Archiv*, **77**, 155–75.

Tinbergen, J. (1992), 'Optimal Redistribution', in *Indian Economic Review*, (27) (special issue), 1–4.

United Nations Development Programme (1992), *Human Development Report 1992*, NY/Oxford: O.U.P.

United Nations Development Programme (1996), *Human Development Report 1996*, NY/Oxford: O.U.P.

United Nations Development Programme (1997), *Human Development Report 1997*, NY/Oxford: O.U.P.

Usher, D. (1968), *The Price Mechanism and the Meaning of National Income Statistics*, Oxford: O.U.P.

Valentine, T. (1993a), 'Drought, Transfer Entitlements, and Income Distribution: The Botswana Experience', in *World Development*, **21**(1), 109–26.

Valentine, T. (1993b), 'Mineral-Led Economic Growth, Drought Relief, and Incomes Policy: Income Distribution in Botswana Reconsidered', in *American Journal of Economics and Sociology*, **52**(1), 31–49.

Varoudakis, A. (1995), 'Inflation, inegalites de repartition etcroissance', in *Revue-Economique*, **46**(3), 889–99.

Veld, R. in 't (1989), *De verguisde staat*, The Hague: VUGA.

Walzer, M. (1983), *Spheres of justice: a Defence of Pluralism and Equality*, Oxford: Blackwell's.

Wazir, R. (1987), 'Women's Access to Land as Owners and Workers: a Stocktaking for five Asian Countries', Paper for ESHL/FAO, Rome, October.

Weicher, J. (1995), 'Changes in the Distribution of Wealth: Increasing Inequality?', in *Federal Reserve Bank of St. Louis Review*, **77**(1), 5–23.

White, H. (1996), 'Adjustment in Africa: A Review Article', in *Development and Change*, **27**(4), 785–815.

Wilfling, B. and W. Kramer (1993), 'The Lorenz-Ordering of Singh-Maddala Income Distributions', in *Economics Letters*, **43**(1), 53–7.

Wolff, E. (1994), 'Trends in Household Wealth in the United States: 1962–1983 and 1983–1989', in *New York University, C.V. Starr Center Economic Research Report*, 94–03.

Wong, K.Y. (1992), 'Inflation, Corruption and Income Distribution: The Recent Price Reform in China', in *Journal of Macroeconomics*, **14**(1), 105–23.

5. Deflation and Distribution: Austerity Policies in Britain in the 1920s

Victoria Chick[1]

1 INTRODUCTION

A policy of austerity and sound money was practised in Britain in the 1920s; the goal was to return to the gold standard at pre-war parity. This goal required a sharp disinflation and then sustained deflation to bring British prices into line with prices abroad. The result was high unemployment and interest rates unprecedented in peacetime. However desirable sound money may seem, these are classic results. The great depression of the 1930s in Britain deepened and continued a condition which had already been going on for a decade. It is the purpose of this paper to examine the redistributive effects of this sound money episode and to draw a lesson for our own time.

Today, the policy of austerity in pursuit of sound money, resulting in high real interest rates, is again being pursued all over Europe. Such a policy follows the example set by the Bundesbank. It was at the core of Conservative policy in Britain after the election of 1979 and is embodied in the convergence criteria for joining a single currency under the Maastricht Treaty. Smithin (1996) has called it the Revenge of the Rentiers.

The British rate of inflation was indeed reduced in the 1980s and has remained low.[2] In fact, inflation has fallen in most Western countries. The most obvious costs of such policies have been high unemployment (partly disguised in the UK by repeated changes in the statistics; see Wells, 1994), increasing pressure on the living standards of those who are at the bottom of the labour market hierarchy, and increasing pressure of work for those in employment.[3]

The other notable feature of the policy in the 1920s – and another similarity with today's economic situation – is historically high real interest rates. These were sustained until 1932, when the largest element of the national debt could be converted at a lower interest rate following Britain's departure from the gold standard in the previous year. (To cover the whole gold standard period, most of our data will extend to 1931.)

Throughout the period, in discussion of the policy to restore the monetary *status quo* either little attention was paid to possible effects on income distribution or the effect on employment was recognized but considered 'worth it'. In this paper we trace the effects on functional distribution. High interest rates, falling prices and a more stable currency favour rentier income. Receivers of rent benefit from falling prices. Profits are hit initially by the deflationary shock and by high interest costs; firms react by 'rationalizing' the use of labour. The net shift toward rent and interest income implies a corresponding relative reduction of real income flows out of productive activity.

Conservative economists and politicians tend to play down these consequences of 'sound money' or attribute them to other factors. Unemployment is attributed to insufficient labour market flexibility, the irresponsible exercise of union power, high wages, generous unemployment benefits on easy terms, a shift in the 'natural rate of unemployment', and structural problems. A legacy of excessive government borrowing and, in the 1980s, expectations of inflation, are blamed for high interest rates. Weak economic growth is attributed to insufficient competition, poor productivity, and poor incentives to work, save and invest.

Reduced inflation, high unemployment, downward pressure on wages and working conditions and high interest rates, all features of the British economy since 1979, are strikingly similar to the experience of the 1920s. There are differences between the two periods: in particular, in the 1920s British industry needed restructuring. Indeed many commentators argue that this structural problem, not the sound money policy, was responsible for the poor performance of the interwar period. Others point to difficulties caused by the loss of monetary hegemony and the lack of international monetary cooperation. These points are correct and important, but they are complementary to the problems caused by deflation, the effects of which are amplified when they fall on firms already weak for structural reasons, and the necessary deflationary efforts were exacerbated by the fact that each country had to find its own way back to gold after the failure of the Genoa negotiations (Eichengreen, 1992).

But the sound money policy itself is instructive, not only as an exercise in economic history: the parallel is sufficiently close to make the experience of the 1920s a cautionary tale for our times. The episode also provides the background for understanding the 'Keynesian revolution' (Keynes began working on the *General Theory* in the early 1930s) and the applicability of

Keynes's theory to today's economic situation and the common currency project.

We shall proceed first with an exploration of the motives for the policy of the 1920s and a Keynesian interpretation of deflation and its consequences, followed by an exposition of the policies pursued and their consequences for prices, wages, interest rates and output and finally functional income distribution. But the *ex post* results are not the whole story; as already hinted, there are adjustments which particular firms can make to shield themselves from the most adverse effects of deflationary policies. We attempt, finally, to estimate the severity of the effect of deflation and the rise of interest rates by a few pieces of counterfactual estimation which abstract from those adjustments.

2 DEFLATION AND DISTRIBUTION: THEORETICAL CONSIDERATIONS

2.1 Prewar Parity: Policy for Recovery or Idée Fixe?

Figure 5.1 shows how far the exchange rate had departed from parity by the end of the War. The desirability of returning to the gold standard at the prewar parity was taken absolutely for granted by nearly all policy-makers and prominent economists, with the notable exceptions of Keynes, Hubert Henderson and Reginald McKenna. The extent to which this was the case is well illustrated by Pigou's evidence to the Macmillan Committee (1931, vol. II of Evidence). He was asked several times, in different ways, whether any alternatives to a return to prewar parity had been considered by the Cunliffe Committee (of which he had been a member) and each time he replied that the only question considered was one of timing: whether to return to gold at the old parity immediately after the war or later. The possibility of devaluation was seen as default and morally unacceptable, and a monetary regime other than a tie to gold was, it seems, unthinkable.

One of the most intriguing elements, now as well as then, is what the policy-makers understood of what they were doing: the question of whether the distributive effects were accidental or conscious. Alford (1972, p. 30) comments:

> It is attractive to depict the episode as one in which villainous bankers, led by Montagu Norman, Governor of the Bank of England, dictated policy to successive governments, regardless of its broader economic consequences, which they did not

understand, and heedless of the social costs, which they considered to be unavoidable.

It is true that Norman, in his evidence to the Macmillan Committee, was at first unwilling to acknowledge the employment effects of the deflation even in retrospect. Whether he or any of the major participants accurately foresaw them is even less clear. But the bankers were not alone; the policy had wide support. Most economists at the time adhered to the theory associated today with Professor Minford, that prices and wages could be forced to change with only a small and transitory effect on employment: their adherence to the classical dichotomy between real and monetary variables leads them to dissociate price and output changes where in Keynesian theory they are inseparable. Thus it is probably fair to say that the social cost of deflation was, at the outset, greatly underestimated.

As the costs of deflation were underestimated, the benefits of monetary arrangements to trade and employment were exaggerated and misplaced. The return to pre-war parity was believed by many at the time to be a policy *beneficial* to trade and employment. The stability of the exchange rate, rather than its level, was thought to be the important issue: stable rates were good for trade; the gold standard ensured stable rates, therefore the gold standard was good for trade:

> [T]he relatively small sacrifices involved in [returning to gold] were much more than counterbalanced by the restoration of international confidence, and by the stimulus given to international trade through the replacement of the pound sterling in its old position as the principal currency of the world's trade. (Cassel 1936, quoted in Cairncross and Eichengreen, 1983, p. 30)

This passage illustrates an important feature of the thinking of the time both amongst City practitioners and amongst academics: successful trade was attributed to Britain's prewar position as the undisputed centre of the international monetary system and to the strength and position of sterling. Very likely it was this sense of power and importance which contributed to gold's allure and encouraged the policy-makers steadfastly to adhere to the restrictive monetary and budgetary policies that an exchange rate of $4.86 to the pound required, despite the serious costs entailed.

The attitude of the Federation of British Industries (FBI) was described by Brown (1929) as complacent towards pre-war parity. At the end of the war their main concern was the threat of credit restriction. By 1924 industrialists were well aware of the deflationary effects of returning to gold in the near future. Nevertheless, their fears concerned the effects of an immediate return; the Federation gave its support to an eventual return to gold. Such opposition as existed, amongst industrialists as amongst politicians, was not about the restoration of a gold standard as such, but only about its timing. There is no evidence of the opposition even of the exporting industries and those facing competition from imports.

Amongst labour, the rank and file, who stood to pay the highest price and gain the least, were, again according to Brown, not interested in the gold question as such, though obviously they were opposed to deflationary policies. However, Philip Snowden[4] was one of the most ardent supporters of a return to gold and fully supported the restrictive budgetary and dear money policies that it entailed.

Keynes understood, even in *Indian Currency and Finance* (1913), that the majority view had got the causality backwards. Sterling owed its pre-war strength to British trade and invisible earnings, not the other way round. Today it is quite widely accepted that key currencies owe their strength to their country's balance-of-payments position and general economic strength, and that the exchange rate is a tool of policy, not an aim.

Manipulation of the level of the exchange rate was not seen as a possible way of increasing export competitiveness, as it later was, to deleterious effect, in the 1930s.[5] The modern perception is the starting point of Rolfe and Burtle, who end the following passage with a telling argument:

> The modern mind finds this effort to return to pre-war parity hard to understand. The dominant concern of the post-World War II generation is with the effects of the exchange rate on income and employment. If devaluation means more exports, more jobs, more income, is this not good? To understand the interwar years, the contemporary mind must understand the interwar values. And except for mavericks or radicals like Roosevelt and Keynes, the dominant motif in the inter-war years was not welfare but rather the restoration of the value of capital assets. (1974, p. 46)

Rolfe and Burtle are suggesting that there was a hidden programme in the return to gold and all that it entailed: a shift of economic power from income-earners to wealth-holders by restoring the domestic and international value of assets.

An argument which is even more arresting is that of Grossman (1990). He argues that the British authorities knew that the end of the 1914–18 war was not the end of hostilities, that there was unfinished business; and the point of going back to the gold standard at prewar parity was, by honouring the debt in full, to maintain Britain's credit rating for future use. This suggestion has a chilling air of plausibility about it.

Both Rolfe and Burtle and Grossman assume that those in power knew exactly what they were doing. The motive inferred by Grossman requires a particularly high level of consciousness. Ideally, we pay politicians to have this consciousness, but it is rarely in evidence, whether because they do not have it or because they do not express it in the public domain. We do not wish to take a firm stand on the motives of the British authorities in returning to gold. Ultimately one cannot establish what were the policy-makers' actual intentions, only what the redistributive effects of the policy actually were. However, the facts are consistent with a similar hidden agenda of redistribution in the policies of the British Conservative governments of the 1980s and 90s and of the Maastricht Treaty. The former is not so surprising: it is one of the functions of the Tory party to champion Capital in the struggle for relative shares. And we have some confirmation in a most unexpected source, the Bank of England *Quarterly Bulletin*, of their conscious intention:

> [I]t would scarcely have been possible to mount and carry through, over several years and without resort to direct controls of all kinds, so determined a counter-inflationary strategy if it had not been for the initial 'political economy' of the firm monetary target. Though not considered at the time, it would have been possible to initiate such a strategy with a familiar 'Keynesian' exposition about managing demand downwards, and with greater concentration on ultimate objectives than on intermediate targets. But this would have meant disclosing objectives for, *inter alia*, output and employment. This would either have been unacceptable to public opinion or else inadequate to secure a substantial reduction in the rate of inflation, or both. (Fforde, 1983, p. 207)

Maintaining the interests of Capital is also traditionally the concern of central bankers. Central bankers and political parties wax and wane in power, and fluctuations in the relative fortunes of different pressure groups are to be expected. The mystery is that enshrining this particular bias in an international Treaty as a permanent arrangement should be acceptable.[6] One possible explanation is the new power of international banking and capital markets, which cannot be voted out of office and will not go away. Another answer comes from America, which as Galbraith has recently written (1996), is 'not all that different [from other rich countries], just a trifle less discrete'. While Fforde, in the early 1980s, spoke of the consequences of a sound money policy being unacceptable, in America, Galbraith tells us, the following view is now openly acknowledged:

> In the modern economy let us say simply that the rich do not want to pay for the poor: that unemployment is necessary and good; that recession can be tolerated, certainly by the many who do not suffer as compared with the smaller number who do. Even mild inflation affects the many as compared with unemployment, which affects the relatively few ... Recession ... is far better than the possible need to pay for the measures that arrest it.

The idea that recessions only hit a minority of the population may be something of an illusion; their effects reach even those who keep their jobs, by keeping wages down and increasing work loads. Even shareholders may suffer until companies have cut their costs. But it is perceptions which matter. Demographic factors also play a role: the position of pensioners vis-à-vis the unemployed is unambiguous, and in the developed world, populations are ageing.

2.2 A Keynesian Interpretation

The restoration of the gold standard at the parity prevailing before the war entailed the reversal of wartime and postwar inflation and repayment of the national debt. These goals dictated fiscal austerity and other deflationary measures, first in preparation for the return to gold and after 1925 in order to maintain an exchange rate which proved precarious.[7] As a whole the decade was characterized by falling prices, falling money wages, high unemployment (Figures 5.1 and 5.2) and interest rates at levels which had only previously been seen in wartime (Figure 5.3), all in the name of sound money.

The deflationary measures employed read like a Keynesian textbook, before 'Keynes' (i.e. before the *General Theory*) and in the opposite direction: the government ran budget surpluses, reduced the absolute size of the government budget, retired debt, and funded debt which they couldn't repay; Bank Rate was kept at high levels and credit was restricted. In the 1920s, neither politicians nor economists had the Principle of Effective Demand, the central concept of Keynes's *General Theory*. Applying the tools of the *General Theory* to the 1920s we have a copybook example of how the Principle works – in the downward direction.

That Principle tells us that lack of demand, whether, as in this case, contrived as a matter of policy or as a result of private sector decisions, first hits sales and profits; then producers defend themselves by cutting back output and shedding labour in the short run. The drop in prices will favour firms whose main markets are abroad, but on the whole firms would like to raise prices, just at the time when it is most difficult.

As the deflation persists and comes to be expected, investment falls and firms have a further incentive to cut back production. They will reduce stocks to lower current labour costs further. They will not replace worn-out equipment. Laid-off labourers reduce their consumption and the reduction in replacement and new investment further reduces demand and confirms producers' pessimistic expectations.

The firms' strategies are rational from the microeconomic point of view, despite their adverse macroeconomic effects. Actions which reduce costs at least improve the share of profits in a reduced level of income, by displacing part of the initial demand shock onto workers, through the fall in the wage bill, and onto the producers of capital goods through the fall in investment orders.

As Keynes repeatedly emphasized in this period, if the object of policy is to reduce wages to establish a permanently lower level of prices, it is only by first creating unemployment that this change can be forced through. Those who remain employed may or may not suffer reductions in real wages.

The classic distribution struggle is that between 'capital' and labour, or the 'two sides of industry'. There are also conflicts within capital. 'Capital' refers to at least two separate and competing groups: those with claims to profit income and the recipients of interest incomes. The shares of these two groups are affected by both changes in prices and changes in interest rates.

While a fall in prices, representing as it does depressed demand, is detrimental to profits, those on fixed incomes, of whom rentiers in this period were an identifiable social class, benefit; more generally, a fall in prices benefits those on fixed (money) incomes at the expense of those on variable incomes. High interest rates also favour rentiers at the expense of producers, for whom interest is a cost. Once again, however, there is a short-period adjustment mechanism by which producers can mitigate the effect on profit: high interest costs produce a further reason for running down stocks; this further diminishes the need for productive workers. In the long run, high rates of interest reinforce the adverse effects of low demand on investment, further deflating demand and eroding firms' longer run productivity and competitiveness.

From a microeconomic point of view, profits are a residual, the least protected of sources of income, vulnerable both to reduced demand and to the high interest rates which are the hallmark of the implementation of a sound money policy. Conversely, rentiers doubly benefit: from deflation, as recipients of contractually-fixed incomes, and from one of the policy instruments used to force the deflation, namely high interest rates.

For rentiers, although *high* interest rates are desirable, *rising* rates are not, as interest earnings and the value of their wealth vary inversely. In the 1920s the Government arranged conversions of government stock at critical moments, accepting selected existing issues at par. This has the effect of protecting rentiers from capital losses arising from higher interest rates. Given that the Government was also determined to minimize its deficits, this implies that rentiers gained also at the expense of the general taxpayer.

There are yet further, more insidious effects of the gains accruing to the rentiers under a high-interest policy. The benefit to rentiers channels financial resources away from productive uses in the hands of the entrepreneurs and inhibits investment, while the reduction in prices increases the real income of a group with a comparatively low marginal propensity to consume, at the same time that the increase in unemployment diminishes the spending power of those with the highest marginal propensity to consume, the working class. The redistribution of income and wealth thus intensifies the slump. The low marginal propensity to consume of this class is reinforced by expectations of continuing deflation. As the matter was put by Sir Henry Strakosch:[8]

> [T]he greater title to goods which the fall of general prices gives to those having fixed money claims remains unexercised. While money appreciates, a reluctance to exchange it for goods is only natural; and that is particularly true of those having fixed money claims, for they can afford it, the greater title to a goods they so acquire constituting, in fact, an increment over and above their accustomed standard of life. They are thus unlikely to exercise it. (Macmillan Committee, Minutes of Evidence, 1931, para. 28, p. 31)

The predicted distributional consequences of a sound money policy are many and sometimes conflicting. In addition, there exist adjustment mechanisms by which erosions of relative shares, particularly the effect on the share of profits, may be reversed. The existence of adjustment processes implies that the true magnitude of the distributive struggle cannot be ascertained from *ex post* observations. In Section 5 we make an attempt to estimate the scale of some of the displacements as they might have been without the adjustments which did occur. To do this we make some counterfactual calculations, to assess the extent to which the fall in prices alone affected distribution, the extent to which the fall in wages and the rise in unemployment were necessary to firms' survival, and the distribution as it would have been with full employment. In these counterfactual exercises, the actual sequence of events, in which firms will typically reduce output and lay off workers first and only later will prices and perhaps also wages fall, is put aside. Nor are the effects of price changes on the real capital value of the securities taken into account.

We take up these points in turn as we discuss the actual data of the period in Sections 3 and 4. The policy actions are outlined first, then their effects. Most of the data is presented by means of Figures; these are presented together at the end of the paper. The data are available on request.

3　A DECADE OF DEFLATION

3.1 The Legacy of War

The 1914–18 war generated inflationary pressures (Figure 5.4) and a considerable volume of public debt (Figure 5.5). It also severely disrupted international trade and the industrial structure of the British economy. And it undermined the very basis of the pre-war international monetary system, based on sterling convertible into gold at a fixed parity.

Even before the war had ended, the Committee on Currency and Foreign Exchanges after the War (the Cunliffe Committee) was set up to ascertain the postwar position of sterling. In its First Interim Report of August 1918, it took the view that:

> Nothing can contribute more to a speedy recovery from the effects of the war, and to the rehabilitation of the foreign exchanges, than the re-establishment of the currency upon a sound basis. (p. 1)

Sound money meant three things: the reversal of inflation, repayment of the debt, and the restoration of the gold standard at the parity prevailing before the war. These considerations dominated policy-making throughout the 1920s, giving rise to fiscal austerity and other deflationary measures, first in preparation for the return to gold and after 1925 in order to maintain an exchange rate which was still overvalued.

Although Britain remained *de jure* on the gold standard until 31 March 1919, the pre-war parity of $4.86 had already slipped slightly by the end of 1914. Convertibility into gold was *de facto* impossible because gold could not be shipped in wartime conditions. The Cunliffe Committee wished an immediate return to gold, though they realized that conditions for the return to gold did not exist in 1918; indeed gold exports were officially prohibited in 1918. When the situation worsened dramatically in 1919, Britain formally abandoned the gold standard, legalizing what had been the *de facto* position despite the Committee's recommendations. Sterling fell quickly, reaching its lowest value of $3.40 in February 1920 (Figure 5.6).

Not to have left gold would have jeopardized the gold reserves, necessitating a restrictive credit policy when the government regarded credit expansion, to encourage a shift in production and employment to meet peacetime needs, as appropriate (Hawtrey in Pigou, 1947, p. 146). The banks responded: advances of the London Clearing Banks (LCBs) rose 81 per cent between January 1919 and April 1920, after which advances turned down (Figure 5.7).[9] Investments and discounts of commercial bills also rose, though less dramatically. The banks became less liquid as credit expanded and Bankers' balances, money at call and loans to the money market declined.[10]

Demand rose sharply; government spending and the pent-up demand for capital and consumer goods provided the driving force, while plentiful money and credit played their enabling role. Howson (1975, chapter 2) follows earlier authors in dating the boom from April 1919 to April 1920 on the basis of unemployment and price data;[11] she estimates, on annual data from Feinstein (1972), that industrial production rose 10 per cent in this year and GDP[12] returned to 1913 levels in 1920. But the rise in retail prices between 1919 and 1920 was more dramatic – a rise of 19 per cent (Figure 5.4), leaving a gap with US retail prices of 24 per cent.[13] We have no data for wholesale prices in 1919, but by 1920 the index stood at 295 in Britain and 221 in America (Figure 5.8).[14] If immediate restoration had been impossible in 1918, it was even more remote after the postwar inflation.

Towards the end of 1919, the priorities of official policy were reversed: the restoration of the gold standard took precedence over demobilization of the economy. The period of rapid deflation began.

Monetary policy was used with vigour to curb the credit boom: Bank Rate was raised progressively to a peak of 7 per cent – a crisis level for peacetime – in April 1920 (Figure 5.9). This rate, however, could only be made effective with the cooperation of the Treasury, due to the volume of existing Treasury bills. The floating debt was already high after the war, and then in the fiscal year 1919–20 the government ran a deficit of wartime proportions, adding 16 per cent to the already-existing glut of Treasury bills,[15] which deprived the Bank of England of control of the market.[16] The Government was thus forced to cover some of its needs through Ways and Means Advances from the Bank of England (£31m was borrowed in 1920;[17] see Figure 5.10 for the composition of the debt in 1920). This borrowing supplied the foundation for an expansion of bank credit, which contributed to the inflationary pressure.

In an era of 'small government', the high post-war levels of government expenditure were a concern in their own right as well as for their inflationary implications. The Committee on National Expenditure, chaired by Sir Eric Geddes, was appointed in 1921 to examine ways to cut government expenditure.

> During the reign of the Geddes Axe, as it was called, parsimony was enshrined as a leading principle of government ... Criticisms of governments for their preoccupation with budget surpluses should be tempered by their recognition of the constraints imposed by the accepted monetary policy. In the absence of borrowing at the Bank of England, public borrowing, or failure to repay loans,

might have entailed higher interest rates and would have produced distributive effects of debatable merit. The most important evil inflicted by the determination to restore the gold standard may well have been the limitations to which it subjected budgetary policy. (Hancock in Pollard, 1970, p. 104)

3.2 Austerity in the 1920s

Deflationary policies were pursued throughout the 1920s, first, and most brutally, to eliminate the disparities between British and American price levels which emerged in the wartime and postwar inflation (Figures 5.4 and 5.8), and then to maintain that parity. The policies undertaken included the running of a budgetary surplus, a reduction in the size of the budget, setting up a sinking fund to retire government debt and lengthening that which remained outstanding, keeping Bank Rate historically high and placing downward pressure on the money supply both through open market operations and also by discouraging advances. Once the deflationary forces took hold, pessimistic expectations would reinforce the policy effects.

The strength and incidence of deflationary policies were not uniform, of course, nor was the response, though high interest rates, persistently high rates of unemployment and falling prices characterize the decade. There are three distinct stages, which can be called Disinflation, Deflation and Overvaluation. The first concerns the years immediately after the war; deflation follows until the gold standard is re-established in 1925; and the adverse effect of an overvalued exchange rate produced low levels of output and employment until the Wall Street crash and underlying weakness of the U.S. economy precipitated the world's slide into deep depression.

3.2.1 The government budget

In 1913 the Budget had shown a surplus of just £200,000. In 1918 there was a deficit of nearly £2 billion,[18] 35 per cent of GDP.[19] The wartime deficit was financed chiefly by debt, the subject of the next section. Between 1920 and 1921 government spending fell by 39 per cent and revenue rose slightly, turning a deficit equal to 5 per cent of GDP into almost as large a surplus (Figure 5.11).[20] The deflationary effect of the surplus was reinforced by a negative balanced-budget multiplier: between 1920 and 1924, both revenue and expenditure were reduced. Absolutely, expenditure was halved, falling by just over £800m; relatively to GDP expenditure fell from 28 per cent in 1920 to 17 per cent in 1925 and remained at roughly that level until 1931 (Figure 5.11).

Surpluses continued until 1925 and repeated in 1928 and 1929, though the data during Churchill's tenure as Chancellor of the Exchequer (1925–29) are unreliable (Winch, 1969, p. 99).[21] The post-1925 Budgets embodied 'the internal contradiction which was to dominate British public finance until 1931' (U.K. Hicks, 1954, p. 8): they were mildly expansionary at a time when the gold standard still required deflation. Churchill recognised the political importance of alleviating the pressure on workers while presenting evidence of a continuing effort to amortize the debt; he was perhaps the first to employ creative accounting to make every effort to show the accounts in surplus; on the available data (Figure 5.11), he succeeded with the exception of 1926, the year of the General Strike, and 1927.

3.2.2 Government debt

The total outstanding national debt rose from £706m in March 1914 to £7,481m in March 1919, of which nearly 1/3 of the latter figure had a maximum life of five years (Figure 5.5).

The most important bond issue of the war was the 5 per cent War Loan 1929/47 issued in 1917 (date of prospectus 11 June) at a price of £95 per cent (thus offering a yield of 5.26 per cent).[22] Throughout the 1920s the 5 per cent War Loan represented roughly a quarter of the total National Debt; it overshadowed both fiscal and monetary policy until Britain left gold. Effectively, it set a floor below which interest rates could not go without jeopardizing the exchange rate.

'The most serious depressing effect of the National Debt in this period ... lay in the Treasury's response to its existence' (Winch, 1969, p. 97) – retiring what it could and funding the rest. Reducing the public debt was a major concern in its own right: these were days before governments – and the informed public – accepted as normal the existence of a large public debt. Whilst the government was regarded as justified in responding to the exigencies of a war-time economy by engaging in heavy borrowing, a balanced budget and a low volume of public debt was understood as the peacetime norm.[23] A policy of setting aside an annual sum as a sinking fund for debt repayment was adopted in 1923 and strengthened in 1928. The policy was maintained until 1934, though abrogated in the year of the General Strike.

The programme of funding and conversions was aimed first at reducing the floating debt and the need for Ways and Means advances. Between 1921 and 1923, Consols and Conversion Loans, repayable at the Government's option only, increased more than 3-fold, while total debt rose by only 2.7 per cent.[24] This action sharply reduced short rates, while keeping long rates at between 4.4 to 5 per cent (Figure 5.12). The Treasury's efforts to fund the debt at lower interest rates were moderately successful despite high Bank

Rate and the overpowering influence of War Loan, but funding added to deflationary influences by reducing liquidity and restoring the capacity of the Bank to pursue deflationary policy. A further series of conversions and new issues began in 1924 to prepare for the potential repurchase of 5 per cent War Loan in 1929.

The higher interest rates introduced in 1920 and the shift to longer maturities increased the cost of servicing the public debt. Interest payments rose from £248m in 1918 to £310m in 1919 and £325m in 1920; it remained over £300m, over 40 per cent of Government expenditure, until 1931 (Figure 5.13).[25] Reduction of the overall debt, therefore, was not only a matter of conforming to the particular ideology prevailing at the time, but was also necessary if deflationary pressure was to be exerted through the budget.

3.2.3 Monetary policy

The restoration of control of the bill market by reducing the large floating debt was a priority in 1920, since Bank Rate was not only an important instrument in controlling domestic credit, but also, in Britain, the traditional governor of the gold standard machinery. As a result of the surplus in 1920–21, £67m of Ways and Means Advances were repaid;[26] floating debt as a whole fell by £300m from March 1920 to March 1922 (Figure 5.10).

The 7 per cent Bank Rate was to be maintained for a full year, until the end of April 1921, well after it was painfully apparent that the back of the boom had been broken. According to Pigou, who by 1947 had dramatically revised his views from the time of the Macmillan Committee:

> If what was aimed at was simply to stop inflation, there was no need to keep discount high once the down-turn had been definitely brought about ... The mistake of the British authorities, if it was a mistake, was not one of technical analysis but one of broad policy, namely the decision ... to restore our currency to pre-war gold parity in the near future. Once that decision was taken, with American prices moving as they did, to allow the monetary slump here to become profound, in spite of the damage thereby done to industry and employment, was a necessary means to an accepted end. (Pigou, 1947, pp. 196–7)

Despite the Bank of England's difficulties, the money base fell by 15 per cent between March 1920 and March 1925 (Figure 5.7).[27] Notes held by the public, of which the bulk were Bank of England and wartime Treasury Currency Notes, fell 17 per cent.[28] Advances of the London Clearing Banks began to fall in the latter half of 1920. They rose again in early 1921 but declined by £10m from March to the end of the year (Figure 5.7). Deposits, both of the London Clearing Banks (Figure 5.7) and all UK banks[29] started their fall later, in early 1922: between February 1922 and March 1925, M3 fell by £452m, 18.8 per cent (Figure 5.7). Bank deposits did not return to their 1921 level until 1929. Interest rates on 3 month bank bills had risen from just under 4 per cent in 1919 to 6.4 per cent in 1920. In 1921 the rate fell slightly but was still over 5 per cent (Figure 5.12).

By January of 1922, the exchange rate had recovered to $4.22 and in that year Bank Rate was allowed to fall to 3 per cent. The exchange rate continued to rise, fuelled by optimism concerning the Genoa Conference, until April 1923. When that Conference failed to produce agreement, Bank Rate was raised to 4 per cent in an attempt to protect the substantial gain (Figures 5.6 and 5.9) and never fell below that level until after the Wall Street crash.

In 1924, parity came to be regarded as a feasible objective in the near term. The return to gold was now urgent, as the Act suspending gold exports expired at the end of 1925.[30] A disparity in purchasing power with the US remained (Figures 5.4 and 5.8).[31] The optimists hoped that inflation in the USA would obviate the necessity for further deflation at home. Fears of deflation were expressed by the Federation of British Industries to the Chamberlain-Bradbury Committee. Bank Rate was made effective at 4 per cent and raised to 5 per cent when the decision to return to gold was taken, overriding the FBI's fears, and despite unemployment of over 1.5m.

The decision to return to gold was taken in March 1925 and announced in the Budget of 28 April.[32] The announcement was followed by an influx of gold to London, which prompted a fall in Bank Rate (Figure 5.9), but Norman's argument that this was temporary optimism was correct. The overall weakness of sterling was evident throughout the period, and Norman kept Bank Rate as high as he could given two constraints: events in New York and the Treasury's concern with the effects of high interest rates on unemployment.

4 THE ECONOMY'S RESPONSE

The effect of dear money and fiscal stringency on prices was dramatic. Feinstein's index of retail prices[33] fell between 1920 and 1922 by 27 per cent, wholesale prices 48 per cent (Figures 5.1 and 5.8). Average weekly wage rates fell by 29 per cent in 1922 and a further 11 per cent the following year and then stabilized until 1930 (Figure 5.1). The extent to which the downward flexibility of wages can be attributed to sliding-scale agreements (indexation) then in place is a matter of controversy.[34] It is clear that they cannot be the whole explanation: real wages fell from 1921 to 1923 and then rose gradually but remained below their 1921 peak until 1931 (Figure 5.1).

The initial effect of deflation fell on aggregate demand and thus on profits, and in response firms cut production and laid off workers. Gross trading profits of private companies fell 45 per cent between 1920 and 1921.[35] Output fell 6 per cent in 1921, then recovered (Figure 5.14). A confident expectation of Feinstein, Table 32. Continued deflation, the high general level of interest rates and the wide gap between short and long term rates brought about by funding discouraged investment. The fall in investment was delayed but sharp (Figure 5.14).

High rates of unemployment characterize the decade. Unemployment data before 1921 are not comparable, so the data begin after the postwar boom had been crushed (Figure 5.2). Feinstein's estimate for 1921 of 12.2 per cent of the civilian working population is substantially higher than the two previous peak rates since 1855. Although the 1921 figure was not equalled again until 1930, unemployment remained high throughout the 1920s – always above 6.8 per cent in Feinstein's estimates and averaging 9 per cent (Figure 5.2). On the data based only on the insured population the rate is much higher; unemployment fell just below 10 per cent only once in the decade.

The Keynesian interpretation of this unemployment naturally focuses on the deflationary policy. There are, however, other factors and interpretations. There was a clear need for structural change, and unemployment was markedly higher in the old, declining staple industries; but unemployment was 5 per cent or more even in the new industries,[36] suggesting a macroeconomic problem in addition to structural obsolescence. There was also a supply shock: in 1919 labour leaders negotiated a fall in the average working week from 54 to 47 hours with no reduction in the nominal weekly wage. Dowie (1975) estimates that this raised unit labour costs 10 per cent between 1919 and 1921. To Broadberry (1986) this cost rise was the main source of interwar unemployment; it surely cannot have helped, but the fall in demand is also real enough.

Wages, retail prices and real wages reached their nadir in 1923, then rose slightly to 1925, despite the continued deflationary policies (Figure 5.1). The unemployment figures also improved from their 1921 peak but remained high. Civil employment rose from its low point in 1921 to 1925 at between 1 and 1 1/2 per cent per year.[37] Prices fell gently but the consensus was that when Britain returned to gold a price disparity with the USA remained; deflationary pressures, therefore, continued, with the exception of a slightly reflationary budget.

Between 1925 and 1930, wage rates fell 3.3 per cent and retail prices fell 10 per cent, bringing real wages back to 1922 levels. Wholesale prices, as before, fell further, by 25 per cent. American wholesale prices were falling much more slowly by this time, and in 1929, for the first time since 1913, the American index was higher than the British (Figures 5.1, 5.4 and 5.8). Parity at last, but too late.

Employment grew faster after the return to gold, at 2 1/2 per cent.[38] But growth was insufficient to bring unemployment below 1.4m,[39] even in the best year of the 1920s. After this miserable decade came something worse, as the world slid into the Great Depression.

5 EFFECTS ON FUNCTIONAL DISTRIBUTION

We shall look at the effects of the return to gold on the distribution of income first following the conventions of national income accounting in treating interest payments within a country as transfer payments. The exception is interest paid by firms, which we have calculated from the appropriation (profit and loss) account.[40] Then in Section 5.4 the question of government interest payments is addressed.

Relative shares are presented in Figure 5.15.[41] (Note that the vertical axis begins at 50 per cent; the bulk of income from employment has been omitted.) We see several effects immediately. As predicted, the impact of the sharp deflation and high interest rates in 1921 is a 'double squeeze' on profits; the share of income from employment actually rose in 1921, and fell in 1922 as firms sacked labour as wages continued to fall. The new share of income from employment was then sustained throughout the period. The share of total labour income also fell but less so, as there was a rise in the share from self-employment. Interestingly, although GDP fell dramatically in the year of the General Strike, relative shares were hardly affected.

At the top of the graph we see the predicted increase in the share of interest paid by firms and also of rent, the other component with a large fixed-income element. There is no contractual obligation to pay dividends, and in a recession there is an incentive to adjust dividends downward, but if firms are to maintain the attractiveness of their shares, dividend yields must follow interest rates. Figure 5.16 shows that dividends remained high; the sum of interest and dividends exceeded gross profits in 1921, 1926, and 1928–31, clearly showing that the second consideration outweighed the first. Interest as a percentage of gross profit rose from 16 per cent in 1920 to 37 per cent in 1931. When taxes on profits are also deducted, profits are uniformly negative throughout the period; the wonder is that the literature on this period is not littered with tales of large scale bankruptcies. Presumably, charges to reserves in the 1920s redressed excess profits earned during the war.

5.1 The Effect of Prices on Distribution

As remarked in the introduction, some attempt will be made to assess the influence of different factors on the distribution which we observe, using some counterfactual analysis. The first area is the effect of price changes on the distribution of relative shares. The effect purely of falling prices can be judged with the help of the ingenious diagram in Sir Henry Strakosch's evidence to the Macmillan Committee (1931).

The Strakosch Diagram (Figure 5.17) illustrates the theoretical effects on income distribution purely of changes in the price level. The diagram is based on the relative shares in 'national production' of five components, estimated as follows for 1924:[42]

Variable incomes:

wages and salaries	49.8%
profit from enterprise	16.8%
'other government expenditure' (i.e. excluding interest payments)	7.0%

Fixed money incomes:

[private sector] interest and rent	16.4%
public debt service, redemption charges	10.0%

Strakosch then shows what would happen to relative shares if prices rose or fell from an index of 100, on the assumption that the national income remains constant – i.e. not allowing for adjustments to price changes by altering output and employment. Thus the diagram illustrates the potential scale of the distributional conflict between fixed and variable incomes created solely by changes in the price level.

Private sector interest payments and public debt service are contractual and thus unaffected, in money terms, by changes in prices. The same was assumed to hold for all rent. Together these elements constitute the economy's fixed money incomes. Their real value therefore increases (decreases) as the general price level falls (rises). The other three categories, i.e. government expenditure excluding interest on National Debt, profits from enterprise, and wages, are the variable component of GDP. Variable incomes, taken as a whole, are treated as a residual; the proportions shown assume that the relative proportions of the three components within the whole remain constant, that is, they share the burden of a price fall (benefit of a price rise) *pro rata.* As with our analysis, Strakosch's main dividing line cuts through the 'capitalist class': profits are variable and rentiers own fixed-money obligations.

Changes in the price level will also trigger conflicts within the variable money-income group, most of all between labour-income and profit. In addition to the results under the assumption of equal shares of the burden/gain amongst the variable-income earners, the two thick lines represent the consequences of constant money wages (the hyperbola) and of constant real wages (the horizontal line). The hyperbola can be interpreted as an indicator of the pressure to adjust money wages in our period. Given the initial distribution of income and the assumed constancy of output, a fall of the price level by only 20 per cent would completely exhaust profits in the absence of a nominal wage adjustment. Real wage resistance (horizontal line) would also squeeze profits, but less harshly. The redistribution in favour of rentiers exacerbates the conflict between profits and wages.

Figure 5.17 shows that a fall of the price level by only 20 per cent would completely exhaust profits in the absence of a nominal wage adjustment, based on 1924 distribution. Profits net of interest were more robust in 1924 than in 1920. Thus any effect we find on profit for 1920 based on the 1924 initial distribution will go forward *a fortiori.* Recall (Section 4 above) that retail prices fell 27 per cent and wholesale prices 48 per cent between 1920 and 1922. Thus Strakosch's diagram shows conclusively that profits net only of interest (i.e. gross of dividends and taxes) could not possibly have remained positive without a fall in money wages. Between 1920 and 1922 money wages fell 23 per cent, and a further 6 per cent the following year (Figure 5.1).

The net fall in real wages between 1920 and 1923 was just 2.3 per cent, so the four years together conform to real wage resistance (Figure 5.1). A 40 per cent fall in prices with real wage resistance would annihilate profit; wholesale prices fell by more than that. In a composite index of wholesale and retail prices a weight of 0.55 to wholesale prices gives an overall fall of 40 per cent.[43] Hence we can conclude that for profits to have remained positive in this period, the fall in wages probably had to be supplemented by unemployment if firms were to retain positive profit.

Figure 5.15 displays the recovery of the share of profits as real wages and employment decline from 1921 to 1923; after that, the share of all labour income stabilizes at around 80 per cent of total domestic income and real wages gradually recover. The other dip in the share of profits, in 1926, is chiefly due to the General Strike – another sudden shock.

5.2 Employment

Another piece of counterfactual calculation shows what would have happened to the shares of profit and employed labour if employment had been maintained. We calculated the income generated per employed worker and applied this to estimated 'full employment', derived from assuming that 70 per cent participation of the working age civil population constituted full employment (thus actual employment in 1920 was 'over-full'). Thus the estimate embodies the wages and prices which actually obtained.

First, following Strakosch and assuming constant income, negative profits would have resulted in 1921, 1930 and 1931 and the rest of the time profits were positive but very small: £13–109m. Of course this calculation is quite unrealistic, as the extra labour would have been producing unsalable output. Nevertheless it gives some feeling for the gravity of the profits squeeze and demonstrates again that the wage reductions of the early 1920s were insufficient by themselves to compensate for the rise in the share of fixed-money incomes: unemployment and/or real wage reduction were necessary as well, if firms were to survive.

The second approach assumes an equal addition to the wage bill and to aggregate income. The absolute level of profits is thus not affected. The effects on relative shares are given in Figure 5.18. Differences appear slight, but the percentage reduction in the share of profit[44] net of interest is 7–8 per cent for most years; the reduction was greater (9–14 per cent) in the years of shock (1921, 1930, 1931). The share of full-employment labour income in potential income in the 'doldrum' years was about 65 per cent instead of the 62 per cent actual share.

5.3 Other Factors Affecting the Company Sector

Once the share of income from employment stabilized, further effects on profits came from the steadily increasing share of rent and interest. High interest rates, as well as being a deduction from profit, can also alter the balance of sources of firms' income. With falling sales and investment opportunities and high interest rates, one would expect firms to expand their investment in securities. The financial side of corporate activity was nowhere near as developed as it is today, where financial departments often seem to overshadow production departments, but nevertheless this protective strategy is attractive. To the extent that firms become rentiers, their action is detrimental to production and employment, though beneficial to profits.

The only relevant data is the proportion of company non-trading income to total company income, which can be assumed to have a large rentier component. Figure 5.19 shows that this proportion rose substantially in the period.

Embedded in the aggregate company accounts are the activities of the banks, which are vehicles of monetary policy. Here, the influence of the rate of interest on the asset and liability sides is more closely matched. Ascertaining the net effect on the banking system as part of the company sector has proved difficult; readers are thus alerted to their inclusion in company data. We see two possible biases on the aggregate net profit position. These are likely to operate in contradictory directions: as banks benefit more from the positive side of high interest rates than do ordinary companies, there is an upward bias, but they were in the 'front line' of restrictive monetary policy and hence their gross profit might have been adversely affected by more than the average company.

5.4 Redistributive Effects of Debt Management

We saw that debt service was a problem throughout the 20s (Figure 5.13). In order fully to assess the redistributive effects of the structure of the public finances, one would need detailed data on the incidence of tax and on personal income distribution at home and the amounts paid to foreign holders. The latter amounted to 35 per cent of payments in 1920 and 22 per cent in 1921 and afterwards were much smaller.[45] Payments to foreigners add to the deflationary force in full.

We have no data on home tax incidence, but Figure 5.13 does show one startling statistic: from 1924 to 1932 income taxes were insufficient to cover interest of the public debt. Some interest income would have been clawed back in tax, and it is believed that the recipients of interest income were more than averagely likely to pay surtax and supertax, but, first, receipts from surtax and supertax never accounted for more than 22 per cent of all taxes on income in our period[46] and second, the aggregate data make it perfectly clear that there was a net transfer from income taxpayers as a whole to rentiers.

5.4.1 War loan

Many of the aggregate effects of the high interest rates have already been explored. We now take a microeconomic perspective, to give some idea of the strength of the rentier's position in the 1920s, using War Loan as the representative security. Data from Pember and Boyle permit the calculation of a matrix of holding period yields on an investment of £100 in War Loan, one yield for each possible end-of-year date at which the stock could be bought and sold.[47] These are presented in Figure 5.1. In addition, two 'real' annual rates of return were calculated, first using Feinstein's retail price index (Figure 5.1) and second, as a rough indication of the international purchasing power resulting from the investment, using an import price index.[48]

The average annual nominal rate of return over all holding periods is no less than 5.16 per cent; excluding 1917–1920 raises this to 5.37 per cent. There is one negative yield after 1920 (buying in 1930 and selling in 1931), but there are also some handsome returns, even in nominal terms. In real terms (retail prices), investors who obtained their stock at the time of the issue in 1917 lost during the inflation of the final war years and the post-war boom. However, any investor who held stock bought at the time of the issue for five years or more earned a real annual return of between 3.6 and 4.9 per cent. Some individual holding period yields were very much higher: 13–36 per cent in the big deflation years. The average of all holding period real yields is 7.4 per cent and after 1920 8.5 per cent.

These high nominal and real yields must be seen against the background of a relatively poor overall real economic performance. From 1916, the year before the issue of War Loan, to 1932, the year of its conversion, the index of GDP at factor cost fell from 108 to 103. From 1916 to 1929, thus excluding the depression years, shows zero growth. Only by using the recession year 1921 or subsequent years as a starting point does one get positive rates of output growth. By comparison, the purchasing power of a £100 investment in 5 per cent War Loan at the time of issue rose to almost £239 in 1932.

Foreign holders fared even better: the estimate of the real value to foreign holders of their purchase of War Loan using import prices as a deflator gives an average annual real yield over all holding periods of 11.5 per cent and over the years after 1920 of 12.7 per cent. Holding to 1932 resulted in an average yield of 13 per cent. If the aim was to keep creditors sweet, especially foreign creditors, these data suggest success.

6 THE END OF THE GOLD STANDARD

The gold standard was suspended on 21 September 1931. The following Sunday saw this comment from Keynes (1931, p. 245):

> There are few Englishmen who do not rejoice at the breaking of our gold fetters. We feel that we have at last a free hand to do what is sensible. ... It may seem surprising that a move which has been represented as a disastrous catastrophe should have been received with so much enthusiasm. But the great advantages to British trade and industry of our ceasing artificial efforts to maintain our currency above its real value were quickly realised.

The release from the gold standard opened the possibility of rescheduling the public debt, in particular, 5 per cent War Loan. The conversion, announced on 30 June 1932, was 'the first major landmark of the cheap money policy which nominally continued until 1951' (Nevin 1955, p. 76). New 3 per cent stock was created only through conversion (ibid., p. 92). A bonus of £1 for every £100 of stock was offered to holders of 5 per cent War Loan who accepted the exchange. 'By the end of September 1932, all but 8 per cent of the £2,086 million loan had been converted, and the remainder was paid out in cash at the end of the year. This successful conversion operation contributed to a fall in debt service as a percentage of national income from 8.3 per cent in 1932 to 4.6 per cent in 1935' (Cairncross and Eichengreen, 1983, pp. 100-1). The annual savings in interest charges for a conversion of £2bn of stock amounted to £30m, more than 10 per cent of the total interest charge on National Debt in 1933.[49]

Interest rates then fell throughout the 30s; the rentier had had his day – for a while.

7 CONCLUSION

There are those who still believe that monetary factors leave real economic relationships unaffected. We believe, in contrast, that neither inflation nor deflation is ever neutral; some sectional interests will always be affected. To demonstrate this, we have examined the deflation in Britain in the 1920s, and shown the considerable redistributive effects, away from labour and net profit toward the recipients of interest and rent, both before and after tax.

There are uncomfortable parallels with the instigation of a 'monetarist' or sound money policy in Britain in the 1980s: the recession of 1980–81 bears a strong resemblance to 1920–21, the settling down to higher-than-normal rates of unemployment is observed in both periods, and finally Britain's subscription to the Exchange Rate Mechanism at an overvalued exchange rate parallels her return to gold in 1925. The joy that Keynes expressed when Britain left the gold standard is an emotion widely felt when Britain left the ERM in 1992. There, mercifully, the parallel ends, as the stock market crash of 1987 has not had the same devastating effects as the Wall Street crash of 1929; nor has the structure of debt played the same role, partly because of the length of intervening years since the Second World War and partly because the moral imperative of full repayment has lost its force. If Grossman's hypothesis is right, this latter fact presupposes that the European War is over. Let us hope so.

The warning that the experience of the 1920s offers is that deflation is not costless, not 'everywhere and always [only] a monetary phenomenon', but that it has real consequences for both the level of output and its distribution. The austerity policies which EU countries have put in place to prepare for a common currency are of a similar nature to the austerity policies of the 1920s. We believe that the analysis of the 1920s provides a good guide to the distributive effects these policies are likely to have.

Table 5.1 War loan, nominal returns

Sold on 31 Dec	Bought on 31 December (year) except first column															
	Issue date															
	1917	1918	1919	1920	1921	1922	1923	1924	1925	1926	1927	1928	1929	1930	1931	1932
1917	3.95															
1918	4.88	6.132														
1919	3.96	4.18	2.38													
1920	2.10	1.58	−0.66	−3.81												
1921	4.30	4.61	4.31	5.57	16.82											
1922	5.39	5.95	6.20	7.88	15.05	14.02										
1923	5.18	5.63	5.80	7.00	11.45	9.32	5.05									
1924	5.12	5.53	5.68	6.66	9.94	8.13	5.55	6.36								
1925	4.85	5.19	5.28	6.05	8.56	6.91	4.86	4.99	3.81							
1926	4.73	5.04	5.12	5.77	7.83	6.41	4.80	4.95	4.45	5.35						
1927	4.63	4.90	4.97	5.54	7.29	6.05	4.73	4.87	4.58	5.21	5.33					
1928	4.58	4.83	4.91	5.42	6.96	5.87	4.78	4.94	4.79	5.37	5.63	6.23				
1929	4.34	4.56	4.61	5.05	6.37	5.36	4.37	4.44	4.25	4.56	4.50	4.29	2.50			
1930	4.38	4.59	4.65	5.07	6.28	5.40	4.55	4.68	4.59	4.97	5.10	5.25	4.99	7.93		
1931	3.98	4.14	4.16	4.49	5.53	4.66	3.83	3.84	3.64	3.77	3.62	3.35	2.52	2.65	−2.49	
1932	4.06	4.24	4.27	4.60	5.58	4.81	4.10	4.16	4.06	4.27	4.28	4.25	3.94	4.63	3.16	9.62

average of all possible holding periods   5.16

average of all possible holding periods after 1920   5.37

101

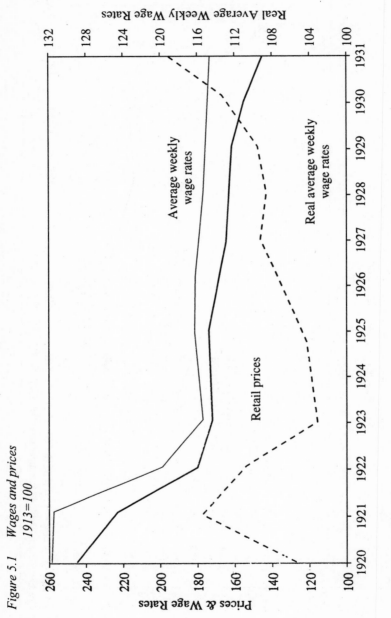

Figure 5.1   Wages and prices
1913=100

Source: Feinstein, Table 65.

102

Figure 5.2   Unemployment

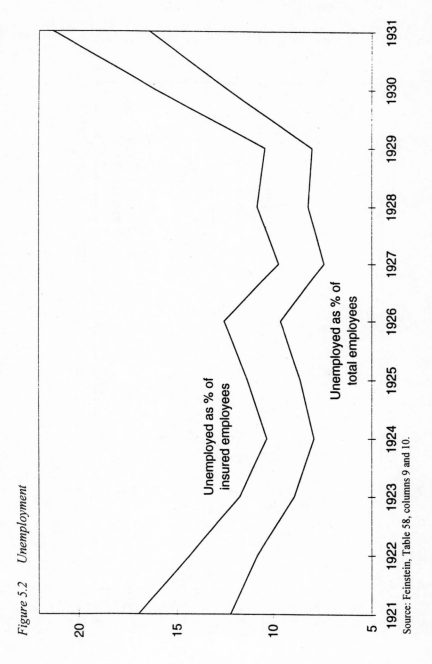

Source: Feinstein, Table 58, columns 9 and 10.

103

Figure 5.3   Yield on consols

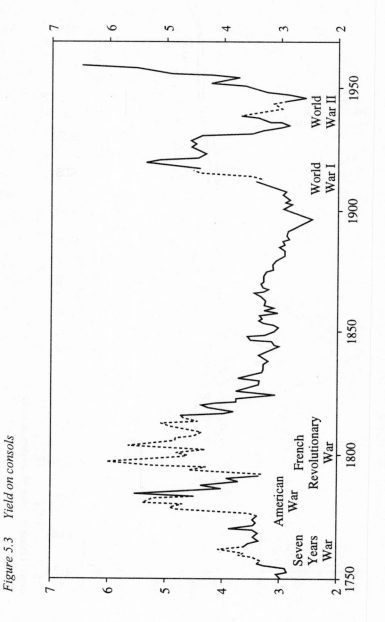

Source: J.R. Hicks, *Critical Essays in Monetary Theory*, p. 84.

104

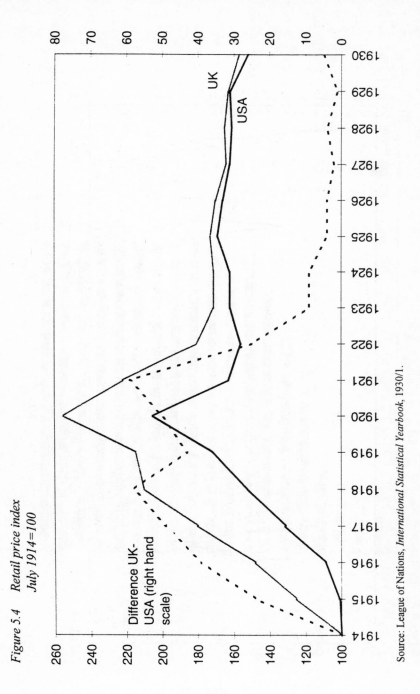

Figure 5.4   Retail price index
July 1914=100

Difference UK-USA (right hand scale)

UK

USA

Source: League of Nations, *International Statistical Yearbook*, 1930/1.

Figure 5.5 The debt

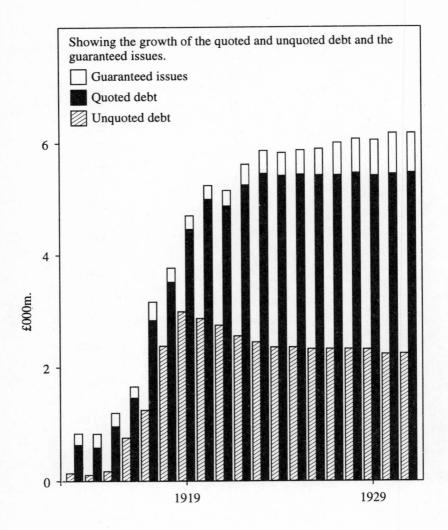

Showing the growth of the quoted and unquoted debt and the
guaranteed issues.

☐ Guaranteed issues

■ Quoted debt

▨ Unquoted debt

Source: Pember and Boyle, p. 563.

Figure 5.6   Exchange rate ($/£)

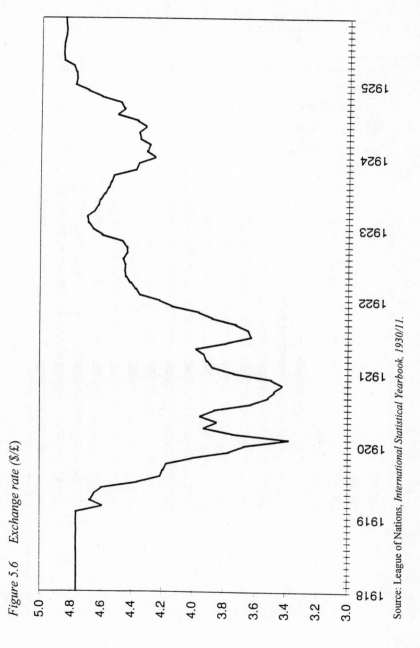

Source: League of Nations, *International Statistical Yearbook, 1930/11.*

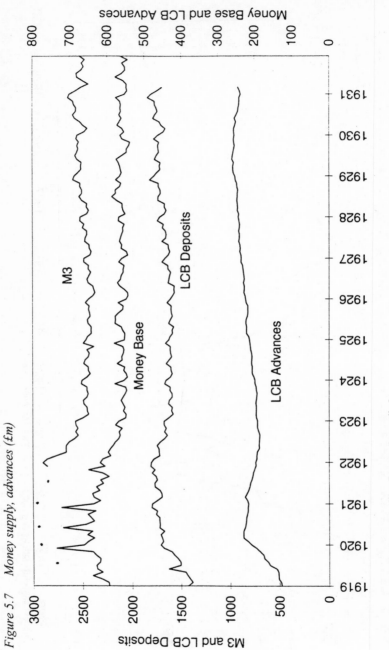

Figure 5.7   Money supply, advances (£m)

Source: Capie and Webber; Macmillan Report, Appendix I.

108

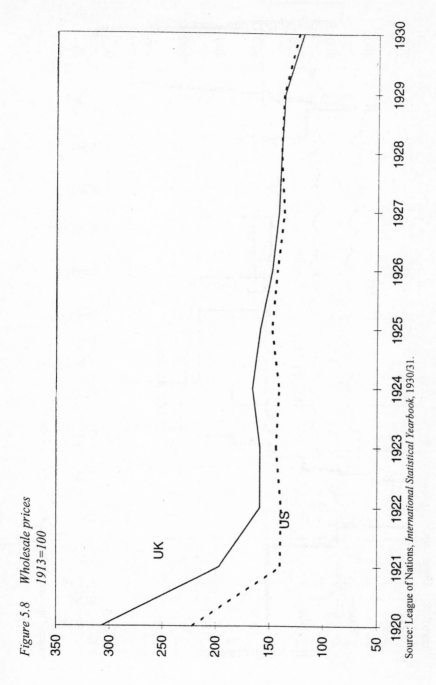

Figure 5.8 *Wholesale prices*
1913=100

UK

US

Source: League of Nations, *International Statistical Yearbook*, 1930/31.

Figure 5.9   Bank rate

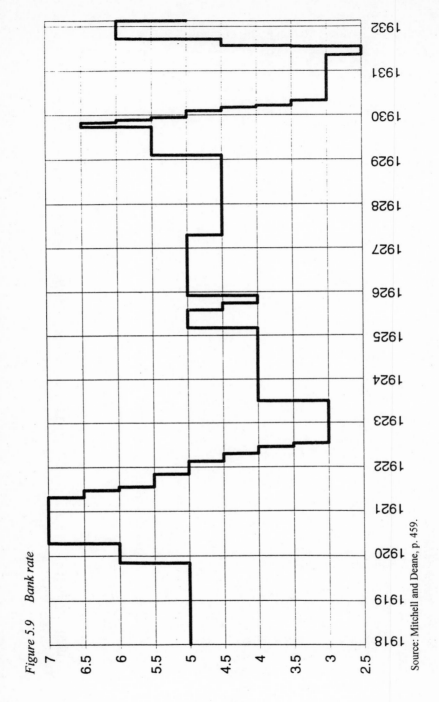

Source: Mitchell and Deane, p. 459.

110

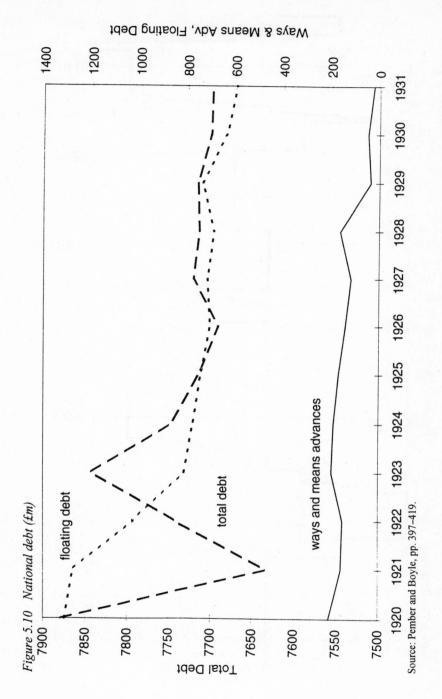

Figure 5.10 National debt (£m)

Source: Pember and Boyle, pp. 397–419.

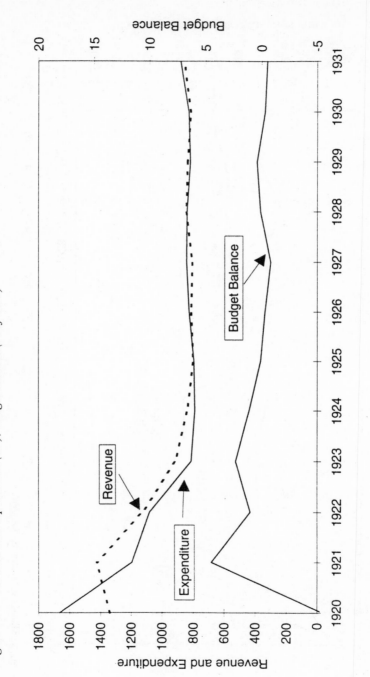

Figure 5.11   Revenue and expenditure (£m), budget balance (% of GDP)

Source: Pember and Boyle, pp. 520–1.

112

Figure 5.12   Interest rates

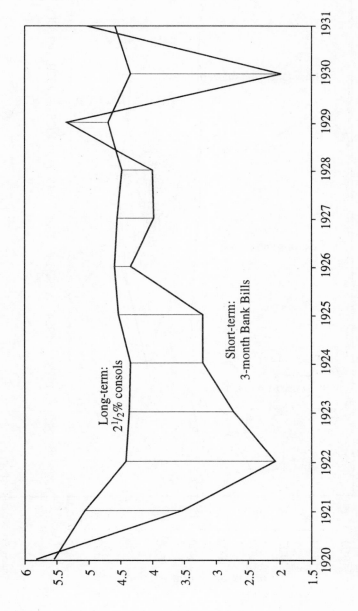

Long-term:
2¹/₂% consols

Short-term:
3-month Bank Bills

Source: Mitchell and Deane, pp. 455, 460.

Figure 5.13   Revenue and debt service

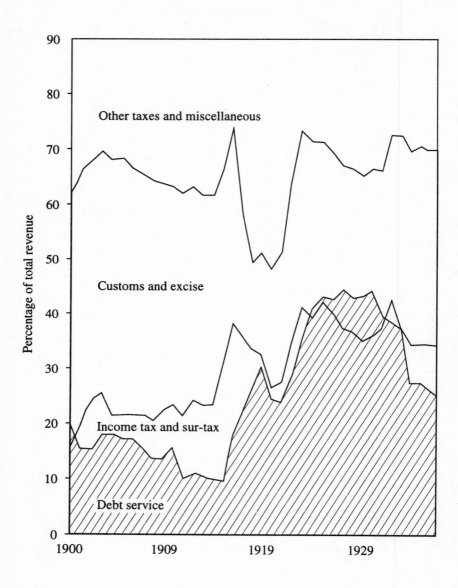

Source: Pember and Boyle, p. 573.

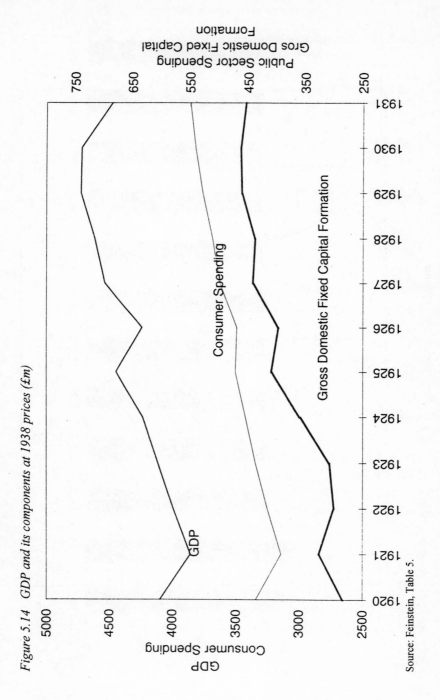

Figure 5.14 GDP and its components at 1938 prices (£m)

Source: Feinstein, Table 5.

115

Figure 5.15 Factor income shares

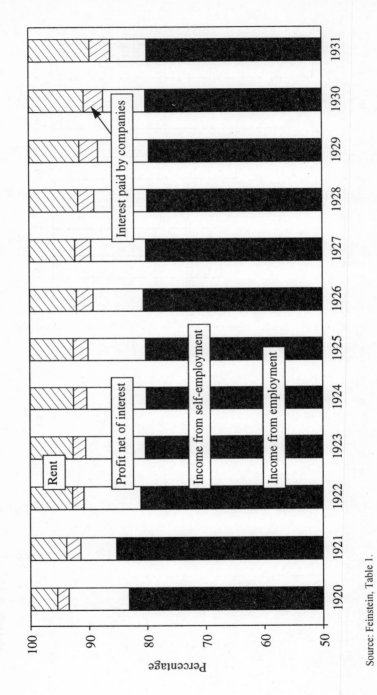

Source: Feinstein, Table 1.

116

Figure 5.16 Interest and dividends as a percentage of gross profit

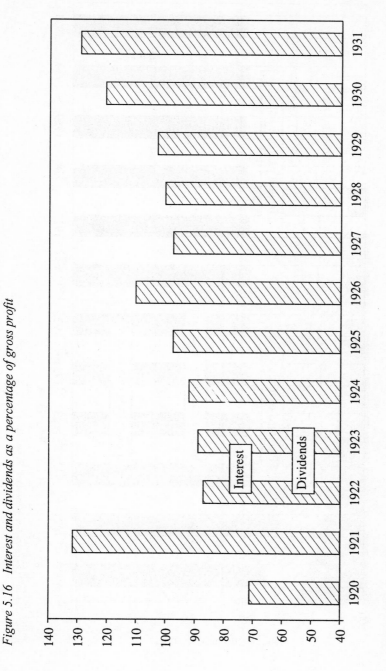

Source: Feinstein, Table 32.

117

Figure 5.17 The Strakosch diagram

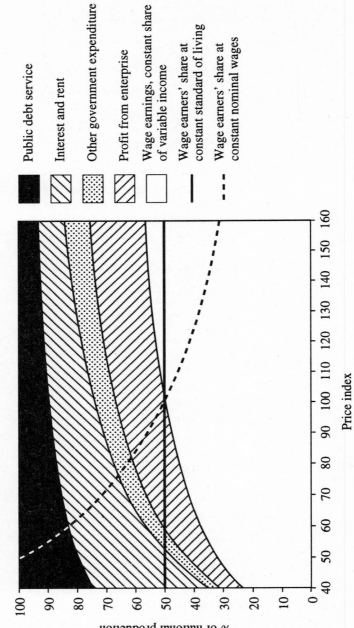

Source: Macmillan Committee Minutes of Evidence.

118

Figure 5.18 Shares of potential income

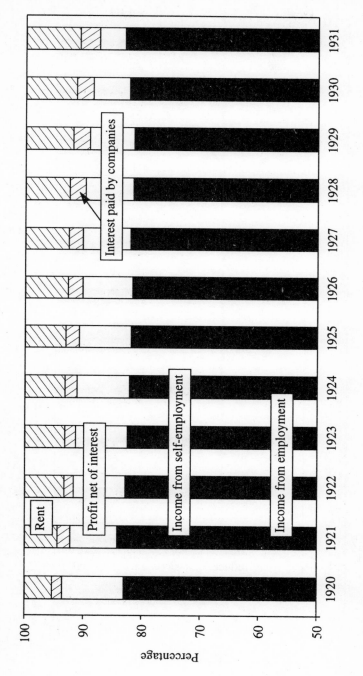

Sources: Feinstein and our calculations.

119

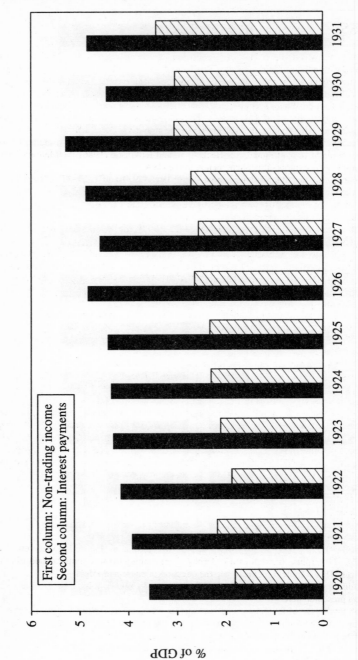

Figure 5.19 Interest payments and non-trading income of the corporate sector

First column: Non-trading income
Second column: Interest payments

% of GDP

1920 1921 1922 1923 1924 1925 1926 1927 1928 1929 1930 1931

Source: Feinstein, Table 32.

NOTES

1. This paper was first presented, without being written up, eight years ago. I am indebted to Ralf Jacob and Jill Pleban for their intellectual and technical cooperation at that time and to the organizers of this conference for the opportunity to revisit these issues. Ralf and Donelle Rowe entered the world of 'retrocomputing' to bring this paper back to life; Ralf, Marco Crocco, Shabih Mohib and Rob Price did the graphs. Sue Howson commented most helpfully on a draft; she is not to be held responsible for the shortcomings remaining. The interpretation put on the data is strictly the author's.
2. Whether restrictive policies or falling oil prices were responsible is a matter of debate; both could have contributed. See Beckerman and Jenkinson (1986); McMahon (1996).
3. Schor (1991) explores this phenomenon in the USA.
4. Chairman of the Independent Labour Party, later (1924 and 1929–31) Chancellor of the Exchequer.
5. Problems of competitive devaluation and of using the exchange rate weapon in a more integrated world economy became apparent later still.
6. Just as this paper undergoes revision (June 1997), the monetarist basis of the Treaty provisions is at last being recognized.
7. There is a debate over whether sterling was actually overvalued in the late 1920s (see the references to Matthews and Redmond). But there is no doubt that the rate was difficult to sustain, whether due to overvaluation or to the altered balance of power between Britain and the US.
8. Strakosch was a financier, Managing Director then Chairman of the Union Corporation, a member of the League of Nations Financial Committee, and Chairman of The Economist Newspaper Ltd (Moggridge, 1992, p. 906).
9. LCB deposits are given in Figure 5.7 to assess representativeness by comparison with M3.
10. Macmillan Report, Appendix 1.
11. The data on advances also support the timing of the end of the boom.
12. Howson (1975, p. 183, n. 5) cautions that the GDP figures of this period are very rough; she suggests a margin of error of +/- 15 to 25 per cent.
13. Assuming parity of prices in 1914, when both indexes stood at 100.
14. The fact that America returned to gold soon after the War made US prices the reference point; it was to the dollar that the pound had to conform. Moggridge (1969) complains that the authorities should have taken European prices into account events as well. The extent of multilateral overvaluation using a trade-weighted basket and retail prices has been estimated (Redmond, 1984) at 20–25 per cent. See also Matthews (1986) and (1989) and Redmond (1989).
15. Pember and Boyle, pp. 394–7.
16. Aldcroft (1970, p. 42); Howson (1975, p. 10).
17. Feinstein, Table 34.
18. I.e. thousand million.
19. Feinstein, Tables 2 and 3.
20. Ursula Hicks (1954, p. 337) warns against overestimating the deflationary effect of the 1920–21 surplus, as much of it is derived from running off war contracts and from falling prices. This comment seems to beg the question of cause and effect.
21. Middleton's (1985) recalculations for 1929/30 and 1930/31 accord quite closely with the data presented here.
22. The total issue of £2,554m comprised £844m cash and £1,709m conversions of previous loans and Treasury Bills. It was repayable at par in 1947 or at any time on or after 1 June 1929 on three months' notice. (Pember and Boyle, p. 296)
23. See Winch, 1969, chapter 6 for an exposition of the thinking of the time.
24. Pember and Boyle, pp. 396–401.

25. Ibid., pp. 522–5.
26. Feinstein, Table 34.
27. March was chosen to avoid the spikes in June and December.
28. Mitchell and Deane (1962), Tables 3 and 6.
29. Capie and Webber, Table I(1).
30. Eichengreen (1992, p. 71, n. 11).
31. See notes 4 and 9 above and Moggridge (1969, pp. 71–9).
32. The whole episode is documented in detail by Moggridge (1969).
33. Table 65.
34. Sliding-scale wage agreements were set up during the War to protect workers from the inevitable inflation. Cairncross and Eichengreen (1983, p. 31) state that 55 to 60 per cent of all wage reductions in 1921 and 40 per cent in 1922 took place under these agreements. Routh (1965) had attributed the fall of wages almost exclusively to these agreements, but Broadberry (1986) argues that Routh's figures are substantially overstated.
35. Feinstein, Table 32.
36. Broadberry (1986, p. 103).
37. Ibid.
38. Ibid.
39. Feinstein, Table 58.
40. Ibid., Table 32.
41. Shares are calculated as a percentage of total domestic income, that is, gross domestic product at factor cost +/- stock appreciation. Gross trading profits includes public corporations and enterprises, though there is no data on interest paid by these entities; thus the Figure overstates the share of net profits.
42. He cites estimates of Arthur Bowley and Sir Josiah Stamp (1927). We could not find this source.
43. Sources as for Figures 5.1 and 5.8.
44. I.e. the hypothetical share as a percentage of the actual share, the shares themselves expressed as percentages of total income.
45. Feinstein, Table 34; Pember and Boyle, p. 522.
46. Pember and Boyle, pp. 520–1
47. Pember and Boyle give the price of War Loan for the last trading day of each calendar year; therefore, apart from 1917, when the Loan was issued, it is assumed that all purchases and sales take place at the end of the year. We assumed that investors do not reinvest the accumulated coupon payments, so we provide underestimates; the more usual assumption, of compound interest, was rejected for the sake of simplicity. The coupon payments are summed, then added to the selling price, thus giving the total amount of cash generated by the investment over the holding period. These are converted into rates of return.
48. Feinstein, Table 64.
49. Pember and Boyle, pp. 422–3, 524–5.

REFERENCES

Aldcroft, D.H. (1970), 'The impact of British monetary policy, 1919–1939', in *International Review of the History of Banking*, **3**.

Alford, B.W.E. (1972), 'Depression and Recovery? British Economic Growth 1918–1939', in *Studies in Economic History Series*, London: Macmillan.

Broadberry, S.N. (1986), *The British Economy between the Wars: A Macroeconomic Survey*, Blackwell.

Beckerman, W. and T. Jenkinson (1986), 'What stopped the inflation? Unemployment or commodity prices', in *Economic Journal*, **96**, 39–54.

Brown Jr, W.A. (1929), 'The conflict of opinion and economic interest in England', in Pollard (1970).

Bullock, A. (1969), *The Life and Times of Ernest Bevin*, Vol. 1, London: Heinemann.

Cairncross, A. and B. Eichengreen (1983), *Sterling in Decline*, Oxford: Basil Blackwell.

Capie, F. and A. Webber (1987), 'A Monetary History of the United Kingdom, 1870–1982', in *Data, Sources, Methods*, Vol. 1, London: George Allen and Unwin.

Clay, H. (1957), *Lord Norman*, London: Macmillan.

Committee on Currency and Foreign Exchanges after the War (Cunliffe Committee) (1918), *First Interim Report*, Cd. 9182 (B.P.P. 1918 (9182), VII, 853), London: HMSO.

Committee on Finance and Industry (Macmillan Committee) (1931), *Report*, Cmd. 3897 (B.P.P. 1930–31 (3897), XIII, 291), London: HMSO.

Committee on Finance and Industry (Macmillan Committee) (1931), *Minutes of Evidence*, 2 vols, London: Treasury.

Cunliffe Committee. See Committee on Currency and Foreign Exchanges after the War.

Dowie, J. (1975) '1919–20 is in need of attention', in *Economic History Review*, **28**(8), 429–50.

Eichengreen, B. (1992), *Golden Fetters*, Oxford: Oxford University Press.

Einzig, P. (1932), *Montagu Norman: A Study in Financial Statesmanship*, London: Kegan Paul, Trench, Trubner.

Feinstein, C.H. (1972), *National Income, Expenditure and Output of the UK, 1855–1965*, Cambridge: Cambridge University Press.

Fforde, J.S. (1983), 'Setting monetary objectives', in *Bank of England Quarterly Bulletin*, **23**(6), 200–9.

Francis, E.V. (1939), *Britain's Economic Strategy*, London: Jonathan Cape.

Galbraith, J.K. (1996), 'The war against the poor', in *The Observer*, Business Section, 29 September, p. 4.

Grossman, H.I. (1990), 'The Political Economy of War Debt and Inflation', in *Monetary Policy for a Changing Financial Environment*, Washington DC: The American Enterprise Institute Press, pp. 166–80.

Hancock, K.J. (1962), 'The Reduction of Unemployment as a Problem of Public Policy, 1920–1929', in Pollard (1970).

Hawtrey, R.G. (1962), *A Century of Bank Rate*, 2nd edition, London: Frank Cass and Co.

Hicks, J.R. (1958), 'The Yield on Consols', reprinted in Hicks (1967), *Critical Essays in Monetary Theory*, Oxford: Oxford University Press.

Hicks, U.K. (1954), *British Public Finances: Their Structure and Development, 1880–1952*, Oxford: Oxford University Press.

Hodgson, G.M. (1984), 'Thatcherism: The miracle that never happened' in E.J. Nell (ed.), *Free Market Conservatism: A Critique of Theory and Practice*, London: George Allen and Unwin.

Howson, S.K. (1975), *Domestic Monetary Management in Britain, 1919–1938*, Cambridge: Cambridge University Press.

Hume, L.J. (1963), 'The Gold Standard and Deflation: Issues and Attitudes in the 1920's', in *Economica*. Reprinted in Pollard (1970).

Keynes, J.M. (1913), *Indian Currency and Finance, Collected Writings of J.M. Keynes*, Vol. I.

Keynes, J.M. (1925), 'The Economic Consequences of Mr Churchill'. Reprinted in *Collected Writings of J.M. Keynes*, Vol. IX, 207–30 and in Pollard (1970).

Keynes, J.M. (1931), 'The end of the gold standard', in *Sunday Express*, 27 September. Reprinted in *Collected Writings of J.M. Keynes*, Vol. IX, 245–9.

League of Nations (1931), *International Statistical Yearbook, 1930/1*, Geneva: League of Nations.

Longstreth, F. (1979), 'The City, Industry and the State', in C. Crouch (ed.), *State and Economy in Contemporary Capitalism*, London: Croom Helm.

Macmillan Committee (1931). See Committee on Finance and Industry.

Matthews, K.G.P. (1986), 'Was sterling overvalued in 1925?', in *Economic History Review*, **39**, 572–87.

Matthews, K.G.P. (1989), 'Reply', in *Economic History Review*, **42**.

McMahon, K. (1996), 'The rise and fall of inflation', in *Prospect*, February, 68–71.

Middleton, R. (1985), *Towards the Managed Economy: Keynes, the Treasury and the Fiscal Policy Debate of the 1930s*, London: Methuen.

Minns, R. (1981), 'A comment on "Finance Capital and the Crisis in Britain"', in *Capital and Class*, **14**.

Mitchell, B.R. and P. Deane (1962), *Abstract of British Historical Statistics*, Cambridge: Cambridge University Press.

Moggridge, D.E. (1969), *The Return to Gold, 1925: The Formulation of Economic Policy and its Critics*, Occasional Papers, 19, Cambridge: University of Cambridge Department of Applied Economics.

Moggridge, D.E. (1992), *Maynard Keynes: An Economist's Biography*, London: Routledge.

Nevin, E. (1955), *The mechanism of cheap money: a study of British monetary policy, 1931-1939*, Cardiff: University of Wales Press.

Overbeek, H. (1980), 'Finance capital and the crisis in Britain', in *Capital and Class*, **11**.

Pember and Boyle (no initials) (1950), *British Government Securities in the Twentieth Century*, 2nd edition, privately printed.

Pigou, A.C. (1931). See Committee on Finance and Industry.

Pigou, A.C. (1947), *Aspects of British Economic History, 1918–1925*, London: Macmillian.

Pollard, S. (1962), *The Development of the British Economy, 1914–1950*, London: Edward Arnold.

Pollard, S. (1970), *The Gold Standard and Employment Policies between the Wars*, London: Methuen.

Redmond, J. (1984), 'The sterling overvaluation in 1925', in *Economic History Review*, **37**, 520–32.

Redmond, J. (1989), 'Comment', in *Economic History Review*, **42**.

Rolfe, S.E. and J. Burtle (1974), *The great wheel: the world monetary system: a reinterpretation*, London: Macmillan.

Routh, G. (1965), *Occupation and Pay in Great Britain, 1906–60*, Cambridge: Cambridge University Press.

Schor, J. (1991), *The Overworked American*, New York: Basic Books.

Smithin, J. (1996), *Macroeconomic Policy and the Future of Capitalism: The Revenge of the Rentiers and the Threat to Prosperity*, London: Edward Elgar.

Wells, J. (1994), 'The missing million', in *European Labour Review*, Summer, 10–18.

Winch, D. (1969), *Economics and Policy: A Historical Study*, London: Hodder and Stoughton.

6. Income Distribution in the Transition: Some reflections and Some Evidence

Jan A. Kregel

1 INTRODUCTION

The theory of distribution is one of the most contested areas of theoretical economics. It is contested by different schools of thought, as well as by different branches of the subject. In Classical theory (which includes Marx) the discussion of distribution concerned its relationship to capital accumulation and growth. It was a question of how the different classes of society might use income to increase capital accumulation and division of labour. It was found that entrepreneurs were much preferable to landowners in this regard. Bound by iron laws and natural proclivities, the worker really did not come into this discussion. It was Marx who pointed out that if all that was required was someone to make investments, the capitalists could also be dispensed with, leaving a workers' state to cultivate the fruits of rapid capital accumulation.

In an unsurprising post-Marxian reaction, neoclassical economics found it prudent to change the subject and shift discussion to indistinguishable individuals blessed with random endowments of resources who joined together to celebrate the simultaneously determination of prices and outputs to the honour of the gods of supply and demand. No one could be held individually, and certainly not morally, responsible for the outcome. In the theory of value and distribution classes thus disappeared, replaced by peculiar individuals, only to be replaced by the even more peculiar 'representative' individual. The question to be answered by distribution theory was thus shifted from what was done with incomes to increase incomes, to how efficiently you distributed incomes in order to avoid wasting them.

After Keynes, distribution became a part of what is now called 'macroeconomics' in the form of 'aggregate' theories of distribution. Social classes were replaced by economic functions, investment and consumption, or more usually aggregate income or output categories, wages, profits and rents. But, the idea that distribution was related to the level of income soon brought back the discussion of the relation between distribution and growth.

Subsequent discussions of the 'microfoundations' of macroeconomics were not only an attempt to reduce Keynesian macroeconomics to general equilibrium theory, they were also meant to return the discussion of distribution to the realm of microeconomics, to emphasize the efficiency of the market mechanism in distributing resources to their most remunerative uses as the handmaiden of growth and development.

Some would argue that these theoretical debates have been sterile, since the facts are the same for any theory. All we really have to do is to record and study them. Leave the theorists to their debates, let's get on with the hard work of measuring the distribution of income. But, what are we going to measure? And once we measure it, what does it mean? And if we don't like it, what, if anything, can we do about it?

Despite the optimism of the applied economist, we have to have some idea about what we are measuring and why. It is only by setting out a theory that we have any idea of what it is important to measure. But, even a clear theoretical specification does not mean that we can get the measurements that allow us to confront the implications of the theory, or to form the basis of policy decisions. The real world capabilities of statisticians do not always correspond to the requirements of theoretical categories. Or the categories may have no real world counterpart, so that they can never be measured except by construction or imputation. Finally, interpretation of the statistical information that is available may be difficult without placing it within the appropriate reference framework.

2 WHAT HAPPENED TO THE DISTRIBUTION OF INCOME IN THE GREAT SLUMP?

For example, Kenneth Boulding (Boulding, 1989, p. 16) notes the seeming paradox that in the US 'in 1932 and 1933, when unemployment was 25 per cent, the proportion of national income going to labour had risen sharply from about 59 per cent in 1929 to 72 per cent in 1932 and 1933 ...' But one would certainly not want to argue that the conditions of workers had improved by a factor of some 20 per cent. Certainly, Boulding notes, workers who managed to retain employment were probably better off, since the fall in national income was concentrated in the decline in the production of capital goods, rather than wage goods. But, for the unemployed, and for labour as a whole, conditions had deteriorated without question, irrespective of what was happening to the statistics which were being reported concerning the distribution of income between wages and profits. The problem is one of relative proportions. The wage share is proportionately much larger than the profit share, so a similar relative decline appears to favour labour.

But, Boulding notes, even this is not quite correct for again paradoxically, 'Interest, ... , as a proportion of the national income almost doubled between 1929 and 1933.' It would appear that both labour and capital were doing well despite the depths of the slump. Here the explanation of the paradox is quite straightforward: the increased real burden of outstanding debt roughly doubled as prices collapsed and fixed interest payments remained unchanged. Here also there were exceptions in the form of a large number of 'creditors', who were never repaid, so within the creditor class those who continued to receive interest were much better off in real terms, while the rest were in exactly the same condition as the unemployed.

It was, of course, the share of profits that had collapsed; profits were negative in both 1932 and 1933. So we finally discover the clear losers, although even within this group there were major exceptions. Realistically, one could not argue that workers, entrepreneurs or rentiers were 'better off', just that some individuals were relatively less badly off.

Boulding provides us with a nice example of the fact that there is no sense in looking at statistics without reference to both micro and macro-economic variables. Without the additional knowledge that national income had fallen sharply, that unemployment had risen sharply, that investment expenditures had collapsed, the figures on functional or personal distribution have little relevance in expressing what actually happened to the economic conditions of the components of those groupings.

Boulding's paradoxes are also of interest because they provide a framework around which I will try to organize the virtually impossible task I have been set by the conference organizers, namely to discuss a subject in which current data is of crucial importance, but which is virtually non-existent in the form required.

I have often suggested that the changes in the economic system which occurred in Central and Eastern Europe in the late 1980s and early 1990s might be thought of as the equivalent of the stock market crash of 1929. Of course, none of these countries had either capitalists, nor operative capital markets, nor was there a cumulative process of price deflation. For these reasons, the traditional functional or class income categories have little application to the problem. And this is part of the difficulties that one faces in trying to assess the changes in income distribution in these countries. It represents a comparison across socio-economic systems, and thus across incompatible distribution categories and theories. However, if we consider the dominant characteristic of the Crash and Slump as the process of debt deflation and the loss of capital values, it is also the case that in most of the Eastern European countries there was a sharp fall in the ability of these assets to produce income, a fall in the net present value of the capital assets under State ownership. State firms went from ersatz 'hedge' financing, to 'Ponzi' financing, and thus so did the State.

Since these assets were owned by the State, analogy with the 1930s would suggest a sharp reduction in the share of the State in national income. Since the major source of State incomes in a planned system is usually a turnover tax, which is roughly equivalent to a tax on corporate gross profits, this also meant an instant fiscal crisis for the State since expenditures could not be cut as rapidly as tax yields collapsed. The result was an attempt to stop the rising deficits by means of decreasing State expenditure on investment. Thus, there was a sharp fall off in investment demand very similar to that in the US in the 1930s.

It is impossible to determine the impact of this change in the government accounts on either labour or interest shares in national income. Analogy with the 1930s would suggest that they should have risen. But, the latter category, rentiers receiving interest, is virtually non-existent, so there is no possibility of improvement in this area. Thus, the share of labour should have increased. Again, we have no simple way of identifying this. All we can do is look at workers' conditions after the transformation, or to look at measures of the dispersion of wage incomes before and after the transition.

3 TRANSFORMATION AND REDISTRIBUTION OF INCOME

The transition in the Central and Eastern European countries has usually been presented as the transition from a 'command' economy to a 'market' economy. I have elsewhere suggested (Kregel, 1994) that a more appropriate way of looking at it was the transformation of the class of state bureaucrats into a class of capitalists. In the real world, everything that is anywhere must be somewhere, and in real capitalist economy, everything that is anywhere must be someone's. The transition was thus more concerned with satisfying the requirement of finding owners for State capital, for the transition of capital owned by the State, to capital owned by private individual capitalists. This is generally represented as the process of privatization. It is usually considered as the transference from one type of management of resources to another, but in reality it has nothing to do with management, but everything to do with ownership. The well-experimented division of ownership and control has been quickly adopted in the transition economies. But, the process of providing ownership via privatization has nothing to do with providing managers to control the operation of assets, nor with the process of building the social infrastructure and institutions required for the successful operations of capitalist firms or a 'market' economy. Thus, if we are looking at the equivalent of what we would call the functional distribution of income between labour and capital, we find it in the privatization of State assets in the transition process, for it is the privatization process which has reconstituted the capitalist's share in national income.

One of the major differences between the 1929 Crash and the subsequent Slump and the conditions of the transition economies in the aftermath of the fall of the Berlin wall was the presence of rapid inflation in most of the countries involved in the latter period. But, as we know, inflation has a relatively clear impact on debtor-creditor relationships. Anyone who has borrowed on fixed terms, or who has fixed assets or natural resources, or the ability to finance the acquisition of fixed assets or natural resources, benefits from inflation and is damaged by deflation. But, officially there were no private 'individual' owners of property under State socialism. The impact of changes in the price level can only affect income distribution in the presence of private contract and private ownership. According to traditional theory, the major beneficiary of the inflation should have been the State, either as the owner of fixed assets, or as a debtor or both. There are a number of reasons why this did not happen. First, the State was not a 'debtor' in the market economy sense, except to the extent of the notes in circulation and savings deposits held by the public. It was the households who were creditors, and who thus suffered the income losses from the loss of purchasing power.

But the most important factor is the one that comes from the experience of the 1920s – the collapse of gross state domestic investment, to coin a term, and the absence of any gross private domestic investment to take its place rapidly. The transformation created capitalists, not entrepreneurs. It created arbitrageurs and speculators in capital assets, it did not create speculators in the production of future incomes. It created new individual wealth, it did not create the ability to make investments. It transformed the party elites into 'free market' elites.

This also makes it difficult to determine whether 'labour' was a gainer or a loser in this process. In one sense, labour was a loser, for the assets which had been held in trust by the worker's state were no longer being operated even ostensibly for the benefit of the workers of the State. This is a question that has been raised before (cf. Kregel et al., 1994) and can be seen in the provision of social overhead services by the state enterprises. These services were paid out of the enterprise budgets, not from the wage funds. When the enterprises are privatized, the new owners are no longer willing to provide these services unless they are counted as a reduction in labour remuneration or are provided on a pay for service market basis. Usually, these 'fringe benefits' disappear without being replaced by government provision of services. As such they represent a net loss in labour incomes.

On the other hand, the process of privatization itself caused a change in the distribution of incomes. When all property is held by the State on behalf of the workers this is equivalent to each individual holding an equal 'share' in the assets owned by the State. It is something like each individual owning a share in a mega index fund which invests in all state assets. The privatization problem could then be seen as dissolving the fund, and distributing the fund's assets to its owners, the shareholders. This is the reverse of the benefits achieved by asset diversification which justifies the existence of mutual fund investment. The transactions costs, indivisibilities, discontinuities and so forth which are reduced by economies of scale of mutual fund investment will now be borne by each individual who as a result will have a lower aggregate value after distribution than before. The voucher privatization programmes were meant to deal with this problem by leaving it up to the individual to decide how these costs would be met. It left the choice of which shares and the concentration of the holding to the discretion of the individual. Or at least this was the theory. Things were rather different in practice.

Consider housing. In Russia the first privatization of housing was to allow each occupier of house room to file for private ownership. Of course, this applied equally to party officials, who received the palatial accommodation they occupied, and to ordinary workers living in one room flats with their assembled relatives. Amazingly, this was initially viewed by most of the population as an equitable distribution of the housing stock.

Now consider the voucher schemes which were supposed to give everyone a similar starting point in terms of the value of their holdings in the index fund. The idea was that each individual could choose how the fund was to be dissolved and distributed. However, not all the state assets were privatized at the same time, and were thus not all available for voucher conversion into direct share holdings. Second, individuals started to buy in vouchers by offering sellers participation in investment groups offering impossible annual returns. Fraudulent financial schemes did not wait for financial markets to be developed and or free market financial regulations to be created to protect individual investors. The problem was aggravated in those cases were an upfront monetary payment was required for participation in the voucher programmes, as speculators simply offered to pay the voucher prices for individuals who did not have the available funds or were risk averse. Some even offered a small premium.

Finally, in the case of privatization by outright sales to domestic residents (sales to foreigners to raise foreign exchange are a different story), in the absence of the favourite assumption of economic theorists of equal access of all individuals to borrow at the risk free rate, this means that those with the highest income and wealth will be those who will participate in the distribution of State assets. Thus, assets which belong to everyone, end up belonging to someone. Again, this should not be a problem in theory if the sales prices appropriately reflect the market value of the assets and the funds received are then distributed by the State. But, they are not. In general they are used to meet budget shortfalls. It is thus virtually impossible to conceive of a market-based system of privatization that does not change the distribution of income by increasing inequality. This should not be surprising, for the nationalization or appropriation of capital assets was originally undertaken with a view to making income distribution more equal, so we need not be surprised if reversing this action should have the symmetrical result of making income distribution less equal.

But, paradoxically, this may not have been the case. This is because the majority of those who benefit from the privatization were those who also benefited from their position in the elite of the socialist economy. It is thus unclear that privatization really brings about a change in the actual inequality of the distribution of income, simply that it is now reflected in market values, whereas before it was reflected in the position in the nomenklatura. All things taken together one should then not be surprised if privatization decreases equality and decreases labour share in national income. Additional reflections on the impact of privatization undertaken by other methods are found in Chilosi (1996).

4 LOOKING AT MACRO DISTRIBUTION DATA

To get some idea of the possible impact of the government spending on distribution, Table 6.1 shows estimates of the share of total product which is now produced by the private sector in some selected transition economies.

The presumption is that the rest is public sector production, which is functioning under the constraint of eliminating budget deficits caused by the write-down of State owned capital equipment. Even in the most advanced countries, the State still account for around a third of total GDP.

Table 6.1   Official estimates of the private sector contribution to GDP 1990–1995

	1990	1991	1992	1993	1994	1995
Bulgaria	9	12	18	25	30	32
Czech	12	17	28	45	56	64
Hungary	25	30	42	50	60	–
Poland	31	42	45	48	70	–
Romania	16	24	26	32	39	45
Slovakia	–	–	22	26	58	65
Russia	–	–	14	21	62	70
Lithuania	–	–	37	57	62	–

Source: ECE, 1996, p. 70, Table 3.2.8.

An alternative way at getting at the wage profit distribution is to look at the production of consumption and investment goods, corrected for trade (Table 6.2). While not perfect, it gives a rough idea of the goods available to wage earners. Here we see a very similar effect to that during the slump in the US, with relatively stable shares of consumption goods, except for the Visograd countries where investment is starting to rise as a proportion of GDP, although most of these countries are now also running trade deficits.

Table 6.2 Composition of final demand in current prices % GDP 1993-1995

	Consumption			Investment			Net Trade		
	'92	'93	'94	'92	'93	'94	'92	'93	'94
Bulgaria	92	88	–	13	13	–	-8	-.6	–
Czech	80	80	74	27	30	26	2	-.4	-4
Hungary	89	85	–	19	20	–	-8	-7	–
Poland	84	83	–	16	16	–	1	1	–
Romania	76	75	79	18	19	22	-5	-2	-5
Slovakia	84	79	78	28	26	25	-6	6	4
Slovenia	76	72	–	18	20	–	3	5	–
Russia	60	69	65	22	25	20	3	–	–
Estonia	77	80	76	24	27	28	-3	-11	-11
Latvia	75	81	81	14	16	17	16	4	2
Lithuania	86	91	85	24	21	15	-8	-6	-.4

Source: ECE, Table 3.2.12

5 THE RETURN OF THE PERSONAL DISTRIBUTION OF INCOME

Theoretically, if we only have one class, then an appropriate measure of income inequality would be the personal distribution as given by the Gini ratio. In effect, even after the transition, this is the most relevant measure, given the weak development and measurement of capital incomes. In this regard the changes in the labour share of income suggested by the stock market crash is that transition should be accompanied by a greater disparity within labour incomes or, more simply, greater wage differentials or wage dispersion. This is not only true because of the difference between the incomes of the employed and unemployed, but also amongst those who have remained employed, a large number of whom are currently not receiving their wages.

About the only way to approach these issues, given the inadequacy of current statistics is through measures of the distribution of gross family incomes or incomes per capita. We should expect such measures to show an increase in income inequality, and the figures that are currently available do not disappoint. As might be expected, all Central and Eastern European countries start the transition process with relatively low income inequality compared with western capitalist countries. (This data is reported by B. Milanovic, 1996, p. 133.) The gini coefficients for the period 1987–1988 are in a range from .2 to .25, with Czechoslovakia showing the lowest inequality and Poland, with a large private sector in agriculture, the highest.

As usual, we must be careful in comparing data across different social systems. A large proportion of the income of the elite accrued as special 'non-income' benefits (to call them non-market is something of an oxymoron) such as preferential access to foreign exchange, foreign goods and travel, and domestic state provided services. None of these are included in the pre-transition income measures. There is thus some validity in the view that there has been no change at all in income inequality, but rather a change in the way these benefits are provided which now shows up in the income statistics.

By 1993 the range of the gini coefficients has risen to .26 to .33, with the figure for Bulgaria rising by a record .10. Hungary and Slovakia however show a reduction in inequality. This may be due to the rather different approaches to privatization that has been taken in the two countries. Milanovic reports that on average gini coefficients for the transition economies as a whole rose about .05 from .22 to .27 over the period to 1993. Data from Torrey, Smeeding and Bailey (1996, reported in Niggle, 1997) report gini values ranging from .189 for the Czech republic to .437 for Russia, with the Slovak republic slightly higher than its new neighbour and Hungary and Poland around .29.

Again, these figures have to be considered with caution as they most probably tend to underestimate the income of the self-employed and the underground economy. However, attempts to estimate this effect show little impact since the majority of these types of income accrue to the top and bottom of the distribution (cf. Niggle, p. 11). There is also great difficulty recording capital incomes, since the figures come mainly from household expenditure surveys and most residents in transition economies still are reticent to provide information to state authorities.

These changes in inequality are roughly comparable to those experienced in the United Kingdom under the Thatcher government over a roughly similar period of time in which the gini coefficient rose from .37 in 1978–1979 to .40 in 1980–1981 to reach .41 in 1984–1985 (cf. Brian Nolan's calculations, p. 131, Table 7.6). Of course, one of the notable characteristics of personal income distribution figures in western economies is their stability over time. The figures reported for the transition economies are thus impressive, not only on account of the size of the changes, but also with respect to the rapidity of the changes.

If we look at the levels of income inequality achieved in the transition economies relative to the capitalist countries other than the UK, the average value for the OECD countries is around .30. Sweden in 1992 had a value of .23, while the US in 1991 had a value of .34. The impact of shock therapy has at least succeeded in introducing Western-style income inequality in the transition economies even if it has done nothing else.

The gini coefficient is an average of changes taking place across all income levels. Nolan, in the paper cited above, notes that the shift in distribution which took place in the UK during the 1980s was largely at the expense of the middle of the income distribution (the percentage of income going to each of the 4th to 8th deciles declined, the first three and the top two increased). For the transition economies, however, the broad picture is one of declines for the bottom quintile and increases in the top quintile, with the middle three quintiles remaining roughly the same. The movements are in some cases dramatic. In Poland and Bulgaria the bottom quintile's share of income fell from around 10 per cent to 6.5 per cent. Since the average real income decline was 10 per cent in Poland and as much as 40 per cent in Bulgaria, the decline in real income for these groups comes out to more than 50 per cent (cf. Milanovic, p. 134). The largest gains in income occurred in the top decile, 'Therefore increasing income inequality is being driven by the rising share of the top 10 per cent or less of the population, the slightly decreasing share of some 60 per cent to 70 per cent, and (in some cases) a strongly declining share of the bottom 20 per cent of the population' (ibid., p. 135).

Earnings differentials tell a similar story. Vecernik (1994, reported in Niggle, p. 12) calculates the changes in the gini coefficient for labour earnings for the Czech Republic and for Slovakia between 1984 and 1992. In the former the coefficient rises from .199 to .263 and for the latter from .194 to .238. A measure of dispersion calculated by the ratio of the top to the bottom deciles moved up from 2.43 to 2.91 and from 2.38 to 2.42 respectively. In the US for 1992 the ratio has a value of 4.57, while in Hungary in 1991 it was 3.64, up from 2.56 in 1984. Austria had a value of 3.49 and West Germany 2.29 for 1992.

Using own estimates for household incomes, Vecernik (1995, cited in Niggle) reports increased gini coefficients between 1988 and 1992 of .29 to .32 in the Czech Republic and a decrease of .29 to .28 in Slovakia. Similar calculations made by Hauser et al. for former East and West Germany show rises from .185 to .216 and .267 to .274 respectively between 1990 and 1993. In Poland, Gorecki gives gini coefficients for household income of .235 in 1987 and .275 in 1992.

Finally, Torrey, Smeeding and Bailey (op. cit.) give the changes in gini coefficients for adjusted disposable household incomes per person for Czech Republic from .192 (1988) to .210 (1992), for Slovakia from .158 (1988) to .173 (1992), for Hungary from .237 (1987) to .295 (1992), and for Poland from .217 (1987) to .243 (1992).

Although none of these figures are strictly comparable, they all show a broadly similar result, which is the rise in gini coefficients towards levels found in western capitalist countries produced over extremely short periods of time.

However, within this broad tendency there are differences with single countries. As Boulding's examples suggest, additional data is often helpful in evaluating distribution data. Table 6.3 gives a better idea of the relative changes across countries. A clear division is discernable between the former CIS and the Southern Med countries on the one hand, and the Visograd countries on the other. These differences can be seen in the declines in industrial production and national income over the period. However, comparison of the figures for changes in the level of employment and changes in industrial production shows that the former is far greater than the latter. On more precise measures (ECE, 1996, p. 91, Table 3.3.3) shows that only in Hungary, Poland and Slovenia has there been an adjustment of employment to match the restructuring in output.

Thus, on our analogy of the Great Crash and Depression, it would appear that employment has fallen far less in the transition economies than it did in the US and that there is still substantial excess labour employed and earning incomes in these countries. This suggests that the distribution figures for the transition countries in fact understate the decline in income shares of labour because of the substantial 'excess employment'. This should also show through in a downward bias to the gini figures. The fall in the share of profits in the US was due to the disastrous fall off in profitability of the private sector and the inability of the Hoover administration to put together a sufficient expenditure programme to offset the decline. But, in the transition economies this fall in profitability will be reflected directly in a rise in the government's expenditure deficit, in large part of it in support of labour incomes. Only as state enterprises are privatized will this deficit be recorded as private sector losses and bring about reductions in employment.

Table 6.3 Selected indicators of transition economy performance 1989–1994

	change in employ. rate 89–94	index real Y per. cap. 1994 89=100	index real wages 1994 89=100	change in Gini ratio 89–94	cum % change in cpi 89–94	cum % fall in GDP 90–94	cum % fall in Industrial Production 90–94
Belarus	-8.4	–	65.4	–	838850	-37.3	-32.7
Bulgaria	-26.1	55.5	62.4	.12	2842	-27.8	-63.3
Czech	-6	82.2	85.8	.03	254	-20.1	-43.6
Estonia	-4.2	–	–	.11	10852	-35.1	-61.2
Hungary	-19	90	88.3	.02	312	-17.0	-20.2
Latvia	-8.5	–	52.5	–	8990	-50.5	-62.7
Lithuania	-10.9	–	32.8	.10	33992	-65.8	-59.1
Moldova	-1.7	30.3	29.0	.13	188955	-61.7	-59.1
Poland	-7.8	91.0	72.5	.05	2926	-7.5	-11.9
Romania	-6	80.7	52.5	.05	7563	-24.5	-59.1
Russia	-7	79.0	63.8	.15	164118	-48.3	-48.7
Slovakia	-16.8	77.1	71.6	.03	274	-19.1	-39.9
Ukraine	-6.4	96.3	28.5	.03	122330	-49	-50

Source: Cornia and Paniccià, 1996.

139

It is thus remarkable that in Russia, where the gini coefficient has risen by 0.15 over five years, the registered unemployment rate is still less than 2 per cent and the fall in employment is only 7 per cent of the working age population, although industrial production has fallen by nearly 50 per cent. On average output has fallen four times the decline in employment. On the other hand this would suggest that the greater stability in income equality in the Visograd countries may be due to their higher levels of labour shedding.

6 CONCLUSIONS

No one will be surprised by the figures reported above. What is surprising is the rapidity of the decline in equality and the extent of the decline in the face of so little industrial restructuring. If income inequality is the key to risk-taking and investment, the process is not very rapid. The example of the 1920s says that we might have expected an improvement in income distribution in terms of income shares. And this is broadly confirmed by the behaviour of the aggregate output categories shown in the accompanying table. However, it is an indication of a worsening in the real distribution of income which can be seen from the figures for the personal distribution. As governments continue to reduce deficits by reductions in transfer payments and sales of state assets, this trend is likely to continue.

In this respect it is interesting to note the apparent continuation of political support for these policies and the absence of political parties aligned according to class interests. It is noteworthy, for example, that in Russia the only class based party which has emerged is that composed of people who have been swindled by one of the large privatization funds. And it was organized to prevent the swindler from being punished. Apparently it was thought that by saving him from punishment the promised returns on their investments could also be saved.

This is reminiscent of the vertical system of social reference found in pre-industrial societies (cf. Brenner, 1979, pp. 79ff) and of the Mafia, in opposition to the horizonal social reference which is the basis for the organization of working groups into trades unions. It is also interesting that this tendency is being reinforced by the formation of concentrated industrial groups formed around combinations of banks and natural resource owners as well as by the formation of criminal organizations, both of which rely on vertical organization. They are also inimical to the development of the forms of competition which are characteristic of capitalism (cf. Brenner, op. cit). This would suggest that both competition between capitalists and between capitalists and worker is at present absent in Russia. It also suggests that attempts to measure the distribution of income by means of these traditional social categories is less than appropriate..

In closing, I cannot resist posing and answering a question. Who came out worst and best in the process of nationalization and denationalization? The answer seems to be (Milanovic, pp. 135–6) 'The transition seems to have affected agricultural incomes more negatively than non-agricultural incomes' while 'Broadly speaking, compared to workers, pensioners seem to have held their ground'. The agricultural peasants, the soul of the revolution, ended up losing in both the creation and the destruction of real socialism.

REFERENCES

Boulding, K. (1989), 'The Implications of Macrodistribution for Personal Distribution', in P. Davidson and J. Kregel (eds), *Macroeconomic Problems and Policies of Income Distribution – Functional, Personal, International*, Aldershot, UK: Edward Elgar.
Brenner, Y.S. (1979), *Looking into the Seeds of Time*, Assen: van Gorcum.
Chilosi, A. (1996), 'Distributional Consequences of Privatisation in the Economies in Transition: An Analytical Framework', in *MOCT-MOST*, **6**(1).
Cornia, G. and R. Paniccià (1996), 'The Transition's Population Crisis: An Econometric Investigation of Nuptiality, Fertility and Mortality in Severely Distressed Economies', in *MOCT-MOST*, **6**(1).
Economic Commission for Europe (1996), *Economic Survey of Europe in 1995–1996*, Geneva: United Nations.
Gorecki, B. (1994), 'Recent Developments in Income Distribution and Social Policy in Poland', paper presented to the Luxembourg Income Study Group Summer Workshop.
Hauser, R., J. Frick, K. Mueller and G.G. Wagner (1994), 'Inequality in Income: A Comparison of East and West Germans before Reunification and during Transition', in *Journal of European Social Policy*, **4**(4).
Kregel, J.A. (1994), 'On the Economic Implications of (Mis)Understanding Markets: The Great Russian Transformation', invited paper to the 1994 Meeting of the Polyani Society, Vienna, November.
Kregel, J., A. Lushin, E. Matzner and L. Specht (1994), 'The Post-Shock Agenda', in M. Perczyński (ed.), *After the Market Shock*, Aldershot: Dartmouth.
Milanovic, B. (1996), 'Income Inequality and Poverty during the Transition: A Survey of the Evidence', *MOCT-MOST*, **6**(1).
Niggle, C.J. (1997), 'Changes in Income Distribution and Poverty Rates in Several Central European Transitional Economies', in P. Davidson and J. Kregel (eds), *Improving the Global Economy: Keynesianism and the Growth in Output and Employment*, Cheltenham: Edward Elgar.
Nolan, B. (1989), 'Macroeconomic Conditions and the Size Distribution of Income', in P. Davidson and J. Kregel (eds), *Macroeconomic Problems and Policies of*

Income Distribution – Functional, Personal, International, Aldershot, UK: Edward Elgar.
Torrey, B.B., T. Smeeding and D. Bailey (1996), 'Rowing Between Scylla and Charybdis: Income Transitions in Central European Households', Working Paper No. 132, Luxembourg Income Study, Syracuse University.
Vecernik, J. (1994), 'Changing Earnings Inequality Under the Economic Transformation: The Czech and Slovak Republics, 1984–1992', Institute of Sociology, Academy of Sciences, Prague.
Vecernik, J. (1995), 'Incomes in East-Central Europe: Distributions, Patterns and Perceptions', Working Paper, No. 129, Luxembourg Income Study, Syracuse University.

7. Income Distribution and Environmental Policy Instruments

Bouwe R. Dijkstra and Andries Nentjes

1 INTRODUCTION

According to the economic textbook, production of collective goods and redistribution of income are different tasks for the government. In the real world distinctions are not so clear. The process of political decision making usually is a struggle between interest groups about the distribution of income, each group trying to maximize its gain and to impose losses on others. The political debate tends to narrow down to a discussion on the distributional aspect, even if the issue was put on the agenda for efficiency reasons; take for example competition policy. If indeed the art of political decision making consists in finding acceptable distributions of gains and losses then efficiency, instead of being the objective of policy, has become more of a side effect and the advice of the economist will not be heard.

An outstanding example is the political discussion about the question which instruments should be applied in environmental policy. Economists have been advocating the use of market instruments, like pollution charges and tradeable emission permits, as the tools of environmental policy that can reduce emissions at minimum cost to society. For that reason they are to be preferred to the command and control methods of direct regulation. A large number of simulation studies has shown that efficiency gains obtained by using market instruments are considerable. For example a recent study for the Netherlands concludes that introduction of a scheme of tradeable emission permits for the fuel-intensive industry in the Netherlands instead of strict regulation would lower costs of pollution control of SO_2 with 25 per cent and of NO_x with 44 per cent (TME et al., 1997).[1]

Economists may be convinced of the scientific correctness of their views, the hard truth is that the economic literature has had hardly any impact on actual political decision making. Market instruments are seldom applied. Command and control methods are the prevailing instrument for curbing pollution.

This observation gives rise to two questions. The first one is whether it is possible to explain actual political decision making, specifically choice of instruments for environmental policy, as the outcome of a struggle about the distribution of gains and losses. If so, the second question is whether such controversies inevitably lead up to choosing inefficient policies, i.e. instruments.

The economists of the classical school were very much aware that the government does not necessarily maximize the aggregate welfare of the whole population. The Dutch economist Simon Vissering remarks: 'how often have we been witness of the weakness of governments, which in that struggle of interests did not put first the question which of these works were most necessary for the common good, but how one could satisfy all these diverging demands most properly' (Vissering, 1867 II; 169, translation by B.R.D. and A.N.). Elsewhere, in defence of international free trade, he points out that the ones who can press the government for protection with best chances of success are the wealthiest and the most powerful.

In our present time Stigler (1971) has provided an analytical framework for the old notion that governments are susceptible to the influence of interest groups and therefore regulation may not be designed to maximize social welfare. Stigler's economic theory of regulation has been further developed by Peltzman (1976) and Becker (1983). Basically their economic theory of regulation argues that a policy that increases aggregate welfare by inflicting large per capita losses on a small group and distributing the gains among a large group (so that per capita gains are small) will probably not be realized. The losing agents have a strong incentive to form a coalition. Moreover, it is easier to organize a small group than a group which consists of many (Olson 1965). The interest group can then put pressure on the government not to implement the policy that is for the common good. It can do so by giving information on the adverse effects, offering campaign contributions, bribes or votes.

The concepts of the economic theory of regulation can be applied to decision making on environmental policy. If the political decision were in favour of a market instrument, say a pollution charge, aggregate cost of realizing a given level of pollution control would be lowest. This is in the general interest. But it might not be in the interest of groups in the sector where the charge is implemented. In our analysis we shall concentrate on the interests of capital owners and of workers in the polluting industry. The management of the firm is modelled as a perfect agent of the shareholders, who are only interested in maximal profits. Workers and their agent, the trade union, go for a maximum wage sum. With the real wage in the sector fixed, this is identical with maximizing employment.

The question then is whether shareholders, who judge instruments on how they contribute to profits, will prefer and lobby for the same instruments of environmental policy as workers, who want a maximum wage sum. Once this problem has been solved, the next question is whether market instruments – being the most efficient ones – make a chance of being chosen. In sections 3, 4 and 5 we tackle the first question. The traditional approach is to analyse the impact of different instruments on profits and wages in a neoclassical model of perfect competition. We shall follow this approach in Section 3. In Section 4 we explore unchartered areas by analysing the impacts of environmental policy instruments in the context of the post-Keynesian model of the industrial firm. As a result of this analysis we are able to derive the preference ranking of shareholders and workers for instruments which will be presented in Section 5. In Section 6 we investigate how the preferences of interest groups can be 'translated' in lobbying activities. Rentseeking theory offers a framework for analysing the impact of lobby effort on the choices that are made by political decision makers. In Section 6 it is shown how the lobby activity of interest groups can be analysed with rentseeking analysis; in Section 7 the results from the theoretical model are confronted with actual experiences with political choice of instruments. Section 8 ends with a summing up and conclusions. But first we will discuss the instruments of environmental policy in Section 2.

2 INSTRUMENTS OF ENVIRONMENTAL POLICY

In this article we will compare the following instruments of environmental policy:

– direct regulation in the form of:
  • standards: a maximum ratio of emissions to output;
  • firm bubbles: a ceiling to the total emissions of a firm;
– market instruments in the form of:
  • emissions charges: a charge per unit of emission;
  • tradeable emission permits: permits for a unit of emission.
These permits can be either auctioned or grandfathered.

The reader may wonder where covenants fit in. Covenants are voluntary agreements between government and one (large) polluting firm or a group of similar firms. The firms agree to reduce their emissions to specified level within a given time period. In return the government promises to abstain from other measures, like imposing standards. Firms have flexibility in choosing how to reduce their emissions. In this respect the covenant resembles an emission bubble for a single firm, or a group of firms. The instrument has been extensively applied in the Netherlands since 1990 and nowadays it is perhaps even more important than direct regulations. The difference between the Dutch covenant and the bubble under regulation is that with the covenant the emission ceiling is not that hard, since firms only promise to make a serious effort to bring down emissions to the agreed limit. This leaves scope for discussions in case firms fail to attain the targets. Covenants on energy use (and CO_2 emissions) are even more flexible by stating the targets in terms of energy-efficiency. In other words: increases in energy use (and of CO_2-emissions) are allowed if output has increased.

We see there are two differences between covenants and direct regulation:

- with covenants, the goal of environmental policy is less 'hard': industry promises to do its best to reach a certain emission reduction, and the government may accept industry's non-attainment of the goal;
- with covenants, one firm may abate emissions more or differently than another firm, if this is more efficient. Direct regulation is more uniform across firms.

We shall abstract from these differences here. It is difficult to integrate the first difference into our models. The second difference is irrelevant to our neoclassical model, because it assumes that all firms are equal. In the post-keynesian model, direct regulation does not take differences between firms into account.

3 THE NEOCLASSICAL MODEL

Buchanan and Tullock (1975) have shown how distributional impacts of environmental policy instruments can be analysed. As their framework they used a neoclassical partial equilibrium model for a single industry, assuming profit maximizing firms and perfect competition. From the analysis it follows that with a pollution tax the firms' profits will be lower than with direct controls. Therefore the industry would lobby for direct controls. Other researchers like Dewees (1983) and Dijkstra and Nentjes (1996) have refined the analysis by making a distinction between the interests of capital and labour and extending the set of instruments to be taken into consideration. They conclude that both interest groups will prefer direct regulation to the financial instruments of an emissions charge and an auction of tradeable permits. However, things change when the set of alternative instruments is broadened; in particular when tradeable permits are included that are distributed for free among polluting firms.

Shareholders prefer permits distributed for free because this instrument provides them with a windfall profit. On the other hand labour will oppose all market instruments. They favour direct regulation (either a standard or a bubble) since product price will be lower and employment higher than it is with a market instrument.

The complete ranking of instruments in the partial neoclassical model is given in Table 7.1. The preference for the instrument is based on its impacts on profits, respectively employment in the short and long run (Dijkstra and Nentjes, 1996). It is assumed that long run employment is proportionate to industry cost. Workers' ranking of the two instruments of direct regulation depends among other things on the elasticity ϵ of long run demand.

Table 7.1   Preferences for instruments in the neoclassical model

Shareholders	Workers	
	$|\epsilon| > 1$	$|\epsilon| < 1$
1 grandfathered permits 2 bubbles 3 standards 4/5 permit auction, charges	1 standards 2 bubble	1 or 2 standards or bubbles
	3/4/5 market instruments	

The upshot of the neoclassical model is that there is a conflict of interest between capital and labour when it comes to a political decision about the instruments of environmental policy. Shareholders will lobby for grand-fathered tradeable permits; workers go for direct regulation. A second major conclusion is that an emission charge or permits that are auctioned will never get a political chance, since none of the two groups will support them.

4 THE POST-KEYNESIAN MODEL OF THE INDUSTRIAL FIRM

The neoclassical model for an industry has been criticized for its unrealistic assumptions. For our problem the most serious blow is the observation that usually industrial firms are not the price-taking agents on a market of homogeneous goods with free entry and exit and zero profits in the long run. For that reason we shall analyse the impacts of instruments on size and distribution of industry income in the context of a more plausible model of industrial firms. We take as our starting point the post-Keynesian model (Kregel, 1973; Robinson and Eatwell, 1973), which has also been applied in industrial economics. The product market is heterogeneous, firms have some degree of monopoly. The margin for gross profits (π) is set as a mark-up on average variable costs of production (avc), which are constant. The gross profit margin covers fixed cost at normal capacity and leaves a rate of profit which depends on actual and potential competition. The firm normally has some reserve capacity that enables it to adjust to changes in demand by way of quantity adjustment, leaving its price constant. A further assumption is that firms stick to the mark-up they have chosen. If average cost rises, the price will be raised by an amount equal to the extra costs. The above model of the industrial firm differs from the neoclassical model of perfect competition in two respects: the market structure is different and the price-quantity decision is not based on maximization of profits, instead the firm practices mark up pricing.

In Figure 7.1 the industry (or target group of environmental policy) is presented. It consists of two firms each with its own demand and cost curve. For simplicity we assume cross price elasticities to be zero. Other properties of the model are: constant rate of interest, constant money wage, constant price of wage goods; employment varies proportionally with output. Since the firm is a price setter output, and employment in the production department, can only change if the firm sets a new price. In Figure 7.1 p_1°, q_1° and p_2°, q_2° are prices and quantities in equilibrium before environmental policy has been introduced.

We add a pollution control department for each firm. Unabated emissions vary proportionately with output. This is an acceptable simplification if the product contains a constant fraction of one or more potentially polluting inputs, like fuels (emissions to air), or agricultural products (effluent). The axis on which emissions e are measured in Figure 7.1 is dimensioned in such a way that with output q_1°, q_2° levels of unabated emissions are at e_1°, e_2°. Marginal cost of pollution control are increasing; for simplicity we have made them linear. If output is q_1°, q_2° then, starting from unabated emissions e_1°, e_2°, pollution can be reduced further at increasingly higher marginal cost (mac), as is shown in Figure 7.1. There are no indivisibilities in pollution control so that we have a smoothly increasing pollution control cost function. We stylize by assuming that abatement cost consists fully of cost of equipment which is bought from producers outside the sector. This assumption means that the employment impact of changing the level of pollution control is negligible within the firm. Of course a higher level of abatement creates employment in the industry that supplies control equipment, but the workers in the firms that buy equipment are primarily interested in their own jobs.

Figure 7.1 No environmental policy

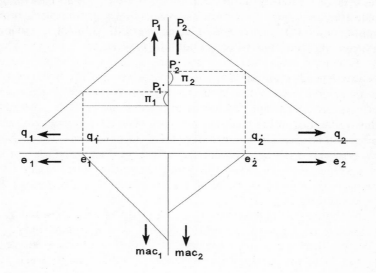

4.1 Introducing an Emission Standard

The traditional approach in environmental regulation is to set the standard as a quantity of emissions per unit of potentially polluting input. Given the assumptions we have made, that the polluting input is a given fraction of output, the standard can be expressed as allowed emissions per unit of output. The standard for each firm is chosen such that emissions in each firm have to be reduced to 50 per cent of the initial unabated emission level e_1°, e_2°.

Figure 7.2 represents equilibrium after the standard has been introduced and firms have adjusted their emissions, prices and outputs. Pollution control increases average cost of the product with the components aac 1 and aac 2; profit margins π remain unchanged by assumption; so prices are raised to the same extent as average cost has increased. Higher product prices induce lower demand for output. Important for the answer to the question of how shareholders, firm management and workers will react, is that lower q, with constant π, leads to lower total profits in each firm. Since employment is proportional with output and real wage levels remain unchanged total wages will also be lower. It follows that neither capital, nor labour see the introduction of standards as being in their interest. The conclusion fits with our casual observation of events in the late sixties and the seventies. However, in the sections that follow we shall take for granted that environmental regulation has been imposed on the sector. The equilibrium with environmental standards will be used as a point of reference that illustrates the impact of direct regulation.

Figure 7.2   Standards

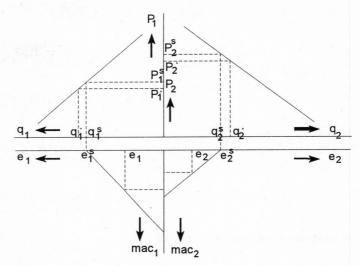

In Figure 7.2 emissions have to be reduced to $0\bar{e}_1$ and $0\bar{e}_2$ respectively. The policy target for total emissions therefore is $\bar{e}_1\bar{e}_2$. Since production has been reduced to q_1^s, q_2^s control of unabated emissions starts from a lower level than depicted in Figure 7.1, that is from e_1^s, e_2^s. Allowed emissions $0\bar{e}_1$ and $0\bar{e}_2$ can be realized by emission abatement $\bar{e}_1.e_1^s$ and $\bar{e}_2.e_2^s$. Marginal cost are mac_1 and mac_2. Marginal costs differ. This indicates that allocation of abatement between the two firms is not efficient under the regime of an emission standard. Total control costs would be lower if firm 1, which has low marginal abatement cost, would increase its emission control (and reduce emissions further), and firm 2, with high marginal cost, would decrease emission control.

4.2 Firm Bubbles

An alternative form of direct regulation is to impose a ceiling to the emissions of the firm, leaving it the flexibility to reduce emissions more, either by way of decreasing polluting inputs (which implies in our model lower output), or by way of controlling emissions at a higher level of input and output. In our analysis the firm bubbles are $\bar{e}_1$, respectively $\bar{e}_2$. Taking output under standards (q^s_1, q^s_2) as point of departure the firm has the option to increase output (by lowering price) and increase control cost to prevent increase of emissions. Such a policy boils down to decreasing the profit margin. If it is profitable to reduce π under the bubble it would have been even more profitable under standard (since it is not forbidden to reduce emissions per unit of output below the standard). But we did not consider this option in the discussion of standards since it was assumed that the firm is neither willing, nor under pressure to accept a lower profit margin. The other option is to reduce output (compared with q^s), raise price and reduce average abatement cost because emissions per unit of output are allowed to be higher than under the standard. The profit margin will then be increased in two ways. However, the action is in contradiction with the assumption that the profit margin cannot be raised without taking the risk of 'inviting' potential competitors to enter.

Therefore it seems appropriate to stick to the assumption that firms set a constant profit margin on average cost. With output at q^s average abatement cost of realizing emissions $\bar{e}$ are equal under standard and firm bubble. Given the constant profit margin prices and output quantity are identical. This means that under the simplifying assumption of a constant profit margin total profits and total wages will be the same under standards and firm bubbles. Shareholders and workers will then be indifferent between standards and firm bubbles.

It should be noted that the above conclusion follow from the restrictive assumptions we made about abatement technology. From empirical research it appears unequivocally that if a firm is allowed the flexibility of a bubble, instead of standards per emission source, large firms can and will use the opportunity to reduce their emission control costs by internal reallocation of emissions between sources within the firm. The saving on abatement cost because of increased internal flexibility can be as high as 25 per cent (TME et al, 1997). Therefore, if we accept the additional assumption that by introducing a bubble instead of a standard the marginal and average cost of realizing $\bar{e}$ is lowered for each level of q then of course the conclusion is that with a firm bubble prices can be lower, given the constant profit margin; output, profits, employment and wages will be higher. For that reason it is to be expected that in the real world shareholders and workers will be more in favour of a firm bubble than of an emission standard.

4.3 Standards and Bubbles versus Charges

In Figure 7.2 it has been shown that if standards or firm bubbles are imposed the marginal cost of abatement differ between firms, indicating that total abatement cost is higher than is necessary. Marginal costs could be equal by accident, or because the environmental authority has full information on cost and price reactions and uses that knowledge to set standards or bubbles which equalize marginal abatement cost. This would be quite exceptional.

If the government uses a uniform emission charge as its instrument firms that try to minimize their cost compare the marginal cost of emission control with the emission charge they have to pay for residual emissions and choose a level of emission control where marginal control cost equals the charge per unit of emission. Since the charge is equal for all firms, marginal control costs of all firms are equal. This is shown in Figure 7.3 where the charge is chosen at such a level that, taking into account all reactions, the same total level of emissions occurs as with standards and bubbles: the distance $\bar{e}_1 \bar{e}_2$ equals $e^c_1 e^c_2$.

In firm 1, which has relatively low marginal abatement cost under the bubble, the charge provokes higher abatement (and lower emissions) than under the standard. On top of that it has to pay the charge for residual emissions, which could be released for free under the standard. Cost per unit of output will rise because of that and price will be higher for these two reasons, compared with bubbles. Output and employment in the production department will be lower and with given π and w both profits and wages are lower than they are with a firm bubble.

In firm 2, with high marginal control cost under bubbles, emission control will be reduced under the charge. Total abatement cost is lower. However, the firm has to pay the charge for residual pollution. Only in exceptional cases will the savings on abatement cost exceed the additional expenditure for charges. Normally the cost for the firm increases if a bubble is replaced by a charge per unit of emission. Product price has to be raised; output and employment will be lower, as is shown in Figure 7.3.

Figure 7.3   Charges

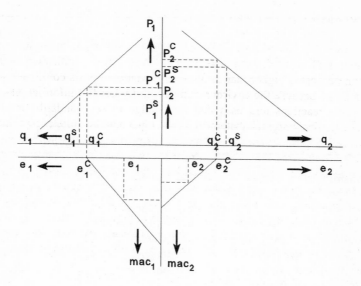

The following numerical example illustrates the difference between a firm bubble and a pollution charge. There are two firms, each with unabated emissions of 100. Marginal cost of emission reduction (r) are $mac_1 = 0.5r_1$, $mac_2 = 0.3r_2$. A firm bubble demands to reduce emissions to $e_1 = e_2 = 20$. Initial quantity is $q_1 = q_2 = 100$ at price $p_1 = p_2 = \$ 100$, profit margin $\pi_1 = \pi_2 = \$ 20$. The demand function has a constant price elasticity of 2. Next a pollution charge replaces the bubble. The charge is set at \$ 27.32 to induce pollution reduction of 160 units. After adjustment the equilibrium is as shown in Table 7.2.

By reallocating abatement from the firm with high marginal control cost to the low cost firm, and by reducing production, total cost of pollution control has been reduced from \$ 2,560 to \$ 1,990. (Compare columns (2) and (5).) This means saving on abatement inputs of \$ 570 or about 22 per cent. However, for each firm the solution is more expensive (compare columns (2) and (7)), because of extra expenditure on charges, and higher level of abatement (firm 2). Product price will be higher, sales and profits will be lower because of charges in both firms.

Although charges are more efficient than bubbles – the aggregate emission target is realized at lowest abatement cost for both firms together –

Table 7.2   Income impacts of bubble and charge

	bubble			charge					
	(1) resid. em	(2) abat. cost $	(3) profits $	(4) resid. em.	(5) abat. cost $	(6) charge exp. $	(7) total exp. (5)+(6)	(8) Δp $	(9) profits $
firm 1	20	1600	2000	37.4	746	1023	1769	3.3	1842
firm2	20	960	2000	2.6	1244	70	1314	4.2	1873
total	40	2560	4000	40	1990	1093	3083		3715

the instrument is opposed by capital owners as well as workers, since it lowers profits and wages. The basic reason is that the benefits for the sector (lower control costs) are swept away by the additional cost of paying the charge. Therefore both interest groups would rather have a firm bubble than a pollution charge. Only in special cases where efficiency gains from charges are very high the firms with high abatement cost might prefer the market instruments and firms with low abatement cost opting for the bubble. There would not be a unified front of shareholders

The same result occurs if tradeable emission permits are auctioned by the government. For the environmental authority the decision problem is less complicated than with charges. It does not need the cost information for calculating the right price per unit of pollution. With permit auction the number of permits is equal to the allowed total emissions and finding the right price is left to the market.[2]

So far the comparison has been between firm bubble and emission charges, respectively permit auction. If it is between standards and charges the choice is a bit more complicated. As we have seen standards are ranked below bubbles because they leave the firm less flexibility to reduce abatement costs. Charges allow firms the same internal flexibility as bubbles and on top of that the flexibility to adjust the emission level; but on the other hand firms have extra expenditure because they have to pay for their emissions. Therefore it is not possible to rank charges and standards. What is clear, however, is that generally direct regulation in the form of bubbles is better for the firm's profits and employment than either standards or charges.

4.4 Grandfathering of Pollution Permits

An alternative way of issuing pollution permits is to distribute them for free among polluters. As a criterion for distributing allowances the authority can take the emission per firm that would be allowed under standards. Firms 1 and 2 of our example in Table 7.2 would receive 20 emission permits per year. This system has been applied in the Sulphur Allowance Trading Program for electricity producers in the US (start January 1995). If emitters have the right to exchange permits then firm 1, with high marginal abatement cost, has and will use the opportunity to buy emission permits and increase its emission by $\bar{e}_1e_1^c$ in Figure 7.3. Firm 2 with low marginal cost will reduce emissions with $\bar{e}_2e_2^c$ and sell its unused emission permits. In a perfect permit market marginal cost will be equalized at the equilibrium permit price. In the example given in Table 7.1 firm 2 sells 17.4 emission permits and increases its emission abatement to 91, whereas firm 1 reduces its abatement to 55 units.

The basic difference with permit auction is that firms receive an initial quota of emission permits for free; just like they have it, although implicitly, with standards and firm bubble. The essential difference is that with a firm bubble and standard the permission to emit cannot be traded; with tradeable permits this is allowed. Starting from the initial quota firms will only buy or sell emission permits if they derive a profit from it. The profit consists in net lower cost of emission control for buyers and net revenue from permits for sellers. Consequently there is a net extra income for firm 1 (buyer of $\bar{e}_1e_1^c$) and firm 2 (seller of $\bar{e}_2e_2^c$) in Figure 7.3. Another way to formulate it is to point out that there is a potential improvement in income since total costs of realizing the aggregate emission target are lower under tradeable permits than they are under a standard and firm bubbles. Realization of the cost saving requires a change in allocation of permits and this is made possible by giving firms the right to trade their emission permits. Comparing column (4) in Table 7.3 to column (2) in Table 7.2, we see that expenditures on environmental measures are lower with grandfathering than with bubbles for both firms.

Table 7.3   Income impacts of grandfathering

	(1) resid. em.	(2) abat. cost $	(3) permit trade exp. $	(4) total exp. (2)+(3)	(5) Δp $	(6) value grandf. permits $	(7) profits $
firm 1	37.4	746	475	1221	3.3	5464	7306
firm 2	2.6	1244	-475	769	4.2	5464	7337
total	40	1990	0	1990		10928	14643

To assess the impact on total profits one has to analyse the impact of the emission permit on average cost of output. It may come as a surprise that the equilibrium in the product market does not differ from the outcome that was derived for a charge and permit auction. It is true that permits that have been grandfathered to firms are for them a free gift, since the permits have market value. It is a potential windfall profit every year a vintage of emission permits is issued. However, a firm that remains in business and uses its emission permits to cover emissions sacrifices the possibility to sell the permits. This forgone revenue is an opportunity cost and therefore it is part of his costs of output as much as permits that he might buy from other firms. Since the price in a permit auction market will not differ basically from the permit price in a market for permits that have been grandfathered and since allocation of abatement between firm 1 and 2 is also the same with auction and grandfathering production cost will also be identical. Consequently price and output quantity are the same with grandfathered and with auctioned permits.

This implies that with tradeable permits the loss on operational profits is equal to the loss under a system of charges as shown in column (9) of Table 7.2. The difference is made up by the 20 emission permits which have been handed over for free but have a market value of $ 27.32 per permit. That makes for a windfall profit of $ 5464 (Table 7.3, column (6)). Therefore there is an increase in profits by having grandfathered permits instead of a bubble, as shown in column (7).

For open economies it is useful to make a distinction between the exposed and sheltered sectors of industry. The exposed firms have to compete on international markets, where foreign competition is intense and for that reason demand highly price elastic. The sheltered sector that produces for the home market, without strong competition of import demand, has a more inelastic demand. In the Netherlands firms in the exposed (export) sector belong to the most input-intensive and therefore potentially most polluting category: oil refineries, basic metal and chemical industry. It should be recognized that for these industries the reduction in output can be considerable when grandfathered permits are introduced and foreign competitors remain under a regime of direct regulation. Grandfathered permits will be attractive only if really large cost savings can be expected.

The conclusion from the neoclassical model that grandfathered permits will be preferred by shareholders over a bubble has to be qualified in the post-Keynesian model. In case of relatively low savings from efficiency and highly elastic demand for output the ranking order can be reversed. The reason is that an increase in average cost and product price then translates into a large decrease in production and operation profits. Emission reduction will largely come about by decreasing production, so that the grandfathered permits are worth less.

Output and consequently employment and wages will be identical under grandfathered and auctioned permits. Therefore workers will make no difference between the various types of market instruments. They will rate them lower than standards that have the promise of higher employment and higher wage sum.

5 RANKING OF INSTRUMENTS

In Table 7.4 the instruments have been ranked according to their impacts on profits, respectively the wage sum. Since standards, although always classified lower than bubbles, are difficult to classify they have been left out. We concentrate on comparing the most efficient instrument of direct regulation bubbles, with market instruments. A comparison with Table 7.1 shows that in the post-Keynesian model the ranking for shareholders is not as straightforward as in the neoclassical model. Yet the ranking orders have much in common: grandfathered permits are always preferred to permit auction and charges; a firm bubble/covenant is always preferred to standards. A major difference is that in the post-Keynesian model if efficiency gains of market instruments are not very high grandfathered permits are ranked first only when elasticity of demand is not too high, whereas in the neoclassical model it is preferred under all circumstances. We think that the post-Keynesian model reflects better the political reaction that can be expected from industry.

For shareholders a second difference with the neoclassical model is that in the case of large efficiency gains charges and auctioned permits can be preferred to bubbles by a part of the industry; in particular the firms with high marginal abatement cost. In the neoclassical model this could never occur. As far as shareholders are concerned the neoclassical model gives a general and strict ranking. But this generality can only be obtained by constructing a sterile model of perfect competition, where all firms have an identical cost structure and where efficiency gains from increased internal flexibility and of permit trade between firms do not exist. This means that essential differences between instruments, which can be observed in the real world, are excluded from the analysis.

The post-Keynesian model is in its ranking for shareholders not unique and strict like the neoclassical model; but on the other hand it has more relevance since it gives a more plausible presentation of firm behaviour and market structure in the industrial sector and pays more attention to efficiency

gains from 'internal' flexibility (bubbles versus standards) next to 'external'
flexibility (market instruments versus bubbles).

Table 7.4   Preferences for instruments in the post-Keynesian model

efficiency gains	price elasticity of product demand	
	low	high
low	1 grandfathered permits 2 bubble 3 charges permits auction	1 bubbles 2 grandfathered permits 3 charges permits auction
	cost of abatement	
	low cost firms	high cost firms
high	1 grandfathered permits 2 bubble 3 charges and permit auction	1 grandfathered permits 2 or 3 bubbles or charges and permit auction

For workers the important resemblance between the post-Keynesian
model and the neoclassical model is that there is no difference between
permit auction (and charges) and grandfathered permits; they are ranked
equally. Bubbles are always ranked higher than standards in both models.
The major difference is that, if efficiency gains from market instruments are
high and especially when on top of that elasticity of demand is low, there is a
chance that even workers will prefer market instruments.

Table 7.5   Workers' preferences in the post-Keynesian model

efficiency gains	
low	1 bubble 2 market instruments
high	1 market instruments 2 bubble

As we have seen in Section 3 the neoclassical model is unequivocal in its
conclusion that shareholders will always prefer grandfathered permits and
workers always rank direct regulation highest (either bubbles or standards).
So there is a conflict of interests under all circumstances. In the post-

Keynesian model the ranking depends on the situational context. The neoclassical conflict of interest between workers and capitalists will emerge only when elasticity of demand is low and the efficiency gains from permit trading are not too high: shareholders will then support grandfathered permits, because of the windfall profit it brings in and workers lobby for a bubble since output and therefore also employment will be highest. With all other conjectures of elasticity and efficiency gains there is harmony of interests. When efficiency gains of permit trading are high product prices can be lower with trade permits than with a bubble and shareholders and workers alike would support trade permits (workers accepting grand-fathering) since both profits and employment would be highest. When demand elasticity is high and cost savings from permit trade are low, shareholders and workers will both favour bubbles. The efficient market instrument, even in the form of free distribution of permits will find no support.

Table 7.6   Harmony and conflict in instrument choice

efficiency gains	price elasticity of product demand	
	low	high
low	conflict shareholders: grandfathered permits workers: bubble	win-win sh. holders: bubbles workers: bubble
high	win-win shareholders: grandfathered permits workers: market instruments	

A conclusion very much like the finding of the neoclassical model is that a pollution charge and auctioned pollution permits will hardly have a chance of being politically accepted. For shareholders they never come on the first place and although workers might accept them when efficiency gains are high, they will rank them equally with grandfathered permits about which workers can make a compromise with shareholders.

Summarizing our findings we can say that the impact on the distribution of income derived form the post-Keynesian model leaves more scope for agreement between shareholders and workers on the choice of instrument in environmental policy than the neoclassical model. This is mainly due to incorporating efficiency gains from market instruments in our post-Keynesian model. In the neoclassical model this aspect was lacking.

6   RENT SEEKING ANALYSIS

The analysis in Section 5 explains which instrument will be favoured by each interest group. A next step is to analyse how interest groups try to influence political decision making on environmental policy instruments and what their impact is on the decisions.

To tackle the question we will use rent seeking analysis (Tullock, 1980; Hillman & Riley, 1989; Nitzan, 1994). Interest groups are modelled as agents that are interested in the political outcome and spend resources on trying to influence the decision. In doing this they try to maximize their net benefits, that is the difference between the expected benefits of a favour political decision for a specific instrument and the cost of lobbying effort. The approach implies that each interest group not only ranks instruments, but is also to make a valuation of the instruments.

In pursuing their aim of maximal net political benefits interest groups are involved in a contest with other interest groups. Rent seeking analysis predicts that the larger the stake, the larger will be the resources the interest groups will spend on promoting a certain instrument. From these effort levels follows the probability that a certain instrument will be chosen. The larger the group's effort level relative to other groups the larger the chance of winning the contest.

Rent seeking analysis has been applied to varying political choice situations, in particular to the choice between free trade and protection, but not to the problem of instrument choice in environmental policy. Central to the analysis is the contest success function (csf), that gives the success probability for an agent as a function of his effort and the other agents' efforts. The most commonly used csf is:

$$\rho_i = \frac{x_i}{x_1 + .. + x_i + .. x_n} \tag{7.1}$$

The contest played according to this function is called an imperfectly dis-criminating rent seeking contest. The probability ρ_i that agent i wins the contest equals the share of his efforts (x_i) in the total of all agents' efforts $(x_1...x_n)$. The contest is like a lottery with one prize, with x_i the number of tickets agent i buys. The agents have to pay for the tickets before they know whether they will win. Suppose three agents each buy 10 tickets. Then the probability that agent 1 wins is 1/3. When agent 1 buys another 10 tickets, his success probability rises to 1/2. Agent 1 can buy as many tickets as he wants, but as long as the other agents also buy some tickets, he can never be certain of the prize. The higher an agent's effort is, the higher will be his cost, but the higher also his success probability. Crucial to an agent's evaluation of his net benefits, or payoff, is his *stake* v_i: how much the prize is worth to him.

It is possible to calculate the effort levels of all agents by defining the Nash equilibrium: each agent sets his effort x_i such that his expected payoff is maximized, given the efforts of the other agents:

$$\max_{x_i} U_i = \rho_i v_i - x_i = \frac{x_i}{x_1 + .. + x_i + .. x_n} v_i - x_i \qquad (7.2)$$

An agent's expected payoff is the probability that he wins the prize multiplied by his valuation of the prize (v_i), minus his effort. From the n first order conditions for the n agents the effort levels $x_1,...,x_n$ can be calculated and next the probabilities ρ_i, expected benefits $(\rho i v_i)$ and the payoffs $(\rho_i v_i - x_i)$.

We shall apply the rent seeking model to the following situation. The political choice is between bubbles and a market instrument. The effects of instruments are determined in the neoclassical model described in Section 3. The workers' difference in payoff between bubbles and a market instrument is 70. This is the workers' stake in bubbles. A financial instrument, either a charge or an auction of trade permits, yields a government revenue of 200. If the shareholders do not receive any of this revenue, their stake in bubbles as opposed to a financial instrument is 60. With grandfathering, the shareholders effectively receive the revenue that would have otherwise gone to the government. Their stake in grandfathering as opposed to bubbles is 200 – 60 = 140.

The numerical example is summarized in Table 7.7, where the interest groups' payoffs from their least favouite instrument is normalized to zero.

Let us first apply the model of the rent seeking contest to the choice between emission bubbles, supported by workers, and trade permits that are grandfathered and are preferred by shareholders. The shareholders have a stake of 140 in grandfathering. The workers have a stake of 70 in bubbles. Using the concept of the Nash equilibrium, the levels of lobbying effort, success probabilities and pay-offs can be calculated. Given the csf (1) the levels of lobbying effort and probabilities to the stakes. Therefore in Nash equilibrium the success probability is 2/3 for grandfathering, supported by shareholders, and 1/3 for bubbles, the workers' favourite instrument. For our analysis it means that although shareholders have the largest interest and organize the strongest lobby they cannot be certain that the instrument pushed by them will be chosen. In the end politicians may decide to implement firm bubbles.

Table 7.7   Shareholders' and workers' payoffs and government revenue

	Workers	Shareholders	Revenue
Bubbles	70	60	0
Market instrument	0	0	200

However, when analysing instrument choice in environmental policy as a rent seeking contest, the contest is more complicated than the one just outlined. One complication is that other interest groups, in particular environmental organizations, can participate in the contest. In such cases a group may decide to pursue its own interest, to free ride on other group's efforts, or to form a coalition and make an agreement on type of cooperation. The problems are to be discussed in Dijkstra (1997); in this article we shall stick to the model with only two interest groups and concentrate on one particular problem we have neglected in sections 3, 4, and 5. Pollution charges and permit auctions bring in government revenue and the use that is made of this money can affect an interest group's preference for the instrument.

It is not all that surprising that shareholders and workers rank the charge or the permit auction so low, because this government revenue 'leaks out' of the industry. Buchanan and Tullock (1975) assume that the charge revenue is used for a general programme, benefiting all citizens. Actually we have made the same assumption in sections 3, 4, and 5. As we have seen in Tables 7.1, 7.4 and 7.5 the shareholders and workers will rank permit auction and charges very low. In that case, the lobby for auctions or charges will not amount to much, because the per capita stake of its proponents (all citizens) is very low.

To illustrate this point with the example from Table 7.6, suppose the choice is between bubbles and an emissions charge. The government spends the charge revenue of 200 outside the polluting industry, where 1,000 citizens benefit equally from it. When the rent seeking agents behave non-cooperatively, only the agent with the highest stake will be active on either side (Baik, 1993). In this case, this means that the workers, with their stake of 70, will lobby for bubbles. The citizens, with per capita stake 0.2, will act as if there were only one citizen with stake 0.2 in the charge. As a result, the success probability of the charge is negligibly low at 0.003.

The strange thing about Buchanan and Tullock's (1975) analysis is that they assume that instrument choice is subject to interest group pressure and revenue distribution is not. Here we will redress this asymmetry by analysing both government decisions as object of a rent seeking contest. More specifically, suppose the choice is between bubbles and charges, and shareholders and workers are the only two agents involved. Both groups would prefer bubbles if they did not receive any of the revenues from the charge. Without distribution of revenue this would be a simple win-win case for bubbles and charges would have no chance since nobody would lobby for them. The situation is different if it is known that the government is willing to distribute the revenue from charges between workers and shareholders. This could be done by lowering the labour income tax and the profit tax.

The political choice consists of two parts: a decision in which instrument to select (I) and a decision on the distribution of revenue, if the charge would be the selected instrument (R). The two government decisions can be made in two following orders and rent seeking can be analysed as a two stage game.

–IR: first an instrument is chosen; then, if charges have been chosen, the revenue distribution is decided upon.
–RI: first, the revenue distribution is decided upon, in case charges will be chosen; then, an instrument is chosen.

With formal analysis (Dijkstra 1997), that will not be reproduced here, it can be demonstrated that the following order of the two decisions affects the outcome. In RI, charges will be the instrument selected; in IR bubbles will be implemented.

We shall try to explain the intuition behind this conclusion with the numerical example from Table 7.7, starting with RI. Suppose the agents enter the game with the idea that it is only about the distribution of the charge revenues. In the contest in which each agent lobbies for a revenue share that maximizes its net benefits, the part of the revenue that goes to agent i is ρ_i. The solution for the Nash equilibrium shows that both agents will make an effort of 50. This makes for equal shares and consequently the charge revenue is split up equally, each agent receiving 100. This means that with the following order RI, each agent's valuation of the instrument of the charge is 100 at the moment when instrument choice is at stake; that is in stage 2 of the contest. At that moment, the lobbying efforts of 50, made in stage 1, are sunk cost; but the revenue will only be obtained if the charge is now selected and not the firm bubble. Remember that the interest groups' valuations for bubbles were 60 and 70. Thus, both shareholders and workers prefer charges, and charges will be selected. The agents' idea that the game would only be about distributing the charge revenues, turns out to be justified. Both interest groups will receive 100 from the charge revenue, for which they have had to spend 50. Thus, charges will be chosen with certainty in RI and both interest groups will have a payoff of 100 – 50 = 50.

In IR, bubbles will be selected. Before the game starts, the agents can look ahead to the second stage of the game. They will play this second stage if the charge is chosen as a result of the first stage. In the second stage, the charge revenue of 200 will be distributed. As we have seen, both agents will spend 50 and receive 100. Thus, their payoff from the second stage is 100 – 50 = 50. At the moment instrument choice will be made (stage 1) both agents' valuation of the charge is 50. This is so because the lobbying effort of 50 for getting a revenue share of 100 still has to be made. Now it is only the net benefit of 100 – 50 = 50 that counts. The agents compare this 50 to their valuations of bubbles: 70 for workers and 60 for shareholders, respectively. Both prefer bubbles, so bubbles will be selected. There are no rent seeking expenditures, because the agents agree that bubbles should be selected, and there are no revenues to be divided. The agent's payoffs are their stakes in bubbles from Table 7.7: 70 for the workers and 60 for the shareholders.

The first and major conclusion from this analysis is that the following order in which the decision on the instrument of environmental policy is made does affect the outcome of the decision process. Secondly, if the government would like to introduce a charge with repayment of revenue to emitters, then it could mobilize support from interest groups by first discussing an appropriate scheme of revenue distribution and postpone the political discussion about which instrument to choose to a later stage. Thirdly, if the shareholders and workers themselves can decide how to play the game, they will choose IR, because it yields a higher payoff for both agents. IR yields a payoff of 70 for the workers and 60 for the shareholders, whereas RI yields 50 for both. The reason for this difference is that in IR, the interest groups can avoid the rent seeking contest for the charge revenue by selecting bubbles right away.

7 EXPERIENCES

In the preceding sections we have shown how the choice of instrument in environmental policy can be analysed as a contest between interest groups for a favoured distribution of income. In this section we intend to complement the theoretical approach with a description of actual experiences with efforts to introduce new instruments of environmental policy.

In the Netherlands a large number of covenants between government and single or groups of firms has been concluded since the first National Environmental Policy Plan (1989): till summer 1994 about 100, of which 23 in industry (OECD, 1995). The covenant is driving out the environmental standard as the major instrument of Dutch environmental policy. This development is in agreement with the prediction implicitly made in Tables 7.4 and 7.5.

The tables also predict that pollution charges will have to face the most fierce opposition; in particular from shareholders' interests. As an example of such resistance one can mention the public debate in the Netherlands in 1992 on the proposal to introduce a CO_2-emission charge on fuels. The Wolfson Committee published its report, ordered by the government, in February 1992. The fuel intensive sectors, like oil refineries, basic metals and chemical industry, organized a very effective campaign to block the proposal. Most of the resistance had already taken place before the Wolfson Committee published its proposal. In September 1991 seven captains of large Dutch international industries like Shell, Akzo, DSM, and Hoogovens, had already written an open letter to the cabinet to protest against another government plan to raise the fuel tax, threatening to leave the Netherlands. A month before the report was published, the Minister of Economic Affairs Andriessen claimed that introducing a regulatory charge in the Netherlands alone was out of the question. According to Andriessen, industry could not take another energy tax rise after the increase of the fuel tax.

As an observer one should admit that selecting fuels as the basis for a charge was the most inappropriate choice the government could make. The fuel intensive industry in the Netherlands is highly export oriented and has to face a highly elastic demand. To make things worse, possibilities to reduce costs by increasing energy efficiency are limited. Elasticities are about -0.1 (Velthuijsen, 1995). Koutstaal (1993) has calculated that if fuel intensive firms pay a fuel charge which raises the basic price of fuels by 100 per cent (from \$ 20 to \$ 40 per barrel of oil equivalent), their expenditure on fuel taxes will be twenty times higher than the cost of improving energy efficiency. Even if taxes would be returned to tax payers by lowering taxation of labour, the fuel intensive sector would hardly be compensated because they are capital intensive. It can hardly come as a surprise that the Dutch government did withdraw the idea of a fuel charge for fuel intensive industries. Instead covenants, voluntary agreements between government and firms to increase fuel efficiency, have become the major instrument for containing CO_2 emissions by industry.

In the late eighties the Netherlands had a similar experience when the government was looking for new instruments to control emissions that cause the 'acid rain' problem. The Boorsma Committee (1988) proposed a peculiar kind of hybrid instrument of permit auction, emission charge and firm bubble. Emitters would have to buy allowances to emit sulphur dioxide, nitrogen oxide and ammonia at a fixed price from an environmental agency. For each firm there would be a maximum to emissions (and therefore also to allowance purchase) to be set by direct regulation. The agency's revenue of selling emission allowances was to be returned by way of subsidies for investments in emission control. The scheme was designed in such a way that it boiled down to a considerable net financial transfer from fuel intensive industries (emissions of SO_2 and NO_x) to intensive cattle farms (emissions of ammonia) and possibly to road traffic. Again this proposal was killed by the strong opposition organized by the fuel intensive industry.

Similarly in the US in the seventies and again in the early eighties government efforts to introduce a SO_2-emission charge for large stationary sources in industry failed because of strong lobbying by the industries that were the target for the charge.

The resistance against charges, or permit auctions, can be undermined and acceptance increased by returning the revenue from the tax or auction to individual firms in such a way that the negative net financial effect for each firm is as low as possible. An example of such a politically feasible charge is the very high tax of SEK 40,000 (approximately $ 5,200) per ton of nitrogen oxide emission from large and intermediate combustion plants which was introduced in Sweden in 1992. The revenue is paid back almost completely to the firms on the basis of their energy production. Since energy and (unabated) NO_x emissions are the joint product of burning fuels one indeed gets a perfect matching of tax payment and repayment, without killing the incentive to invest in NO_x-emission control equipment. Again the acceptance of this type of tax is in agreement with the outcome of the theoretical analysis in Section 5.

The most enlightening example of a political process culminating in the choice between standards and grandfathered emission permits is the public debate in the US in the late eighties about how to control SO_2 emissions from electricity producers. Once it was accepted in the eighties that acid rain was not just a European and Canadian phenomenon but also a problem in the US, particularly the North East, the question was how to deal with sulphur emissions. Since the electricity sector emitted 70 per cent of all SO_2 emissions the debate focused on this industry. The first plan proposed to control emissions in the traditional way by setting standards for emissions. Cost was to be expected to be high and, as can be expected, the electricity industry and members of Congress with constituency in regions where high sulphur coal was mined were strongly against. Environmental organizations campaigned against the proposals since in their view the proposed reduction of total emissions was too low. The stalemate was broken when model simulations demonstrated that the costs of emission reduction could be reduced by as much as 40 per cent if more flexible solutions were chosen; in particular if a scheme of trade sulphur allowances were introduced with grandfathering of allowances among established electricity producers. Resistance from the sector dwindled. Environmental organizations took the chance by stating their willingness to support the trade permit scheme if simultaneously the total of allowed emissions would be considerably lower than in the original plans had been proposed. In this way the benefits (lower costs and larger reduction of emissions) could be shared between two major interest groups and a majority of votes in Congress had been won. The Clean Air Act Amendments, of which the sulphur allowance trading scheme is a part, was accepted with 411 votes against 24 in Congress and 89 against 10 in the Senate; total annual emission per year from 2000 on are about 20 per cent lower than in earlier plans. The programme started in January 1995 (see for an assessment Klaassen and Nentjes, 1997). It should be noted that the electricity sector in the US produce for the home market which makes it more easy to pass on the costs of the scheme to electricity consumers.

The prediction implied in Table 7.4, that to be politically accepted trade permits have to be grandfathered, leaving no scope for auctions, is supported by the observation that all existing schemes for trade quotas are based on free distribution of permits among established producers. For the Netherlands we can mention: trade quotas for milk, fish and manure. The support of vested interest groups for the trade permit scheme has been obtained by offering them permits for free as a compensation. The potential entrants to the sector can be viewed as victims, since they will not get the permission to pollute for free (which they would have received under direct regulation). However, the potential entrants are not organized to defend their common interest as the established firms are and consequently they can politically be ignored.

The case stories presented so far all suggest that our model perfectly predicts the instrument that will be chosen in the real world. However, it is not as simple as that, since we did find a counter-example. In Sweden a very high charge on sulphur emissions of SEK 30,000 (about $ 3,900) per ton was introduced in 1991. The revenue is not paid back to the industry. The charge is meant to support new and more stringent direct regulation by giving emitters a financial incentive to implement the stringent regulation faster. In this the charge has been reasonably successful (Lövgren 1994). Such a very high charge, in particular in combination with direct regulation contradicts the ranking in Table 7.4, derived from the analytical model. Perhaps the 'anomaly' can be explained by particularities of the situation, about which we have no information.

A charge with the appearance of a counter-example is the Dutch water pollution charge. In the literature it is often cited as the success story of a market instrument. But it really is not. The charge is basically a payment for the purification services of public waste water treatment plants offered for firms that emit their effluent on the sewerage system. The revenue is earmarked for covering the costs of the public plants and the level of the charge is dictated by the level of these costs. When the scheme started in the early seventies it was not foreseen that costs could rise as high as they have done over the past twenty-five years, pushing up the charge. Since it is politically unfeasible nowadays to subsidize firms for having their waste water treated there is no other choice than to raise charges. Large industrial emitters have reacted by purifying waste water in their own installations. The reduction of emissions is an unintended effect. The charge has not been introduced with the intention to do so and it cannot be considered as a counter-example to our ranking of instruments.

8 CONCLUSIONS

In the introduction it was proposed that to understand why a certain instrument of environmental policy is chosen one has to investigate its impact on the incomes of shareholders and workers. Next we have analysed what the income impacts are if different types of instruments are implemented in an industry where firms behave according to the assumptions of post-Keynesian theory. Our major result was that there are win-win cases where workers and shareholders have a common interest in either grandfathered permits, or bubbles. Market instruments will receive general support if their efficiency gains are really high. A particular case arises when savings on abatement cost of market instruments are not that spectacular and product demand is very price elastic. Capital and labour will then form a united front against any form of market instrument.

It has been shown that in cases where interests do conflict rent seeking analysis can be applied to assess for each group the chances of winning the contest. Since the theory of the rent seeking contest is a young theory, it is still in need of further development to make it better applicable to relevant problems. We gave one example of such an extension by showing why returning revenue from charges or permit auction may not work to win sufficient support for these market instruments. However, much work remains to be done. One of the gaps that should be filled in is the role of political parties, ministers and the civil service. Nentjes and Dijkstra (1994) make an attempt to analyse the problem, but it needs further elaboration.

The relevance of our analysis can be illustrated by making a prediction. In the second half of 1997 there will be a discussion in the Netherlands whether or not to introduce trade emission permits for four fuel intensive sectors in the Netherlands. Three of the sectors (oil refineries, chemical industry and basis metals) are export oriented and price elasticity of product demand is high. The exception is the electricity sector which produces for a sheltered home market. Although efficiency gains are high compared with standards (25 per cent for SO_2 and 47 per cent for NO_x) they are lower relative to firm bubbles (20 per cent SO_2 and 27 per cent for NO_x). Guided by our model of the post-Keynesian polluting firm we predict that the managers of the firm will express their satisfaction with the existing system of covenants (firm bubbles and sector bubbles) and will declare that they see no need for trade emission permits. We also predict that trade unions will not oppose the firm's management on this issue.

NOTES

1. See also Baumol and Oates (1988) and for an up to date survey Klaassen (1996).
2. This supposes a perfect permit market. A survey of permit market failures is given in Koutstaal (1996) and Koster (1996a,b).

REFERENCES

Baik, K.H. (1993), 'Effort levels in contests: The public-good prize case', in *Economics Letters*, **41**, 363–7.
Baumol, W.J. and W.E. Oates (1988), *The theory of environmental policy,* Cambridge University Press, Cambridge.
Becker, G.S. (1983), 'A theory of competition among pressure groups for political influence', in *The Quarterly Journal of Economics*, **98**, 371–400.
Buchanan, J.M. and G. Tullock (1975), 'Polluters' profits and political response: direct controls versus taxes', in *American Economic Review*, **65**, 139–47.
Commissie Boorsma (1988), *Een anti-verzuringsfonds*, Publikatiereeks lucht en energie, Ministerie van Volkshuisvesting, Ruimtelijke Ordening en Milieubeheer.
Commissie Wolfson (1992), *Eindrapportage Stuurgroep Regulerende Heffingen*, Den Haag.

CPB (1992), *Economische gevolgen op lange termijn van heffingen op energie*, 's-Gravenhage.

Dewees, D.N. (1983), 'Instrument choice in environmental policy', in *Economic Inquiry*, **21**, 53–71.

Dijkstra, B.R. (1997), 'The political economy of instrument choice in environmental policy', Ph.D. dissertation, University of Groningen

Dijkstra, B.R. and A. Nentjes (1996), 'The political choice of instruments in environmental policy', Paper for the ESEE Conference, May 23–25, Université de Versailles Saint Quentin-en-Yvelines.

Hillman, A.L. and J.G. Riley (1989), 'Politically contest rents and transfers', in *Economics and Politics*, **1**, 17–37.

Klaassen, G. (1996), *Acid rain and environmental degradation*, Edward Elgar Publishers Ltd.

Klaassen, G. and A. Nentjes (1997), 'Sulphur trading under the CAAA in the US – an assessment of first experiences', in *Journal of Institutional and Theoretical Economics*, **153**, 384–410.

Koster, M. (1996a), 'Market failures and trade emission permits – a survey', Research Memorandum 13, Department of Economics and Public Finance, Faculty of Law, University of Groningen.

Koster, M. (1996b), 'Regulated and public firms facing environmental policies: A survey', Research Memorandum 15, Department of Economics and Public Finance, Faculty of Law, University of Groningen.

Koutstaal, P.R. (1993), 'Verhandelbare CO_2 emissierechten in Nederland en de EG', *Beleidsstudies DGE 1*, Ministerie van Economische Zaken, Den Haag.

Kregel, J.A. (1973), *The reconstruction of political economy. An introduction to post-Keynesian economics*, Macmillan, London and Basingstoke.

Lövgren, K. (1994), 'Economic instruments for air pollution in Sweden', in G. Klaassen and F. Førsund (eds), *Economic instruments for air pollution control*, Kluwer Academic Publishers, Dordrecht/Boston/ London, pp. 107–122.

Nentjes, A. and B. Dijkstra (1994), 'The political economy of instrument choice in environmental policy', in M. Faure, J. Vervaele, A. Weale (eds), *Environmental Standards in the European Union in an interdisciplinary Framework*, Maklu, Antwerpen, pp. 197–216.

Nitzan, S. (1994), 'Modelling rent-seeking contests', in *European Journal of Political Economy*, **10**, 41–60.

OECD (1995), *OECD environmental performance reviews: Netherlands*, OECD, Paris.

Olson, M. (1965), *The logic of collective action*, Harvard University Press, Cambrige, MA.

Peltzman, S. (1976), 'Toward a more general theory of regulation', in *Journal of Law and Economics*, **19**, 211–40.

Robinson, J. and J. Eatwell (1973), *An introduction to modern economics*, McGraw-Hill, Maidenhead.

Stigler, G.J. (1971), 'The theory of economic regulation', in *Bell Journal of Economics and Management Science*, **2**, 3–21.

TME et al. (1997), *Emissies: kiezen voor winst*, Den Haag.

Tullock, G. (1980), 'Efficient rent seeking', in J.M. Buchanan, R. Tollison and G. Tullock (eds), *Toward a Theory of the Rent Seeking Society*, Texas A&M Press, pp. 269–82.

Velthuijsen, J.W. (1995), 'Determinants of Investment in Energy Conservation' (diss. RUG), Groningen.

Vissering, S. (1867), *Handboek van de praktische staathuishoudkunde*, 2e druk, Amsterdam.

8. Looking Back

Yehojachin S. Brenner

A farewell address seemed to me a good opportunity to look back at the ideas I have held and elaborated in the course of the twenty-four years I worked at Utrecht University. I began from my inaugural lecture and then, in chronological order, passed in review the books which I believe most representative of my thoughts on economic theory and practice. When I committed my notes to paper the result became too long for an oration. I therefore decided to read a shortened version and present the longer as an article for those wishing to know the arguments behind my hypotheses.

1 1973: THE INAUGURAL LECTURE

In my inaugural lecture I defined *economic progress* as the augmentation of freedom of choice. I said, or rather my wife who stood in for me because I was in hospital said, that with mankind's increasing ability to satisfy its material needs more fully and with less effort, this freedom was increasing.[1]

The year was 1973. Abject destitution appeared to have been banished from the *Welfare States*, and the student movement's call for a 'march through the institutions' was still reverberating through the land. I said that increasing productivity allows people greater freedom to choose between leisure and the satisfaction of desires which could not be satisfied before, but I cautioned that the decreasing material constraints give rise to new constraints because a more complex economic and social environment imposes new restrictions. I explained that there is no freedom without economic security, and that economic security depends upon progress in both the natural and the social sciences. Society's institutions determine the pace and direction of technological advancement, and scientific and technological achievements determine which forms of social reorganization are possible and which illusory. Science and technology delimit the material wants which can objectively be satisfied, and the culture of societies demarcates the nature, diversity, and extent of these wants and the techniques employed to satisfy them. As all living is action, and human living implies choices that, whether free or circumscribed, are choices to prefer one action rather than another in the hope that they will lead to one rather than another kind of future (Bronowski, 1951, p. 109), I was optimistic. I trusted in people's good sense and in democracy's provisions to make their wishes known at the ballot box and as far as practicable democratically elected governments to fulfil them.

After all, we have formulated a theory of gravity which enabled us to find a way to reach the moon; an atomic theory of matter which enabled us to split the atom and obtain sources of energy more powerful than ever known before; theories in chemistry about the composition of substances enabling us to synthesize and form compounds more suitable for our uses than nature has provided; genetic, biological and biochemical theories enabling us to interfere with natural growth. We even envisioned abstract theories as far removed from sense perception as Einstein's about space, time, energy and matter. Why, then, should we not be able to restructure our social institutions to banish involuntary unemployment, poverty and destitution for all time?

As said, I was optimistic, too optimistic. I underrated the power of old *'habits of thought'* – the tenacity of old ideas and institutions. I forgot Keynes's admonition that the difficulty lies not in new ideas, but in escaping from old ones which ramify into every corner of our minds. I did not sufficiently realize that norms of conduct communicated to the young by elders and teachers persevere long after their original causes lost their earlier rational justification. Convinced that the relentless pursuit of gain before the coming of the *Welfare State* was the product of individuals' dire need to forestall poverty and destitution, I overlooked the possibility that in spite of the objective waning of this need the old notions would linger on.

In the climate of social engagement of the late 'sixties and early 'seventies, I simply could not imagine that the new affluence, which relieved the young from the fears of earlier generations and provided them with a chance to create a new more equitable social order, would give rise to trite materialism. I listened to their vocal denunciations of 'false wants' and to their calls for a new agenda for society, but turned a deaf ear to their other slogan: 'We want it all, and we want it now!'.

2 1979: LOOKING INTO THE SEEDS OF TIME

In 1979, in my book *Looking into the Seeds of Time* (1979) I returned to the theme of the relationship between economic developments and social mechanisms. But my optimism had been damped. I chose the title of the book advisedly because it dealt with the question whether we could interpret the signals from the past and present them correctly without bias.[2] We know that the past and present hold clues about the future, but do we know which clues are relevant and which are not? And even if we know, are we then free to choose our future or are we destined to follow a predetermined path? Moreover, how can we tell if our conception of a good future is shared by others and if it will be shared by coming generations?

In my work before I came to Utrecht I explained that economic growth provides nations with the opportunity, but no more than the opportunity, to choose the kind of society they wish to have (Brenner, 1966, 1969, 1971, 1972). I illustrated how capitalism 'created more massive and more colossal productive forces than have all the preceding generations together' (Marx and Engels, 1848, p. 4). But I also showed that the mechanism which accounted for this wonderful achievement, namely competition, was powered by constant fear. Employers afraid to be driven out of business and reduced to the ranks of the proletariat, and workers fearing destitution and starvation. It was a two-pronged mechanism: competition between entrepreneurs for their respective shares of the market, and competition between employers and workers for their share in the fruits of production. Fearful of being driven out of business by more efficient competitors, entrepreneurs were inexorably driven to search for and introduce superior technological and organizational methods of production; and facing an increasingly well-organized and powerful labour force they were pressed to introduce improvements which helped them to raise output per worker sufficiently to maintain the necessary profit to finance the innovations which compensated them for the rising wages. Though not the exclusive driving force, and not always functioning smoothly, this dual mechanism was not only the dynamic but also the progressive element in old-style capitalism. It increased mankind's ascendancy over nature and gave it the power to produce the material affluence with which the citizens of the technologically-advanced countries are still endowed.

I showed that with all its economic merit the system also had a darker side. It imposed a state of mind that made *acquisition* the purpose of almost all endeavours. In fact, the spirit of acquisition seized not only upon all phenomena within the economic realm but reached over into the entire cultural sphere, including social relations, and established the supremacy of business interests over almost all other values. Enterprises took on a separate intelligence and became the locus of economic rationality quite independent of the personality of their owner and staff. It imposed on society a utilitarian valuation of people, objects and events. The motives of entrepreneurs could be many: the desire for power, the craving for acclaim, the impulsion to serve the common good and the simple urge to action. But by virtue of an inner necessity they all became subordinate to profit-making, because without economic success almost none of these desires could be attained (Sombart, 1935).

What I was trying to explain in *Looking into the Seeds of Time* was why the pursuit of narrow materialistic self-interest continues to govern people's lives in the *Welfare State* although it ceased to be a dire necessity, and why the spirit of relentless economic competition perseveres. But I was still convinced that given time this demon would eventually waste away. I reasoned that just as by the end of the Middle Ages faith continued for a very long time to be an area of life with boundaries extravagant to overstep even in science and business dealings, in which reason was only gradually taking the place of revelation,[3] so in the end would unbridled materialism also gradually taper off.

I was aware that when social values, and the associated modes of conduct, communicated from one generation to the next become habitual, they seem to be intuitive – to be 'human nature'. But I believed that in the end reality is stronger and the old *habits of thought* eventually fade out. Alas, the process appears to be more protracted than I thought. In the era of pre-war capitalism the need to compete successfully in order to survive invested egoism with almost moral quality. At home and in school, practically everywhere, competitive success met with approval and failure with contempt. Competition in all spheres of life became 'human nature'. During the first decades of the post-war era it continued to determine people's conduct in spite of the fact that in many spheres of life the need to compete lost its earlier context. Having become 'human nature' it practically justified anything: providing African children with unsuitable milk-powder, selling arms to combatant nations, the pollution of air and water, and eventually also massive unemployment. All became 'understandable' to most people when done in the name of competition.

It is not this alone that sustains the old regime. Capitalism has an ability unmatched by any previous system to socialize opposition by presenting a relative mobility of individuals within the system as an illusory image of social progress. It allows individuals to find their place in society on the basis of competitive ability, while the system as a whole remains immutable. This is a kind of running on the spot and leading nowhere in particular. Blue jeans and long hair, which autocratic regimes, like the Greek colonels, forbade because they regarded them a symbol of opposition, are tolerated by liberal capitalism. They are simply turned into a fad – a fashion which often only the rich, who have the least reason to challenge the existing order, can afford. Similarly in the sphere of ideas, it does not disallow opposition but emasculates it by integration. When Copernicus suggested that the sun was at the centre of the solar system his hypothesis was suppressed; when Galileo made his heliocentric theory plausible, he was banned by the Church, made to recant and placed under house arrest for the remainder of his life. Under capitalism, Germany's *Berufsverbote* and the British *Official Secrets Act* are exceptions. On the whole, such measures are superfluous. Studies which do not agree with commercial interests are simply seldom funded. Substantial criticism of the system is either not published at all or printed in journals which are seldom read by anyone but the converted, and in books with too small circulation to be influential. There is no sinister conspiracy, only the logic of the market. Serious unconventional ideas are hard to sell; they seldom promise substantial profit to publishers and, naturally, offer little incentive for the establishment to subsidize their dissemination. It is the same as in industry. When a pharmaceutical firm with limited resources faces the choice whether to produce a medicine against river blindness which afflicts millions of poor Africans, or a new kind of perfume that will please a few thousand rich Europeans, the decision will be in favour of the perfume. Not that the firm's managers are lacking in humanity, but because the cure for river blindness is less financially rewarding. Shareholders neither know nor care what is produced with their investments, but they are well aware of the returns; and a management which does not make the customary rate of profit will not remain management for long.

In short, in spite of the achievements of the Welfare State the system continued to be held together by a universal pursuit of gain which permeated society to the last individual. It provided each individual with an illusion of security of life and property which led him or her to approve of arrangements, such as the legal system, that enabled him or her to enjoy what earnings or property they had but left them unmoved by the fact that it prevented them from obtaining true economic security which could be an alternative to the Marxist requirement of obtaining the full value of their work. By immediate notions of self-interest it led workers to approve of one type of insecurity in order to be protected from another. It turned all people into the system's unconscious protectors, and denied them the security they were actually striving for. It made the competitive pursuit of gain a necessity for survival, and the wish to survive a necessary rationale for accepting it – a vicious circle with an inescapable internal logic, an internal consistency that made it unassailable from within, permitting it to last long after the objective reasons which originally gave rise to it ceased to be valid.

3 1984: CAPITALISM, COMPETITION AND ECONOMIC CRISIS

In 1984 my earlier optimism was turning into trepidation. In *Capitalism, Competition and Economic Crisis* (1984), I showed at some length how corruption was undermining the positive achievements of the *Welfare State*. I described how democracy was losing its socially emancipating powers and remedial control over the Free Market system.

For most people in the industrialized countries living standards in the late 1970s were higher than ever before, and the social security system still seemed steadfast, but dark clouds were gathering on the horizon. Concentration and accumulation of wealth was giving rise to monopolistic or near-monopolistic business conglomerates with world-wide connections that enabled them to determine not only supply but also the structure of demand. Relatively high and rising taxes and wages, as well as political considerations,[4] led to the removal abroad of low-skill labour-intensive enterprises and sometimes of entire industries. Increasing unemployment frightened workers, and the inability of governments to mitigate inflation after the oil crises scared small savers. The scramble for investment funds to finance costly technological process innovations, and the growing public debt, raised interest rates. But the crisis had also another reason.

Classical capitalism had made a clear distinction between legitimate and illegitimate means of acquiring wealth. Thieves, swindlers, embezzlers, forgers, and the rest of that ilk, were excluded from free enterprise society. This was still so in 1984, but the frontiers of social disapprobation receded and the modus operandi changed. In their new form these practices were less easy to prosecute and more socially tolerated. Respectable businessmen increasingly regarded tax fiddles as peccadilloes and even bragged of them among their friends, and more and more working-men were also taking undue advantage of the state. In fact capitalists, workers, civil servants and self-employed ceased to regard misappropriation of company property, and public funds, as malfeasance. People collected unemployment benefit and conspired with others who needed workmen to defraud the state. The 'moonlighter' obtained an income on top of his social security benefits and the employer saved the money he had to pay the state.

The effect was disastrous. At one time or another almost everybody came face to face with these malpractices and decent people felt fooled by society, and began to resent paying taxes and national insurance contributions, and to work responsibly and honestly for normal wages, while 'smart alecs' were much better off. The old fears were still simmering in the background, but no longer as impelling as they used to be. Workers took longer sick leave, prolonged their tea-breaks, worked less diligently and responsibly, allowed more time to pass between leaving one position and finding another, and like employers they were tempted to resort to all manner of stratagems to misuse facilities provided by the state. To be sure, dishonesty was no new phenomenon, there had always been corrupt individuals, but the threshold which divided what is and what is not acceptable became lower. The old sense of decorum was waning. But without this sense of decorum – without working-men's feeling of responsibility taking the place of the old fears of unemployment and destitution, there is little left to maintain the necessary level of efficiency to sustain a highly complex industrial society and to assure the living standard it affords.

Worst of all, people lost interest in politics and confidence in political leaders. After the war democracy was meaningful and Keynesian economics placed much of income and wealth distribution in the hands of representative governments. People voted on issues which related to the welfare of the majority of citizens. Political parties were committed to programmes which clearly stated how they intended to solve the problems facing their electorates. But gradually this changed. The voice of high social, business and academic position gives access to television, radio and the press, and the voice of economic advantage being louder was regularly mistaken for the voice of the masses (Galbraith, 1981). In the 'seventies and 'eighties democracy was practically drowned by a flood of factually true but misleading information. The failure of labour's leadership to acknowledge what was common knowledge, namely that not only capitalists but also workers were abusing the provisions of the *Welfare State,* made this worse. It prevented prime of place being given to efforts to correct this situation, and afforded the oligarchy the opportunity to revive some features of the pre-war social and economic system, while ignoring others. In short, the combination of these moral and political crises, with persistent unemployment and inflation, afforded the foes of the *Welfare State* the long-awaited opportunity to stage their comeback.

The economics profession must share the blame for this. Unwilling to abandon the metaphysical foundations of the Enlightenment's 'Grand Design' – the all pervasive regulating mechanism of the 'invisible hand', which provided capitalism with a veneer of 'scientific' and moral justification, economists greatly assisted the drift toward the restoration of the pre-war social and economic conditions. Not prepared to abandon the neat models of Adam Smith and Léon Walras they never took on board the thought that an egalitarian society which incorporates everyone in a shared moral citizenship and high culture, without poverty, oppression or arbitrariness, and with perpetual economic and cognitive growth, is not inscribed into any historical plan. They were simply ill-equipped to see that a stored surplus needs to be guarded and its distribution enforced and that no principle of distribution is either self-validating or self-enforcing (Gellner, 1988). Educated in the neoclassical mechanistic paradigm they excluded the long-term dynamic processes of complex economic life from their studies by labelling them 'exogenous' or lumping them together in empirically untraceable 'proxy variables' to obtain rigour by quantification.[5] They did not deny the influence of technological innovation, changes in social conduct, the emancipation of women, the increasing alertness to environmental hazards, but treated them as if they were not themselves also influenced by the economic system. Economists assumed a one-way traffic and ignored the fact that most of the variables which they labelled exogenous do not develop in an economic vacuum. They simply disregarded the mutual influence of social and economic factors, and introduced unrealistic assumptions such as 'ceteris paribus', which may well be expedient for the prediction of short-run microeconomic processes but become a travesty where long-term macroeconomic processes are concerned. They transformed macroeconomics into scholasticism, and found good answers to the wrong questions. The point is that although good scientists' philosophical background seldom influences their answers it does determine their questions, and the final outcome can depend on this.[6] Even the work of such brilliant economists as Hicks, Hansen and Samuelson, was tainted by 'habits of thought' which led them to ask how best Keynes's *General Theory* could be incorporated as a 'special case' in the old conception, rather than to see it as a break with it, as a step on the road to a new scientific paradigm free from the myth of the eternally valid full employment-seeking equilibrium.

The result was that economists, instead of addressing themselves to the real causes of the malaise that since the early 'seventies had plagued the Welfare States directed their efforts to finding remedies for its symptoms. By this they inadvertently helped to create the public climate which paved the way to the social, economic and moral morass into which Thatcherism and Reaganomics led us. They attempted to contain inflation by monetary measures and by cutting back government expenditure, and hoped to create employment by reducing production costs and wages in particular. As this came from renowned economic experts, and as it had little access to other views, the public was persuaded that this was *the* way out of the depression. Keynes's proposition that it is employment that generates savings and induces investment, and that the level of employment determines the height of *real* wages, was simply ignored. That the entire economic structure of capitalism was in a process of rapid transformation was simply disregarded.

What our profession overlooked was that since the eighteenth century the rising productivity in agriculture was matched by a more or less equivalent fall in the real prices of farm produce. The fall in food prices increased real incomes and allowed people to spend more on industrial goods (Brenner, 1969). In this way the falling demand for labour in agriculture was compensated by a rising demand for labour in industry. Later, when productivity in industry also increased, and the demand for labour in this sector began to flag, and competition reduced the price of industrial products, a growing demand for services made good the loss of jobs in industry. In other words, for as long as competition remained sufficiently powerful to pass on the benefits of technological progress to consumers, a diminished demand for labour in one sector gave rise to an increased demand in others. This sequence lasted well into the 1960s, and led social scientists to believe that the rising demand for services would sustain full employment also in the future (Dettling und Herder-Dorneich et. al., 1977, p.66). This seemed to be a plausible prognosis because several important services can hardly be improved by labour-time-reducing innovations as they require the simultaneous attendance of consumer and provider (for example patients and doctors and pupils and teachers) and their quality depends on their duration.

Again it appeared as if an 'invisible hand' were leading the economy toward full employment equilibrium, but it was an illusion. Old and new monopolistic practices prevented prices falling in line with labour input and in many services, such as banking, insurance and even marketing, the expected new employment opportunities fell prey to *automatization*. In comparison with the cost of the goods where the new technologies could be applied, the cost of services where labour-time could not be reduced greatly increased. Obviously if two cars can be produced with the labour input previously required to produce one, and the time required by a hairdresser to serve a customer remains as before, the cost of a haircut becomes expensive if compared with the cost of a car. But the trouble with this was that this relative rising cost happened mainly in the services which have to be funded by the state.

In other words, relative to the decreasing costs of goods produced by the private sector, the public sector became dearer. This was one cause for the rising cost of the *Welfare State* – for the relatively high taxes associated with state regulation and for a good part of the growing public debt. But the real reason for the rising cost was that the general affluence of the 'sixties transformed society by placing with the state many of the obligations which traditionally rested with the family. The customary responsibility for the infirm and aged, and for health-care and education, shifted from the household to the public sphere. This became the most visible addition to the costs imposed by the increasing complexity of the economic system, like the construction of new national communication networks (that at least initially were too costly to be constructed and maintained by private enterprise alone) and the protection of the public from epidemic diseases and from pollution of air and water, not to mention the defence budgets. Together, they made government more costly than it had ever been before.

However, a society accustomed to assign social status to private ownership of property found it difficult to appreciate the intangible returns it was receiving from the state. Such a society tends to forget that even if all these needs were met by private enterprise the share of the national income allocated to their satisfaction would still be high and rising. The aged and infirm would still have to be housed and fed; teachers would still want to be paid; communication systems would still need to be constructed and maintained, and epidemics and pollution would still have to be prevented. In this respect the difference between a regulated and deregulated economy is inconsequential, but the distribution of the burden is significantly different. Under a system of *progressive taxation*, the rich as individuals are obliged to pay more than the poor to maintain the provisions of the *Welfare State*, while they are the least dependent on its services. This then, is the crux of the matter. The rich are allergic to subsidizing the 'undeserving poor'.

In practice, though the poor did indeed benefit from the provisions of the *Welfare State*, it was the large middle class which gained most. Tax-deductible mortgages to purchase houses; tax-deductible expense accounts; the free use of company vehicles; free or almost free health-care; redundancy pay; state pensions; free education including higher education, all these were only a few of the most direct advantages to which the middle class had better access than the poorest members of society. Yet the cultural legacy of old-style capitalism prevented the majority of the members of this class from recognizing this. Their eyes were focused on taxes and other deductions from their incomes.

Coming mainly from a rich background, or from the deluded middle class,[7] most politicians genuinely believed that the interests of individual business enterprises and those of the state must always coincide – that what is good for General Motors must always also be good for the American people. They were easily convinced that high taxes and wages were the causes of inflation and tenacious massive unemployment, and mainstream economics, dominated by the study of the private profit-maximizing firm and its trust in the distributing powers of the 'invisible hand', provided them with 'expert' justification. Moreover, even if politicians did understand that the pursuit of the public's interest required a different attitude from that which suited the pursuit of private business, being dependent on votes they never dared say that to assure the future affluence of the industrial societies taxes must from time to time be adjusted or raised.

In reality however, the new situation required a judicious reallocation of the fruits of the technologically generated economic growth. Such a reallocation of the added value does not imply *less* to the rich. All it means is that the poor receive a little more, and the rich a little *less more*. In other words, what was needed was state intervention to sustain effective demand in line with growing productivity, and measures to provide sufficient capital to allow innovative investment to continue. With stringent measures to reduce abuse of social security, tax evasion and the ill-use of public funds, this could probably have been achieved with little or no inflation. But instead of doing this, governments adopted *supply side economics*, and ignored that the object of private investment is profit, and that profit can be obtained from a growing consumer demand as well as from a fall in production cost. This is because there are two types of innovation: *Product innovation* and *Process innovation*. Both types usually go together, but in periods of increasing consumer demand, as was the case in the 1960s – in the era of the 'false wants', more capital is attracted to the former, while in periods of stagnating consumer demand more capital is attracted to the latter in an effort to sustain profit by reducing the cost of production. Oblivious to the fact that the preference of the latter led to a new form of competition,[8] governments feather-bedded the rich in the hope that easy money would encourage investment and revitalize demand for labour. The result was that investment continued to increase, but only in *process innovation* – in the replacement of human labour by machines, and production was scaled down in line with the resulting diminishing consumers' effective demand, thus increasing unemployment.[9]

4 1991: THE RISE AND FALL OF CAPITALISM

In 1991 I published *The Rise and Fall of Capitalism* where I tried to explain why in the new market structure competition was no longer functioning in the way it did before and why without state intervention massive unemployment becomes chronic. I tried to explain why this new structure of capitalism is accompanied by a kind of *industrial feudalism* which threatens to demolish the achievements of the market system, and destroy most of the capitalists themselves. I predicted that the adopted economic policies will cause society to disintegrate and result in something like South American conditions.

The often recited reason for the failure of the market system to distribute the fruits of innovation in a manner which relates consumer purchasing power to production is monopoly or oligopoly. With limited success, monopoly has been subjected to a great volume of corrective legislation, but even firms acting independently are aware of their mutual interdependence. Most businesses have a good notion of their competitors' sales, production, investment and even advertising plans, and make decisions on the basis of their rivals' expected behaviour. This was recognized by neoclassical economists who developed models designed to take account of co-operation and collusion. Neoclassical price theory did not ignore *monopoly* and *oligopoly*, but treated them as the exception, not the rule. Yet oligopoly is no longer an anomaly.

The power of monster conglomerates is well known and needs here no elaboration.[10] But while there is little new in the tendency toward monopoly, the stimulus it received in the 1980s from technological developments made it different because it ushered in a *new market structure*. Corporations manufacturing production technology, together with changes in the world economy, and *Computer Integrated Manufacturing* (CIM) caused a revision of large corporations' market strategy.[11] From being companies in many countries, important *multinationals* became *global* concerns; and their new managerial watchword became *globalization*. This new type of globalized monopoly exorcised the odium of malpractice and illegality from a great many monopolistic and oligopolistic practices.

The most obvious reasons for this change were the growing capital-intensity of manufacture; the accelerating momentum of technologies; the emergence of a growing body of universal users; and the spreading of neoprotectionist pressures. Since the late 1980s the pursuit of economies of scale was increasing the capital-intensity of manufacturing, and the increasing capital-intensity of manufacturing was, and will probably continue to be, a major source of 'globalization' in spite of the spreading of *flexible manufacturing systems* (FMS) which provide cheap short production runs. The accelerating pace at which new technologies are discovered and applied causes the costs of *research and development* (R&D) to soar, while the diffusion of new technology through the industrialized countries is advancing so rapidly that it has become difficult to sustain technological advantage. This forces companies planning to penetrate Japanese, American and European markets with new products to invade the entire zone simultaneously rather than gradually, country by country, as they used to do. Finally the emergence of an unprecedented massive body of universal users is also pushing companies in this direction.

Coalition-forming is the specific type of cooperation which accompanies globalization. It has become *the* new strategy of large enterprises. Coalitions differ from mergers and takeovers because they allow participants to retain relative independence. Their *raison d'être* is that they provide the opportunity for establishing positions in strategic markets. They have a synergistic effect by recruiting partners to fill gaps in each other's operations and to increase the possibility for exploiting economies of scale. They lead to cost and risk spreading and help to arrive at new standards.[12] This type of alliances and coalitions, especially favoured by capital-intensive industries with high R&D costs and a broad technological basis, practically dominates production in aviation, electronics and increasingly also motor vehicles. Even the largest enterprises feel that they can no longer afford the independence which previously they jealously protected. The choice of coalition partners depends on the companies' *core activities*. To maintain international standards large enterprises need to specialize in order to reduce the cost associated with the increasing complexity of their operations. They must avoid the risk of destroying competency by diversification, or from engaging prematurely in activities outside the technological and market paradigms with which they are familiar. This concentration on core activity, globalization and coalition-forming, is the salient feature of new strategic planning. It introduces a new *market structure* dominated by something close to what used to be known as *natural monopolies*. In conclusion, although price competition continues to play an important role in wholesale and retail trade, its influence on large-scale producers has been waning. The enormous and continually rising costs of breaking into markets makes prospective entrepreneurs shy away from competition with established businesses even when they are very profitable. The greater the cost of innovating the more even well established large producers tend to concentrate on what they consider to be their *core* activities. Rather than competing, they prefer to cooperate, amalgamate, buy up each other's shares, or form coalitions.

The new market structure implies the presence of a near monopoly in certain semi-finished goods and in particular production processes. If in any of these industries a new investment leads to a greater output than an equivalent investment did before, and oligopolistic structures prevent prices from falling, then consumer demand cannot increase in line with rising productivity, and profits can no longer be made in the market place. The result is that producers turn to *process innovation* because in an inert or shrinking market the way to preserve or increase profitability is to reduce production costs. With this, competition shifts from markets to innovation. The most efficient process innovator makes the highest profit. As process innovation usually involves high R&D expenditure and costly new equipment, the new structure strengthens the near monopoly of successful producers. It facilitates the determination of prices in line with investment plans with little regard for market competition – variations in the volume of demand do not influence prices but determine the volume of production; it replaces familiar market competition by a scramble for investment funds, and since *process innovation* is normally associated with a reduced demand for labour it increases unemployment. The final outcome is growing unemployment together with rising rates of interest. This is the phenomenon known as *stagflation*.

With this becomes questionable the entire theory by which prices, wages and the rates of interest, are said to regulate the economic system towards full employment equilibrium. If prices are determined by investment plans, then the latter determine the volume of demand, and income effects thwart price effects.[13] Effective demand remains the final arbiter of production, but instead of influencing prices it determines the volume of employment. Inflation, rates of interest and economic growth all rise together, but the volume of employment dwindles. In other words, the *new market structure* allows large enterprises, or practically compels them, not to pass on to consumers the advantages of innovation by reducing prices, and with this the entire full employment equilibrium-restoring mechanism at the root of mainstream economic thought becomes a travesty. State intervention to regulate income distribution becomes an unavoidable necessity.

The reason why neither the technological achievements of the last decades nor the new markets opened by the disintegration of the communist block can break this vicious spiral by which the western economic progress is slowly grinding to a halt, is the spreading of a new managerial culture. I called this culture *industrial feudalism*. The old *Captains of Industry* were owner-managers who operated with their own money, or with borrowed funds for which they staked their good name. Their wealth determined their position in the social hierarchy. It reflected what was taken to be evidence for their economic sagacity. The new *'Captains'* of large enterprises are managers whose personal wealth and attainment is less directly tied to their businesses' profitability. Shareholders, the *owners* of the enterprises, are of course interested in profit, but they have only indirect control over the businesses in which they hold their shares, and they compete in a quite different market from the managers.

In the 1950s and 1960s top professional management was mainly recruited on the basis of the candidates' prior scientific, technological, or otherwise professional capability. This was the Galbraithian *technostructure* (Galbraith, 1967, Ch. VI). The more recent managerial oligarchy receives its education in schools of management which provide useful social contacts.[14]

Its members' positions are determined by their social connections.[15] Once holding managerial position, managers' true ability can hardly be assessed because the test of business perspicacity depends on a great variety of circumstances from which the role of management can seldom be disentangled. Naturally, even today there are some very competent managers, but unlike the owner-managers of the past, the least competent are less likely to be weeded out by business competition. Their economic acumen is not the most decisive factor which determines their rewards. It is the other way around, their rewards, their salaries and perks, determine their position in the social hierarchy. Business success will enhance their prestige and earning capacity, but failure need not signal their ruin. Unlike the owner-managers, they can abandon a failing enterprise and become directors in another. Such managers form a new stratum of society which has more in common with a feudal estate than with a capitalist class. They exercise *power over people*, but hold this power by virtue of position, not wealth. This vests status with a new significance. Status becomes a rival to wealth in a competitive scramble for distinction.

Controlling large funds which are not their own, the members of this new élite are less careful than their forebears to avoid unnecessary costs when this can strengthen their personal prestige. Provided such expenditures can be correctly booked as business costs, or tax deductible, they will be incurred regardless of whether or not they are really necessary for the business. Wealth continues to bestow numerous advantages on those who own it, and company profits remain an indispensable necessity, but the role of salaries and profits is reversed. Not current business profits but the height of his personal remuneration reflects the manager's social status. This means that the new utility-maximizing 'Captain of Industry' is no longer Adam Smith's profit-seeking entrepreneur who is willy-nilly promoting business efficiency, but an individual who constantly weighs his own against the enterprise's best advantage. With this the concept *utility*, as it is conventionally applied in economics, no longer reflects economic reality, and if given a more realistic definition the concept undermines the premiss that the market structure is a self-sustaining economic growth-promoting mechanism.[16]

The *'Feudalization'* of the modern economic system does not affect top management alone. It penetrates the entire structure of most large scale corporations in both the public and the private sectors. As the vertical and horizontal integration of businesses progresses and more and more firms amalgamate to achieve greater market control, their management becomes increasingly bureaucratized and hierarchical. Top managers delegate tasks and responsibilities to sub-managers, to heads of branches, departments and sections. Each of these strata is assigned its own responsibilities and status.

Beside its appropriate wage or salary, the holder of each rank is also given its specific privileges – expense accounts, official or business vehicles, housing allowances, etc. The higher the rank the greater the perks. This is a natural concomitant of the growing size of corporations. But the newfangled type of competition, the scramble for position and status, introduces an economically debilitating element.

With personal status the object of attainment, each head of department or section becomes more interested in his own part of the organization than in the achievements of the business as a whole.[17] Within each department or section, the worth of an employee is more often measured by his contribution to the activities of his particular department than by his value to the organization as a whole. Sometimes it is not even the employee's actual efficacy which determines his employment and position but the impression that his particular section is functioning without a hitch. In this way promotion becomes less a reward for good performance and more for acquiescence, obedience, and personal relations between inferior and superior members of the organization. Criticism which does not suit the personal interests of the direct superiors upon whom an employee's advancement depends is muted. Step by step not capability but the quasi-feudal nexus, 'who one knows and who one serves', becomes the overriding factor for personal advancement. In this way a new vertical relationship is forged by which the whole hierarchy is held together. The lower ranks protect the higher since their positions depend upon their superiors' standing; the higher ranks protect the ones below, since by holding higher responsibility any mistakes made by their inferiors eventually come to rest on their own doorstep. As each member of the hierarchy has little to gain personally by questioning the value and efficiency of his organization but good reason to fear jeopardizing his chances for promotion by it, and as all members of the organization will be adversely affected by outside criticism, little is left to stimulate personal responsibility and general efficiency.

This Feudalization is however not the only debilitating factor which disturbs the efficient functioning of the new market system. The growing size of enterprises makes 'bookkeeping supervision' almost the only means of financial control. This provides many opportunities for dubious practices, and not only in the production, purchase and sale of public goods which are shrouded in secrecy, such as military equipment or space technology. The funds involved in most transactions are not the property of those who disburse them and it is hard to ascertain whether they are well spent or not. All that can be checked is if the receipts match the claimed expenses. Consequently not only public enterprises but individuals in all firms fall prey to temptation, and corruption undermines the confidence which used to be a fundamental constituent of traditional capitalism.[18] Confidence was an essential ingredient of transactions, and the demise of this ingredient is therefore not only a moral matter but a real threat to the proper functioning of the economic system. Not that traditional capitalists never indulged in shady practices, or that present-day managers are all corrupt, but the opportunities for engaging in dubious practices were more circumscribed under traditional capitalism. Few self-respecting capitalists would ever have admitted to have, for example, given or received a bribe. This is no longer so and herein lies another source of social and economic entropy.[19]

The position of the scientific and technological research units in the large enterprises and public institutions is somewhat different. Characteristically scientists are motivated by curiosity and peer appreciation. They are therefore less keen than administrators to obtain the kind of status which comes from power and control of people. Often their successes and failures can be tested by experiments and are immediately visible. Therefore, unlike administrators whose status is determined by their level of remuneration, scientists' and technologists' remuneration only *reflects* their status which is in fact determined by their genuine achievements. It is this special position of Research and Development which permits economic growth in spite of managerial inefficiency and rising unemployment. But even here the feudal culture takes its toll. When a section head is offered a new idea which deviates from well established principles he faces a dilemma. If the idea proves to be successful the acclaim is reaped by the person who suggested it or by the top managers of the organization, but if it turns out to be a failure it is he who will be blamed. It therefore becomes safer for heads of sections to avoid spending money on new or unconventional ideas.

Unfortunately this debilitating culture is rapidly spreading also to public research institutions, such as universities. Worse than this, the penetration of commercial interests into the world of science has led to a confusion between profitability and social relevance. Scientists still register tremendous achievements, particularly where science has a high degree of technological applicability, but they have lost control over the direction of their work. They push back the frontiers of ignorance but leave the decision which frontiers to push back in the hands of industrialists and bureaucrats and thus relinquish their moral obligation to society. This submission to the material interests of industry not only caused the public's currently spreading flight from science and reason, and the resort to all kinds of 'alternative medicine' and other metaphysical beliefs, but depreciated the role and social status of science to the point that many gifted young people prefer to become managers rather than scientists.

For several decades, well into this century, science played a major role in the promotion of welfare and economic growth. This gave scientists a special position in society. The majority of people romanticized their work and regarded scientists as selfless servants of human progress and truth. At the same time the scientists themselves developed a sub-culture of their own in the midst of an otherwise profit-dominated social environment. They found their ideal in the advancement of true knowledge and put this before the pursuit of material advantage. Not that there was a lack of people in the scientific community who were keen on money, but these did not determine either the principles of scientific practice or the public image of the scientist. Many students of medicine, engineering and the natural sciences, as well as of economics and sociology, chose their studies out of strong social commitment. Even those studying just to obtain a well-remunerated job with social status, or because their parents just wanted them to go to universities, did not escape the influence of the sub-culture's value system. In recent years this is no longer true – the scientific community is losing its soul; it is becoming part of the commercial enterprise, and apart from some exceptions has forfeited its public esteem. Together with the spreading of the feudal structure, this makes scientists less and less able to produce new ideas and find financial backing for their testing and application. But just as the loss of confidence in a businessman's word is not merely a moral decline but a real threat to the proper functioning of capitalism, so this loss of the traditional scientific spirit – the search for truth – is a real hazard for the proper functioning of the new market economy, because new ideas is precisely what western society needs to sustain a humane face and what industry requires to keep ahead of its new Asian industrial competitors.

5 1996: A THEORY OF FULL EMPLOYMENT

In *A Theory of Full Employment*, which I wrote together with my wife and we published earlier this year, I reviewed the current drift toward a society which I find neither economically expedient nor morally attractive (Brenner and Brenner-Golomb, 1996). My wife discussed the risks involved for science and society in the newfangled sophism hiding behind some of the post-modern ideas and 'political correctness', and I the need for a revival of the public's political engagement and for a revision of economic theory to restore to society the humane perspective which inspired the founders of the *Welfare State*. What we described in economics and in philosophy are the symptoms of a loss of direction. For centuries the West, and particularly the west of the West, had turned its eyes to the morrow and eagerly embraced change, perceived as progress, and by this it marked itself off from earlier and alternative cultures. From the 1950s onwards much of this intellectual energy spent itself in practical achievements, from town planning to the Welfare State. The subsequent loss of momentum gave people the impression that the wheel is motionless – that it fails to carry them upward, as they previously believed, or downward, as they try not to fear. They immerse themselves in their daily business and immediate circle, and turn their back on the political parties who until now claimed to command the levers of change.[20]

In the dark days of World War II, Albert Einstein declared that whatever science 'will produce depends entirely on the nature of the goals alive in this mankind. Once these goals exist, the scientific method furnishes means to realize them. Yet it cannot furnish the very goals. The scientific method itself would not have led anywhere, it would not even have been born without a passionate striving for clear understanding. But perfection of means and confusion of goals seem to characterize the age. If we desire sincerely and passionately the safety, the welfare, and the free development of the talents of all men, we shall not be in want of the means to approach such a state.'[21]

Einstein's statement is as true today as it had been when he made it, but a society nurtured on individualism interpreted as materialistic self-interest is ill equipped to choose goals and pursue policies designed to promote *social* safety, *social* welfare and the *free* development of talent; and a scientific community which regards *expediency* as its guiding principle is ill equipped to deal with truth. Nobody is against safety, welfare, and the development of talents, but events have given these desires a different meaning from those supposed by Einstein's generation to be self-evident.[22]

Unlike the depression of the 1930s, which affected the lives and hopes of millions of people from almost all classes, the depression of the 1980s had a discriminatory effect. The incomes of the employed did not diminish, as had been the case in the 1930s, but separated society into reasonably well remunerated employed people and the unemployed, poor and destitute members of the community. In the USA it led to ghettos and 'no go' areas. In most countries of western Europe this disintegration of society was delayed by the social security system of the Welfare State, but is now rapidly moving in the same direction. Ideas like the *New Deal* lost their attraction for politicians because these can no longer secure them an electoral majority. They realize that even if all the unemployed were to cast their votes for an updated similar proposition the total number of their votes would not suffice to balance those of the employed.[23] To obtain power in a democracy one must win elections and this places politicians in a dilemma. They feel that they cannot take their electorate into their confidence, and dress up their decisions in what seem to be plausible arguments. They place their trust in rhetoric rather than in truth. The result is that people lose confidence in politics as an instrument of change. The worst is that major parties lull the large middle class into false confidence and do not alert it to its impending fate. For a long time this middle class, which nowadays comprises the great majority of all the gainfully employed, was *the* main beneficiary of the Welfare State. Even those able to pay for it themselves enjoyed government-assisted housing, free health care and education, and many other material advantages, and if necessary even unemployment pay. Many European sociologists believed this middle class interest to be a safeguard against a return to the pre-war misery. But their confidence was misplaced. Since the late 1970s increasing unemployment has progressively, salami-like, sliced off the lower tiers of the middle class and thereby increased the number of people no longer merely enjoying but actually depending on the social arrangements of the Welfare State. At the same time, fewer and fewer working members of the class were obliged to pay more and more for sustaining those sliced off from the bottom tiers of the salami. But the politicians of the Left refused to look this process in the eye. They simply took the easy way out, and did not warn the decreasing number of employed, who make up the majority of the middle class, of the risk of approaching unemployment. Instead they used a whole array of plausible half-truths borrowed from the right wing of the political spectrum to convince the public that the malaise is only temporary, or that it is a kind of unavoidable natural disaster.

However, as long as there is no real shift of policy to address such structural issues, the salami-slicing process will continue. And as the number of the unemployed continues to increase and the number of those able to sustain them to diminish, a choice will eventually be forced upon industrial society. It will either have to accept South American conditions, that is its separation into a small group of affluent citizens and a large majority of poor and destitute people, or it will have to take collective political action.

Unfortunately, the virtual monopoly of the establishment over the media of public information makes the explanation of the necessary choice practically impossible.[24] It excludes the possibility of presenting *alternatives* to the 'received' recipe for solving the unemployment problem, as the New Deal had purported to be. Moreover, although the survival of the achievements of the Western World crucially depends on education, education as distinct from training is anathema to obedience and compliance, and these are the attributes the new oligarchy requires to ensure its hegemony. Hence, the new oligarchy has most to lose by supporting the free development of talents. The denial of the traditional role of the study of history and literature in the widening of the concept of 'humanity' ignores the traditional wish for progress associated with modernity. If the term human progress can be given any meaning at all it means the extension of equal rights to an increasing number of people.[25] Democracy promoted equal rights for all irrespective of colour, religion and sex, though unfortunately they were never fully attained. The hallmark of progress is the search for what is common to mankind, and the hallmark of reaction is the stressing of differences.[26] Striving for equality is not antithetical to individuality. Characteristically, modern science searches for the unifying principles behind events, but it also makes the distinction between facts and values. Equal *rights* provide the basis for the opportunity to realize individual aims and desires. But the attempt to regard pure self-interest as a unifying principle behind all behaviour, as if it was a scientifically established fact, and in the political sphere equating it to individualism, turned success itself into a kind of vindication of almost all means by which it is obtained. This attitude is more evident from day to day.[27] There is nothing new in the fact that politicians are corruptible; and it is a good sign that the press still finds corruption in high places newsworthy, because it indicates that decorum is not yet altogether dead. What is new is that in the public's mind high office is increasingly becoming synonymous with corruption. If the alternative to a drift to a South American situation is collective political action, then herein lies the real danger for the future: distrust in *politicians* is leading to distrust in *politics* and hence to disbelief in the possibility of obtaining desired ends by means of the ballot-box.

Collective political action must take account of the fact that economic *policy*, and not only economic *conditions*, influence the conduct of society, and the conduct of society influences the economy. This means that to be successful any attempt to revive the progressive economic policies called Keynesian must take note of its possible effect on people's conduct. It is an illusion to think we can provide economic security without deliberate, powerful and costly measures to restrict corruption. It is certainly not enough to introduce half-heartedly some legislation to prevent corruption. But to fight the abuses of the economic security provided by the Welfare State by its abandonment, as the Thatcherites attempted to do, can only end in social and economic disaster.[28]

6 WHAT IS TO BE DONE?

Having reviewed my work of the last quarter of a century, I cannot help asking myself how the new generation can find its way out of the present wasteland of the spirit. I do not presume to offer a route map out of it. I have been describing the charts which have been used to shepherd us into it, and the dangers of continuing to use them. All I can now do is to indicate the main considerations which may point to a possible exit, and hope that others be persuaded to move towards it.

The first thing to realize is that the era in which *economic growth* automatically engendered more employment has passed. The time when unskilled labour could quickly be absorbed into the industrial labour force, by 'on the job training' is gone. Second it must be acknowledged that the modern mode of production requires a growing volume of ancillary services which have a public rather than a private character. Third it must be understood that there are services which can be and services which cannot be made less costly by technological innovations.

When these changes are taken into account it becomes self-evident that economic policy needs reconstruction. Instead of holding on to the idea that economic growth provides employment, and 'small government' is good for financial stability, it must be recognized that growing employment produces economic growth and that financial stability depends on the judicious regulation of income distribution. Hence, the prime objective of economic policy should be *full employment*, in the conventional sense of this term.

Taking this as their point of departure, governments will have to create employment by making low-interest finance available for innovating enterprises; and by investing where private enterprise fails to meet this need. As a result new incomes and savings will be generated and effective demand for goods and services in the private sector will also be increased. The investments in the public sector will improve the functioning of the private sector and reduce some of its costs, and the savings on social security together with the additional tax revenue from the greater volume of employment will reduce government deficits. If all this is not to remain a fantasy the state must reveal to the large middle class that it risks South Americanization unless it is prepared to accept tax increases *if* such increases should become necessary. It must explain to those still gainfully employed that such a levy is then not merely a matter of solidarity (though the revival of solidarity is also important in itself) but that it is perhaps the only way to prevent the 'salami-like' process continuing slicing off more and more employed workers and bringing the risk of unemployment and misery closer to everyone. All who are objectively threatened by the demise of the achievements of modern western civilization – the poor, along with all but the most privileged members of the middle class, must be recruited. Intellectuals and students, socialists and churchgoers, ought to be shown that nowadays more unites them than divides them[29]; that they need to cooperate and be politically engaged in a combined effort to save the humane elements in our common cultural heritage – Judaism's principle of justice, Christianity's of compassion, and Socialism's of solidarity.

For this, it is absolutely necessary to make clear that it is not mankind's objective *inability* to sustain full employment and abundance for all but perverted institutions which prevent it. It is necessary to make clear to all that the social and economic system to which we have become accustomed, and whose assumedly inevitable laws we take for granted, is based on misconceptions.[30] David Ricardo saw already that the *distribution* of the economic product of society is inextricably related to its growth, and must not be ignored or relegated to the automatism of some assumedly self-validating mechanism. This does not mean that on the microeconomic level there is no market mechanism which adjusts supply to demand by the variation of prices and profits, but why should the outcome of these profit-regulated adjustments be best for society at large? On the macroeconomic level there are other and often more important objectives than those indicated by individual short-term profit and loss accounting. On the macroeconomic level there are the problems of the *distribution* of the national product between consumption and investment, between the public and the private sector, between the supply of goods and of services, between the satisfaction of present wants and aspirations for a better future, which are all beyond the automatism of the market, and require taking of decisions.

There is no reason why an informed public should not understand that the economic process functions in two separate sectors, the private sector where markets determine wages, prices and the allocation of resources, and the public sector where decisions determining the long term future of the society are made. The latter sector has no mechanism and depends on the culture of societies – on their aspirations and political power structure. The only *objective* factor which limits its freedom of decision-making is the society's level of technology. The rest depends on *values* and on the political will to sustain and improve desirable institutions and abolish or adjust those which hinder progress towards responsible economic growth and greater social stability and equity. If this is understood, the public will be willingly recruited for the protection of the humane values in our heritage.

To the elderly it needs to be explained that the economy is not 'a zero sum game', where everyone's gain is somebody else's *real* loss. It needs to be made clear to them that if an economy is growing, as it has done for decades and thanks to technological progress continues to do, it is the distribution of the *added* output they need to be concerned about, and not the ability of the economic system as a whole to sustain a larger so-called inactive population. People must be reminded that the arguments which are nowadays employed to explain why the aged are becoming an 'unbearable burden' for the economy are no different from the arguments used in the past against the shortening of the work-day to eight hours and the loss of child-labour when compulsory education was introduced, neither of which have resulted in catastrophe. The truth is that as long as productivity continues to increase, and unemployment is not allowed to soar further, there is no reason to fear that the relative growth of the 'inactive' part of the population must cause a real fall in the welfare of the gainfully employed.

The young and the old must understand that if they do not want to restore the responsibility for the aged and infirm to the family, the alternative services must be paid for. Indeed, this implies higher taxes, but it also implies more employment and fewer people depending on welfare payments.

The single issue groups ought to be reminded that their objectives are better served by common effort with all the others whose vital interests are adversely affected by the current trend than pursued in isolation. Feminists ought to recognize that not all our modern cultural heritage is 'white male dominance' but a mixed bag of elitism with emancipatory tendencies. They must understand that focusing attention on their problems to the exclusion of all others' is not the most promising way to solve them.[31] At best they achieve the inclusion of some of their members in the new 'class' while the rest will join the new army of those discriminated against, namely the majority of people. Environmentalists must cease to regard *economic growth* as an adversary, and learn to understand that it is not economic growth which needs controlling but the *direction* it is taking. They need to realize that economic growth represents no more than a positive change in the relation between the money-earnings and spending of a community during a determined length of time; that its measurement is no more than a statistical representation of a positive change in certain economic indicators such as the National Product which tells nothing about the activities from which the money was earned and what goods and services it was spent on. An increase in the National Product may just as much reflect an increase in the number of factories producing sweets, as the increase in the number of dentists employed to repair the tooth decay caused by the sweets. A rise in the GNP may reflect an increase in the number of new installations to purify the water and the air as much as an increase in the number of air and water polluting factories. Environmentalists must also understand that without economic growth the Third World is doomed to poverty and the rich countries are condemned to continual unemployment.

All the single issue movements have good reasons for being discontented, but discontent alone is dangerous. It tends to create a climate in which the *symptoms* of ills become the focus of attention while the underlying causes are ignored. Worse than that, discontent precipitates conditions which can be exploited just as well by reactionary forces as by those who are genuinely committed to elimination of the ills.[32] Discontent does not guarantee changes for the better. It can just as well lead to hopelessness and resignation as to action, and when it leads to action it may just as well engender fascism and reaction as it may promote democracy and the assertion of human dignity and rights.

Today both these tendencies are well discernible in most parts of the western world. One hears people speak of the 'end of history' and of the 'end of the great stories' – the post-modern ideologies that doubt the unity of science and the inherent unity of mankind, which lead to the conclusion that 'anything goes', and that truth is no more than good rhetoric. While the rich remove their homes to regions where they are separated from the rest of society, and hire private security guards to protect their houses and their businesses; while solidarity among workers is transformed into passive membership of Trade Unions, and political engagement becomes a visit to the ballot-box every few years, to cast a vote *against* some party or politician whom one dislikes, rather than *for* a party programme which holds a promise of real change; while the poor and unemployed are written off as 'losers' and 'free riders' who deserve no better than their lot; while all this is taking place, post-modern philosophers speak of a tolerant society where each individual can, or should be able, to do his or her 'own thing'.

But there are also manifestations of a different kind. The very existence of the single issue groups; the growing anxiety of churches and humanists about the loss of 'norms and values'; the persistent concern for Third World populations and for refugees from overtly terrorist regimes and ethnic massacres reflect the other tendency.[33] It bears witness to the fact that old-fashioned decorum is not yet extinct. This may show the young that the conversion of truth into expediency and the transformation of 'good connections', rather than excellence, into a source of personal advancement, is not 'the way of the world' but the product of the culture which a perverted establishment imposes on society.[34]

The essence of all this is that the fate of the humane values of western civilization is still in the balance – the battle for a more decent world is not yet lost. What is required from us – from economists, is to provide a plausible *alternative*. Discontent, and efforts to correct specific wrongs alone, cannot reverse the drift towards despondency. A realistic alternative, the vision of a future worthy to be struggled for, is indispensable. Without it discontentment breeds desperation, reaction and disaster. But given an alternative people find *hope*, and hope is the great antidote to despondency and fear.

Our social and economic system is in the process of reorganisation, and the final outcome of any system's reorganization is always unpredictable. But our decisions may influence its future. As for me, I am considered too old, or I am really too old, to carry on the struggle, but I can call on you, the younger generation, not to miss these opportunities to try to build a better world.

NOTES

1. Brenner, Y.S. (1973), *Economic Progress*, Inaugural lecture delivered at the State University Utrecht on May 7th, on the occasion of the appointment of Y.S. Brenner as Professor of Economics in the Faculty of Social Sciences, Geography and Prehistory.
2. I borrowed the title from the scene in Shakespeare's *Macbeth* where Banquo asks the three witches to foretell him his destiny: *'If you can look into the seeds of time, And say which grain will grow, and which will not, Speak, then, to me, who neither beg nor fear Your favours nor your hate. '* and from the scene at the end of the play, when Macbeth comes to realize that predictions *alter with us in a double sense. That keep the word of promise to our ear, And break it to our hope!'*
3. And thereby restricted the pursuit of riches to ingenuity and business acumen and contained rapacity within legally conceded confines.
4. For example, some Third World governments made the sale of certain products conditional on their production or assembly locally.
5. The reference here is to terms like 'real national output per head' or 'capital-labour ratio'.
6. This, as Heisenberg pointed out, is also true for other sciences. *Vide* W. Heisenberg [1975], 'The Philosophical Background of Modern Physics'. Lecture notes from Dubrovnik seminar.
7. In *Capitalism, Competition and Economic Crisis* (1984, p. 21), I gave several examples to illustrate this.
8. To which I turned in my next book and which is discussed in the following paragraph.
9. The explanations given by the economic 'experts' for the failure of employment to revive were various and many. It was blamed on the flight of industries with a large low-skill labour input to the Third World, on the new technologies, on competition from the Asian Tigers, etc. But as my colleague A.J.C. Manders has shown, none of these explanations is substantiated by the facts (1995).
10. For example, in the 1970s, five Dutch conglomerates directly employed 18 per cent of the working population, and indirectly many more. These five controlled electronics, metallurgy, food processing, chemicals and oil. In Germany, some 2000 businesses employed about 50 per cent of the total labour force. In the USA some 2000 corporations controlled about 80 per cent of all resources used in manufacturing. By 1994, their share in employment had fallen more steeply than the fall in overall employment, but their grip on all other resources had increased. Globalization had added an entirely new dimension to the familiar problem of economic concentration.
11. The process was triggered by three developments in the production sphere: 1) in computer-aided manufacturing (CAM), flexible manufacturing systems (FMS) and robotics; 2) in computer-aided design (CAD) and paperless knowledge work; and 3) in the increased understanding of physical phenomena. The combination of all three provided the basis for computer-integrated manufacturing (CIM).

12. Kenichi Ohmae in *Triad Power: The Coming Shape of Global Competition* (1985) listed several examples for this type of cooperation. In *aero engines:* General Electric and Rolls Royce; Pratt and Whitney-Kawasaki-Rolls-Royce. In *motor vehicles* (components and assembly): GM and Toyota; Chrysler and Mitsubishi; Volkswagen and Nissan; Volvo and Renault. In *consumer electronics:* Matsushita and Kodak; JVC and Telefunken and Thorn, Philips and Sony. In *computers,* AT&T and Olivetti; Hitachi and Hewlett-Packard; Fujitsu and Amdahl and Siemens and ICL; IBM and Matsushita.

In The Netherlands, André Manders tells us in *Sturing van produktie-technologie (Decision-making on Production Technology)* (1990), that Philips cooperates with Sony in the field of compact-disc players and with Matsushita and Yamaha in efforts to establish a standard for interactive CD and in seeking a standard for CD-video. A detailed study of the technological alliances into which Philips had entered by 1989, and of the multiplicity of relationships with other companies working with it in tandem (with five or more cooperation agreements) lists 27 agreements with Siemens, 11 with Thomson, 10 with Matsushita, 8 with Bull, Olivetti and Sony, 7 with AT&T and Bosch, 6 with DEC and Nixdorf, 5 with Alcatel (CGE), Hewlett-Packard and STC (+ICL). Of the listed inter-company agreements, 43 per cent were finalized between 1986 and 1988. During the same period the proportion of alliances in professional products and in the systems sector (including production automation) rose from 10 per cent prior to 1986, to more than 13 per cent in 1989.

13. Whether this has always been the case because, as Post-Keynesians believe, production antecedes sales, and producers only learn ex-post from the movement of prices if their estimations of the markets were correct, or if this is a new phenomenon, is here irrelevant. The point is that the new market structure practically forces large producers to adjust their volume of output to demand and not their prices; and that it obliges them to increase expenditure on technological innovation even more when markets are stagnating or reducing than when they are expanding.

14. Without going into the question whether or not such schools equip their graduates with much learning that is really functional for the efficient management of enterprises, it is obvious that unlike the Galbraithian members of the technostructure the new managers can seldom show prior evidence of competence in any sphere, not to mention professional capability.

15. Above all by the prestige of the particular institution where they received this education.

16. The conventional concept of *utility* becomes too narrow to reflect conflict between personal and corporation interests, and if it is extended to include craving for status it is too broad to sustain the causal mechanisms at the root of neoclassical theory.

17. This comes to light, for example, in the constant squabble between the heads of sales departments and research divisions in large enterprises.

18. It can of course be argued, as various socialist ideologists do, that by any moral standard, except by that of the capitalist system itself, the system has always been unethical, but this is beside the point. The point is that old-style capitalists even when they were not noted for their honesty, unlike their modern peers, were at least aware of it. When they transgressed the unwritten rules of their society they did their best to hide it. To be found out meant social disgrace and often economic ruin. The reason for this was that the entire system rested on trust and confidence. 'My word is my bond' was the slogan of the Stock Exchange; 'The Bank of England promises ...' was printed on the British currency and was sufficient to make it acceptable as a medium of exchange.

19. When the US agency Business International questioned the managers of 55 multinationals about their experiences with bribery it was told that bribes are taken practically everywhere. When a study group to investigate corruption was organized by the United Nations Social and Economic Council (ECOSOC) and the American delegation suggested that all payments to persons involved in the arrangement of contracts should be made

public to avoid corrupt practices, this suggestion met with the strongest opposition.

20. In these doldrums, in Britain for instance 80 per cent of the population reject a grey prime minister, a greedy top management and greasy politicians familiar with the slush-fund and the sleaze of pocket-filling deals. In this atony, this dystrophy of civil society, people live materially from day to day and intellectually from hand to mouth.

21. A broadcast-recording for the Science Conference in London on September 28th, 1941.

22. The director of a plant generating atomic energy may be very much concerned for his and his family's safety but less troubled by hazards facing the rest of the community. He will move his home as far as possible from his enterprise but not shut it down because other families which do not have this option are living in its immediate vicinity. Nor will the state (barring extreme circumstances) close down the power-plant if it is deemed necessary for maintaining the country's competitive economic position. Similarly, irrespective of class and social status, many people will deplore cuts in social benefits, but they will not be prepared to reduce their own income even if they are or can be convinced that this is the only way to secure the welfare of society as a whole and in the long run possibly also their own.

23. Even an unlikely combination of environmentalists, communists, old-age pensioners, the unemployed and their dependents, and the genuinely religious-motivated supporters of a less profit-centred policy, all these would together not muster more than 20 per cent of the votes in the Netherlands. In the USA, where most of the deprived do not even bother to register for elections, the percentage would probably be smaller.

24. There is nothing sinister in this and there is no conspiracy to hide the truth, but there is the simple fact that the information given to the public is usually selected by people who do not consider themselves experts in the field of knowledge they report, and that they rely for their information on what they believe to be the best established sources. The very nature of their work allows them little time to analyse the press releases and government communiqués which they receive. Their task is to report the news, and an official press release is news. In the Gulf war reporters were in fact prevented from obtaining first-hand information, and had to rely only on press releases, and this practice is not confined to matters of defence alone. Often reporters also do not know the *true origins* of the news they are reporting, and the measure of its import on the public mind. For example, if they report information provided by an international organization such as the OECD, they may not even be aware that it is based on the material supplied to the organization by member governments and therefore reflects no more than these governments' official policy. But by broadcasting the news the media are creating the impression that they convey independent international confirmation for the ruling point of view. The public, learning of the OECD report, finds that it conforms with what their government is saying, and concludes that what the experts have been telling them is right. The public stops thinking. If the 'experts' and everyone else agree that the world is flat, it must be true. Even the ministers and experts who originally supplied the material upon which the international report is based forget the doubts they may initially have had, and feel that their views have been confirmed.

25. Ancient Rome regarded slaves as 'speaking instruments'; feudal society distinguished people with blue from red blood; early capitalism abolished slavery and 'blood' but transformed workers into 'hands'; and late capitalism allowed workers to rise on the basis of individual competitive ability but did not provide them with equal opportunities.

26. Nazi Germany separated mankind into superior and inferior races, as has always been done by all who do not wish to see others equal to themselves. The new oligarchy does so by claiming for itself a superior understanding which it denies to others.

27. Hardly a week goes by without the newspapers reporting some new political scandal. In the USA, Senators and even Presidents are deservedly or undeservedly reported to be or to have been involved in financial or sex scandals. In Britain, the term *sleaze* has practically

become a byword for politics. In Belgium, Willy Claes is accused of accepting bribes to finance the advancement of his party. In Italy the country's seven times prime minister Andreotti is charged with links with top Mafia boss Toto Riina. In Holland, when large scale reorganizations are taking place even Trade Union leaders are suspected of making arrangements in favour of their members by circumventing the law of last in first out. The public figures whose involvement in scandals is spreading distrust in politics are too many to be mentioned here by name, but a few will suffice to illustrate the drift. In Britain the names of Jeffrey Archer, Neil Hamilton and Tim Smith spring to mind; in Italy Silvio Berlusconi, Bettino Craxi, Francesco de Lorenzo; in France Alain Carignon, Henri Emmanuel, Gerard Longuet, Michel Roussin, Bernard Tapié; in Belgium the Vice Prime Minister F. Vandenbroucke, Guy Coëme, Guy Mathot, Guy Spitaels; in Spain Alfonso Guerra, Mariano Rubio; and in Germany Jürgen Möllemann, Franz Steinkühler and Max Streibel.

28. I tried to explain how it can be done in the last chapter of *A Theory of Full Employment* (1996).

29. Even intellectuals have no substantial quarrel with either Church or socialism. The time when Galileo was excommunicated is long gone, and with few exceptions which do not worry the Church alone (such as genetic manipulation and abortion) religion puts little restriction on scientific research. In their rise socialism and scientific positivism were interlocked. It is not the Church that should worry true intellectuals, but the abandonment of the search for truth in favour of expediency, and the funding of research which is likely to be financially rewarding for certain people rather than serving mankind's needs. What intellectuals ought to be weary of is the intrusion of false advertising into their domains which sows a climate of public distrust in science and in the integrity of scientists.

30. Since 400 BC, or even earlier, people have seen kites gliding through the air, but in spite of birds and kites people took it for granted that Man could not fly. Those who dared to try made themselves wings and flapped them up and down imitating the motions of the birds. Their efforts failed. But Man *can* fly. When Cayley, Lilienthal and Chanute abandoned the old *habits of thought* and ceased flapping wings, a new conception, aerodynamics was born. The myth that people cannot fly was dead. The point is that before people abandon their old misconceptions they cannot see things they could have seen which remained unnoticed or appeared to be irrelevant. Therefore, as long as people persist in the belief that a deregulated market provides the best mechanism for promoting economic growth and equitable distribution, they simply ignore alternatives. Like those who had attempted to fly by flapping wings, their efforts to 'correct' the economic system will land them flat upon their faces.

31. As a single issue movement, women can achieve high positions for *some* women, and raise certain *legal* obstacles to advancement, but this will not really solve the problem for women as a whole. To conduct the struggle in a climate of *them* (men) and *us* (women) not only alienates a large number of potential supporters, but does not help to create the climate necessary for achieving true equality and mutual respect between the sexes. It introduces a whole spectrum of unnecessary divisive and debilitating factors into the struggle and provides numerous openings for opponents to exploit. As long as there is poverty and unemployment, employers (including women) will always find specious arguments justifying sex-discrimination which evaporate in times of full employment, such as difficulty and cost in finding temporary replacements for the pregnant. When there is massive unemployment these arguments sound convincing to male workers fearing for their jobs, and provide employers with a mass support for the revival of discriminatory practices against women. This culture of discrimination is reinforced by arguments that working women neglect their children, and that it is in the public interest to exclude married women from the labour market.

32. The rise of Nazi Germany and the coming of the Welfare State illustrate the two outcomes. Nazism did not solve the problems which gave rise to discontent in pre-war Germany, but it diverted attention from its sources which it was neither able nor willing to remove. It offered surrogate answers to the symptoms of the ills and presented them as solutions. Only the major catastrophe brought people back to their senses – a catastrophe that cost the lives of millions and left Germany in ruins.

33. In the USA President Clinton, in his election campaign, promised to make health-care more accessible. He did not manage to implement it, but the fact that he made the promise shows that the majority of American people favour it. Though the old and the poor were only a small segment of its traditional electorate, the Labour Party of the Netherlands lost a very considerable part of its traditional support and was practically wiped out when it ceased to care for them. Even in Britain, where the process of social disintegration is the most advanced in Europe, Lady Thatcher had massive media support for her handling of the miners' strike and for the dissolution of the Welfare State particularly from characters like Maxwell, but since then has been deliberately turned into a non-person to try to save her party.

34. The question whether human conduct is more influenced by genetic factors than by the social environment is a red herring. It is enough to accept the obvious, that at least part of human conduct is environmentally determined, and since human environment is basically social environment, it can therefore be swayed to serve the common good.

REFERENCES

Brenner, Y.S. (1966), *Theories of Economic Development and Growth*, London: Allen & Unwin.

Brenner, Y.S. (1969), *A Short History of Economic Progress*, London: Frank Cass.

Brenner, Y.S. (1971), *Agriculture and the Development of Low Income Countries*, The Hague / Paris: Mouton.

Brenner, Y.S. (1972), *Introduction to Economics*, Ankara: Middle East Technical University.

Brenner, Y.S. (1973), *Economic Progress*, Utrecht: Utrecht University.

Brenner, Y.S. (1979), *Looking into the Seeds of Time*, Assen: Van Gorcum.

Brenner, Y.S. (1984), *Capitalism, Competition and Economic Crisis*, Brighton, and Kapitan Szabo Publishers, Washington, D.C.: Wheatsheaf-Harvester Press.

Brenner, Y.S. (1991), *The Rise and Fall of Capitalism*, Aldershot (UK) and Brookfield (USA): Edward Elgar.

Brenner, Y.S. and N. Brenner-Golomb (1996), *A Theory of Full Employment*, Boston, Dordrecht, London: Kluwer Academic Publishers.

Bronowski, J. (1951/1968), *The common sense of science*, Harmondsworth: Penguin Books (reprinted).

Dettling, W. und P. Herder-Dorneich et. al. (1977), *Die Neue Soziale Frage und die Zukunft der Demokratie*, München, Wien: Olzog (2nd edition).

Galbraith, J.K. (1967), *The New Industrial State*, New York: Houghton Mifflin Company.

Galbraith, J.K. (1981), 'The Conservative Onslaught', in *The New York Review of Books*, January 22.

Gellner, E. (1988), 'Introduction', in J. Baechler (ed), *Europe and the Rise of Capitalism*, Oxford: Blackwell.

Manders, A.J.C. (1990), *Sturing van produktie-technologie (Decision-making on Production Technology)*, Zeist: Kerckebosch.

Manders, A.J.C. (1995), 'Facts and Fiction: Wage Levels and the Relocation of Production' in *International Journal of Social Economics*, **22**(V), 15–27.

Marx, K. and F. Engels (1848), 'The Communist Manifesto', in D. McLellan (1977), *Karl Marx: Selected Writings*, Oxford: Oxford University Press, 221–46.

Ohmae, K. (1985), *Triad Power: The Coming Shape of Global Competition*, New York: Free Press.

Sombart, W. (1935), 'Capitalism', in *Encyclopedia of Social Sciences*, III, New York: Macmillan.

Index

Abduh, M. 52
Adelman, I. 34, 64
Aldcroft, D.H. 121
Alesina, A. 36
Alexeev, M. 36
Alford, B.W.E. 79
Andreotti, G. 201
Andriessen, J.B. 65
Archer, J. 201
Atkinson, A.B. 3, 10, 32, 34–6
Ayres, C. 22

Baik, K.H. 162–3, 171
Bailey, D. 136, 138, 142
Bassin, B. 50
Baumol, W. 11, 169
Becker, G.S. 144
Beckerman, W. 34, 121
Bentham, J. 43, 45
Bergeijk, P.A.G. van 4
Berlusconi, S. 201
Bhagwati, P.N. 51
Biddle, J. 26
Blank, R. 38
Blitz, R. 36
Boorsma Committee 166
Boulding, K. 128, 129, 138
Bowley, A. 122
Boyle 97, 106, 111–12, 114, 121–2
Brabant, J. van 6
Brenner, Y.S. 1–3, 7, 9, 11, 15, 36,
        140, 175, 181, 190, 198
Brenner-Golomb, N. 190
Broadberry, S.N. 92–3, 122
Bronfenbrenner, M. 2–3, 13, 15
Bronowski, J. 174
Brown, C. 27, 72, 81–2
Brown, W.R. 80–81

Buchanan, J.M. 146, 162–3
Burtle, J. 81

Cairncross, A. 80, 91, 99, 122
Capie, F. 108, 122
Carignon, A. 201
Cassel, G. 80
Chai, J. 66
Chai, K. 66
Chaubey, P.K. 37
Chick, V. 2, 5
Chilosi, A. 133
Chowdhury, K. 33
Churchill, W. 88–9
Claes, W. 201
Clark, J.B. 18
Clarke, G. 35
Clinton, W. 202
Cloutier, N. 65
Coëme, G. 201
Colander, D. 27
Commons, J.R. 16–17
Conrad, C. 65
Cook, P. 36
Copernicus, N. 177
Cornia, T. 139
Craxi, B. 201
Crocco, M. 121
Cunliffe Committee 79, 86

Davidson, P. 20
Davies, J. 65
Deane, P. 110, 113, 122
Dettling, W. 181
Dewees, D.H. 146
Dijkstra, B. 2, 7, 146–7, 162–3, 169
Dowie, J. 92
Drèze, J. 61

Dror, Y.   41

Eaton, B.   40
Eatwell, J.   148
ECE (UN-Economic Commission
    for Europe)   134–5, 138
Edmundson, W.   32
Eichengreen, B.   78, 80, 99, 122
Einstein, A.   191
Ekes, I.   30
Elson, D.   62
Ely, R.T.   16
Emmanuel, H.   201
Engels, F.   175
Ergas, Z.   57

Falk Moore, S.   41, 42–3, 46–7
Falkinger, J.   34
Feinstein, C.H.   87, 91–2, 94–5, 98,
    102–3, 115–17, 119–22
Fforde, J.S.   82
Fisher, R.   36
Fitzsimmons, E.   66
France, A.   45
Frank, R.   36
Frick, J.   138

Gaay Fortman, B. de   2, 4–5, 30, 40,
    44–5, 50, 55, 63–5, 67
Galanter, M.   55
Galbraith, J.K.   82, 179, 186
Galileo, G.   176, 201
Gallaway, L.   35
Gasparini, L.   66
Gasper, D.   65
Geddes, E.   87
Gellner, E.   180
George, H.   12
German, H.   66
Ghai, H.   41
Giariato, L.   36
Glaeser, M.   16
Goldman, Ph.   63
Goldsmith, O.   14
Gore, Ch.   60
Gorecki, B.   138

Graver, H.P.   51
Grossman, H.I.   40, 81–2, 99
Groves, M.   16
Guerra, A.   201

Haggerty, M.   27
Hamilton, N.   201
Hancock, K.J.   88
Hanmer, L.   30, 37–8
Hansen, A.   180
Harrod, J.   54
Hauser, R.   138
Hawtrey, R.G.   86
Heisenberg, W.   198
Henderson, H.   79
Hepple, B.A.   59, 64
Herder-Dorneich, P.   181
Herrnstein, R.   10
Hicks, J.R.   104, 180
Hicks, U.K.   89, 121
Hilhorst, J.G.M.   65
Hill, C.   61, 72
Hillman, A.L.   160
Hobbes, T.   41
Hoeven, R. van der   36
Hoff, K.   35
Howes, S.   33
Howson, S.K.   87, 121
Hoy, M.   65
Hume, D.   17, 125

Jackson, R.H.   57–8
Jacob, R.   121
Jenkinson, T.   121
Johnson, C.   27
Johnson, H.   12
Johnson, P.   37
Jolly, R.   64
Jones, R.   22

Kaganovich, M.   36
Kaldor, N.   2
Kalecki, M.   2
Karst, K.L.   44, 53, 61
Kelsey, T.W.   1, 4, 16, 29, 31–2,
    42–3

Keynes, J.M. 7, 23, 61, 78–9, 81, 83–4, 98–9, 127–8, 174, 180
Khan, A. 66
Killingray, D. 58
Kim, M. 48
Klaassen, M. 167, 169
Kleene, G. 23
Knight, F. 26
Knoedler, J. 27
Kohli, J. 58
Kolkhuis Tanke, P. 67
Kortekaas, C. 67
Koster, M. 169
Koutstaal, P.R. 165, 169
Kramer, W. 65
Kregel, J.A. 2, 5–6, 130–131, 148
Krongkaew, M. 33
Krugman, P. 62, 66

Lamb, G.S. 48
Langemeijer, G. 45
Lapidus, G.W. 63
League of Nations 105, 107, 109
Letelier, L. 34
Levy, A. 33
Lewis, J.L. 3
Linden, J. van der 15
Linder, S.B. 11
Lindert, P. 3, 10
Longuet, G. 201
Lorenzo, F. de 201
Lövgren, K. 167–8
Lushin, A. 131
Lyon, A. 35

Macmillan Committee 79–80, 85, 90, 94–5, 118
Maital, S. 63
Malthus, T.R. 17, 22
Manders, A.J.C. 198
Marshall, A. 18
Marx, K. 127, 175
Mathot, G. 201
Matthews, K.G.P. 121
Matzner, E. 131
McAllister, I. 66

McKenna, R. 79
McKinley, T. 66
McMahon, K. 121
Medema, S.G. 15, 20, 26
Mercuro, N. 15
Middleton, R. 121
Milanovic, B. 136–7, 141
Mill, J.S. 13
Milner, B. 63
Minami, R. 36
Mitchell, P.R. 110, 113, 122
Moggridge, D.E. 121–2
Mohib, S. 121
Moll, T. 33
Möllemann, J. 201
Mueller, K. 138
Murray, Ch. 10

Nader, L. 55
Nentjes, A. 2, 7, 146–7, 167, 169
Nevin, E. 99
Niggle, C.J. 136–7
Nitzan, S. 160
Nolan, B. 136–7
Norman, M. 79–80, 91
North, D. 40, 169
Nozick, R. 3, 10–11
Nuti, D.M. 6

Oates, W.E. 169
Odink, J. 66
OECD 165
Ohmae, K. 198
Olivier, P.J.J. 66
Olson, M. 144
Oorschot, W. van 67

Paniccià, R. 139
Parijs, P. van 35
Peach, J. 27
Pearson, B. 45
Peltzman, S. 144
Pember 97, 106, 111–12, 114, 121–2
Pen, J. 2
Perotti, R. 34, 36

Persson, T. 34–5
Pigou, A.C. 79, 86, 90
Pleban, J. 121
Pollard, S. 88, 125
Price, R. 121
Pyatt, G. 30, 37–8

Ram, R. 34
Ramprasad, V. 31
Rawls, J. 3, 10, 35
Redmond, J. 121
Ricardo, D. 17, 22, 26, 194
Riina, T. 201
Riley, J.G. 160
Robbins, L. 18, 24, 28
Roberts, A. 36
Robertson, D. 23
Robinson, J. 2, 148
Rolfe, S.E. 81
Roosevelt, F.D. 81
Rosberg, C.G. 57–8
Rose, R. 66
Rosen, L. 57
Rosenn, K.S. 44, 53, 61
Rothschild, E. 59
Round, D. 36–7
Roussin, M. 201
Routh, P. 122
Rowe, D. 121
Rubio, M. 201
Ruiz-Castillo, J. 65
Ryscavage, P. 65

Saith, A. 54, 59
Samuels, W.J. 1–4, 15, 20, 22–4,
    31–2, 41–3, 45
Samuelson, P. 180
Santos, Th. Dos 56
Sarmiento, E. 34
Scargill, A. 13
Schaffer, B.B. 48
Schmid, A.A. 15, 20
Schor, J. 121
Schott, R. 54–5
Seers, D. 54
Sen, A. 4, 31, 37, 39, 43, 51, 61, 65

Shackle, G. 20
Shaffer, J.D. 15
Shakespeare, W. 198
Siegfried, J. 36, 38
Silber, J. 36
Simon, H. 11
Sinderen, J. van 4
Smeeding, T. 136, 138
Smith, A. 40–41, 179
Smith, T. 201
Smithin, J. 77
Snowden, Ph. 81, 121
Sombart, W. 176
Specht, L. 131
Spengler, J. 17
Spitaels, G. 201
Sraffa, P. 12
Stamp, J. 122
Statius, C. 40
Steinkühler, F. 201
Stewart, F. 36
Stigler, G.J. 144
Strakosch, H. 85, 94–6, 121
Streibel, M. 201
Swaan, A. de 47, 58
Szekely, M. 36

Tabellini, G. 34, 36
Tapié, B. 201
Tarifa, F. 63–4
Tchernina, N. 63
Thünen, J.H. von 18
Tinbergen, J. 34–6
TME 143, 151
Todd, H.F. 55
Torrey, B.B. 136, 138
Trebing, H.M. 15
Tullock, G. 146, 160, 162–3

Usher, D. 54–5

Valentine, T. 33
VandenBroucke, F. 201
Varian, H. 11
Varoudakis, A. 34
Veblen, Th. 22

Vecernik, J.   137
Vedder, R.   35
Velthuijsen, J.W.   165
Vissering, S.   144
Vries, B. de   4

Wagner, G.   137
Walras, L.   179
Walzer, M.   58
Wang, L.   66
Webber, A.   108, 122
White, W.   40
Wicksell, K.   23
Wilfling, B.   65
Williamson, J.   3, 10

Weber, M.   23
Wells, J.   77
White, E.   36
White, H.   30, 37–8
Williamson, O.   11
Winch, D.   89, 121
Witte, E.   17
Wolff, E.   66
Wolfson Committee   165
Wong, K.Y.   36

Yeltsin, B.   64

Zaslavsky, V.   3
Zilberfarb, B.Z.   36